The Harry Potter
Generation

D1594317

The Harry Potter Generation

Essays on Growing Up with the Series

Edited by EMILY LAUER and
BALAKA BASU

McFarland & Company, Inc., Publishers
Jefferson, North Carolina

Library of Congress Cataloguing-in-Publication Data

Names: Lauer, Emily, editor. | Basu, Balaka, editor.
Title: The Harry Potter generation : essays on growing up with the series /
edited by Emily Lauer and Balaka Basu.
Description: Jefferson, North Carolina : McFarland & Company, Inc., 2019 |
Includes bibliographical references and index.
Identifiers: LCCN 2019000474 | ISBN 9781476670034 (paperback :
acid free paper) ∞
Subjects: LCSH: Rowling, J. K.—Criticism and interpretation. |
Potter, Harry (Fictitious character) | Fantasy fiction, English—
History and criticism.
Classification: LCC PR6068.O93 Z695 2019 | DDC 823/.914—dc23
LC record available at https://lccn.loc.gov/2019000474

British Library cataloguing data are available

ISBN (print) 978-1-4766-7003-4
ISBN (ebook) 978-1-4766-3552-1

© 2019 Emily Lauer and Balaka Basu. All rights reserved

No part of this book may be reproduced or transmitted in any form
or by any means, electronic or mechanical, including photocopying
or recording, or by any information storage and retrieval system,
without permission in writing from the publisher.

Front cover image © 2019 Shutterstock

Printed in the United States of America

McFarland & Company, Inc., Publishers
Box 611, Jefferson, North Carolina 28640
www.mcfarlandpub.com

For Chris and Daniel and
most of all for Mary Cotter: may you grow up
to have the heart of a Hufflepuff,
the courage of a Gryffindor, the wit of a Ravenclaw,
and the fashion-sense of a Slytherin

Acknowledgments

Our work would not have been possible without the help of our families, friends, students, colleagues, contributors, and fellow Harry Potter fans. We are indebted to Gary Mitchem at McFarland for his ongoing support of this project, to our peer reviewers for their thoughtful and perceptive comments, and to our wonderful contributing authors for their provocative and insightful essays and their patience as we steered this collection towards completion.

We are immensely grateful to our first readers, Carrie Hintz and Katherine Broad, for their keen eyes and useful advice. We'd like to thank our parents, George and Laurie Lauer and Sumita and Dipak Basu, for their confidence in us not just for this project but also throughout our lives. Our partners, Chris Cotter and Daniel Clark, came happily along for the ride as we lived and breathed Harry Potter for the past several months. We especially thank Daniel for managing our document and for his painstaking work in preparing the manuscript for delivery.

Our colleagues at Suffolk County Community College–SUNY and the University of North Carolina at Charlotte have been invaluable sources of support, particularly Audrey Delong, David Clark, Lizzie Harris McCormick, Mark West, and Paula Connolly.

The inception of this book project was a panel at the Northeast Modern Language Association (NeMLA) conference in 2014. We would like to acknowledge this conference's friendly, productive atmosphere, which makes it seem so exciting and achievable to collaborate. Thank you, NeMLA.

Finally, we'd like to thank J.K. Rowling for creating the wizarding world and for allowing us and a generation of fans to grow up at Hogwarts with Harry and his friends.

Table of Contents

Introduction

Learning from the Harry Potter Generation

EMILY LAUER *and* BALAKA BASU

When J.K. Rowling introduced the world to Harry Potter[1] in 1997, she gave us not just a character and a novel, but a zeitgeist. For those who love books, that act has become the stuff of legend. In an article for the *Wall Street Journal*, titled "How Harry Saved Reading" (Lebrecht 2011), the author—like many others—gives this ultimate accolade to the series: before Harry, children's books simply "did not sell"; in contrast when the fourth novel of the series, *Harry Potter and the Goblet of Fire*, was published in 2000, midnight release parties sprung up in bookstores all over the nation to give readers access to the new installment as early as legally possible. As Lebrecht points out, suddenly "On trains, in airport lounges, in parks and on beaches, everywhere one went, everybody seemed to be reading Harry Potter." It didn't end there; children's authors who had been publishing for many years previously were suddenly being pushed forward by book-sellers who claimed readers would like them because they loved Harry. The 2001 edition of Diana Wynne Jones' 1980s Chrestomanci series, for instance, had a cover blurb which read: "Mad about Harry? Try Diana." It was a heady, game-changing time for adults in the publishing industry, but for the generation of children born in the late 1980s and early 1990s, it set the standard by which all other fictions and narratives would be measured.

Those children, now adults, came of age in a world where Pottermania was as defining as Beatlemania had been for their grandparents. Unlike Beatlemania, however, which frequently divided young people from the adults in authority, Pottermania matured with its readers, as the main characters, the readers themselves, and the franchise all grew up together. What does it mean to interact with this generation of readers, students, and authors who came of age alongside Harry? As they've matured over the last decade, the Harry Potter generation has watched a series of books thoroughly permeate the landscape of popular culture. Due to the intense cultural saturation of these books, movies, imagery and merchandise into almost every aspect of their lives, children of this generation have had their ideas about education, romance, friendship, family, and narrative shaped by the Harry Potter stories.

The effect of the series on this generation—and the effect of this generation on the world—is profound. As professors, we can now reflect on the ways we have encountered this generation in college classrooms, and it becomes apparent that their conception of themselves as independent readers begins with Harry Potter. As many of the authors in this volume make clear, because of the series' crossover appeal to adults as well as children, it has created a fan space where the boundaries between children and adults are blurred, which has been foundational for the generation's conception of adulthood. Rowling's flawed, three-dimensional adult characters who behave in similar ways to her child characters bring together adult and child fans of the series letting them interact with one another at midnight releases of books and movies as well as on the internet in fan communities. In fact, the series has even helped to erase distinctions between child and adult readers, with YA novels now being regularly cross-marketed to both demographics. Further, because of its global media saturation, the Potterverse has helped to give rise to our current culture of participation and fandom, where people of all ages can discuss and disseminate ideas with each other in both authorized and unauthorized fan spaces. Intergenerational appreciation and multimedia participation have shaped the Harry Potter generation who grew up with a cultural phenomenon that had the potential to inflect every aspect of their lives.

As all of this fan activity surrounding the series indicates, Rowling's creation is one that offers a substantial reward for investment. The Potterverse imbues the quotidian experiences of a child's life with magic, as activities such as shopping for school supplies or taking a train ride are shared by the lives of the readers and fantasy characters. This blend of the magical with the mundane also inherently supports the notion that the fictional lives of its characters should be extended beyond the borders of the novel. Naturally the owners of the Potter franchise are attempting to cash in on this phenomenon with the release of the film *Fantastic Beasts and Where to Find Them* (and its four planned sequels) and with the authorized release of a two-part play that continues Harry's saga: *Harry Potter and the Cursed Child*. Even these authorized expansions of the Potterverse are competing with their own originating material, just as the children's book industry continues to do the same; in what we might call a post–Potter era, Rowling's success has created a benchmark for new authors to strive for and Rowling's story and world have also shaped the expectations of the industry and the readers, as we discuss in the first essay of this volume. To be clear: this era is post–Potter in that Potter already exists, not because Potter has ceased or diminished.

In this collection, we examine the Harry Potter generation as our students in the classroom, as the authors publishing the fiction we read in the bookstore and on the internet, as community builders, and ultimately as the makers of a very near future. How do they understand history and politics? Do they learn differently from those who came before them? Are they indeed any different from the mythologized scores of fans who met the boat carrying the latest installment of Dickens' *The Old Curiosity Shop* in New York Harbor, screaming, "What happens to Little Nell?"

We begin this journey with our prologue, "Reading Harry Potter in Context," which discusses the tradition of British children's fantasy that Rowling draws upon for her series, now a hallmark of the genre, as well as the influence that the Harry Potter novels have had on a new generation of stories that have begun to sprout, inspired by her work.

The essays that make up our first section, "The Phenomenon," examine the myriad ways in which this influence, the series' overwhelming ubiquity and popularity, has permeated this generation's identity formation. In his essay, "Yours to Keep: Owning Harry and Hermione," Isaac Vayo uses celebrity theory to discuss the role Daniel Radcliffe and Emma Watson have had on the generation that grew up alongside them as they portrayed Harry and Hermione, suggesting "between them, Radcliffe and Watson provide an object lesson in self-creation." In contrast, Dion McLeod and Elise Payne suggest in their essay, "Loony Lovegood and the Almost Chosen One: Harry Potter, Supporting Characters and Fan Reception," that more than just the famous trio of Harry, Hermione, and Ron, supporting characters like Luna and Neville provide readers as much or greater possibilities for identifying with and thereby engaging with the narrative. McLeod and Payne argue that the series gives resisting readers, unwilling to be swept along by the author's preferences, room to fit within the novels' context. Moving beyond identification with characters and the actors who play them, Emily Lauer optimistically argues in "Harry Potter and the Book Burners' Mistake: Suppression and Its Unintended Consequences" that a brief Christian fundamentalist denunciation of the series at the turn of the millennium resulted in reaffirming its position as an icon of reading-as-resistance, a position supported by the actions of fan groups like the Harry Potter Alliance who continue to work for social change within their communities long past the series' end. Marian Yee closes the section by examining the way in which the contemporary reality of modernity—in the form of Harry, Hogwarts, and wizarding bureaucracy—

must eventually triumph over pre-modern forms of magic. In "The Disenchantment of Harry Potter: How Magic Died and the Wizard World Became Modern," Yee argues that the Harry Potter generation need not see this "death of magic" as a loss, since through the course of Harry's adventures, Rowling manages to successfully merge the wizarding world with the one her readers live in.

Our second section, "Cultural Memory and Identity," examines sites of cultural memory—the symbolic heritage, history and even trauma that is embodied in texts, celebrations, rituals, objects, and other media—for the Harry Potter generation both in and out of the novels. In "Cloaked in History: Magical Heritage Sites in the Harry Potter Series," Emily Lohorn examines the development of what she calls "magical heritage sites" within the series, arguing that Rowling's blend of magic and anachronism adds both historical and ahistorical layers to the series, intervening in the Harry Potter generation's understanding of history itself as potentially accessible and applicable to everyday life. Dennis J. Siler's "Wizarding World Tourism: Numinous Experiences of the Harry Potter Generation" studies how the Wizarding World of Harry Potter theme park attempts to realize Harry Potter as cultural memory within a real-world physical play space for a generation of fans. Heather Urbanski expands this view of collaborative understanding as she explores the concept of fan memory in "Filling in Memory Gaps with Love: Harry Potter on Tumblr." She argues that fan memory and knowledge of both canon and fan production are "situated within complex social and collaborative endeavors," suggesting that the blurred boundary between fan and producer makes its way into the collective memory of the readership, shaping the way the Harry Potter generation may read—not just Harry Potter, but also other popular texts. Balaka Basu concludes the section with "Magic from the Margins: Harry Potter and the Postcolonial Experience," in which she examines the way the British setting of Rowling's series subtly marginalizes and disenfranchises certain characters and readers, potentially teaching this generation to be more conservative than it is usually imagined to be.

The essays of our third and final section, "Pedagogy," seek to understand the Harry Potter generation as college students: how can they and the students following them be more successfully taught, since we as instructors and professors know that their exposure to literacy frequently begins with Harry Potter? Amber B. Vayo argues in "Fandoms as Classrooms: Harry Potter Online Communities as Social Intellectual Spaces" that because the students in this generation are digital natives, fandom's social media spaces become "a place for analytic depth" where ardent members of the community are able to "help each other re-engage into the educational process" through the development of what Vayo calls "social intellectualism." In "Harry Potter and the Male Student Athlete," Julia D. Morris explains how Harry Potter can function as a gateway to achieving literacy within a typically uninterested student demographic. In the context of teaching Harry Potter as literature, Christina A. Valeo's essay, "Lumens and Literature: Teaching Harry Potter in the College English Classroom," argues that the series' immense popularity means that while only some of her students arrive in the course already "experts" on the series, all of them are inherently interested in the basis of the phenomenon, which motivates them to gain similar expertise on the literary, social, and historical aspects of the novels. We conclude with "'Harry Potter changed my life': Students and Educators Reflect on the Harry Potter Generation," by Lauren Hammond and Linda Pershing, along with Harry Potter generation members Allison Bianco, Rachael Dohrn, Cathy Gutierrez, Shelby M.M. Kacirek, Harmony Owen, Angelo John Reyes, and Erin L. Southam. Here, Hammond and Pershing present members of the Harry Potter generation speaking in their own words about what the series has meant to them, how they experience a world where a series of books about a boy wizard and his friends have created spaces where heritage site and amusement park, fandom and social activism, literary and children's fiction all may meet and easily combine.

Our contributors frequently disagree with each other about the particulars of their topics: the worth of fandom, the series' treatment of time, and whether or not a future in the hands of this generation will be progressive, among other issues. However, we all agree that this series has shaped the generation that grew up with it, in ways that are still reverberating outwards as the Harry Potter generation takes its place as the world's adults.

NOTE

1. Within the collection, Rowling's novels will be parenthetically referred to as follows: *Harry Potter and the Sorcerer's Stone* as *SS*; *Harry Potter and the Philosopher's Stone* as *PS*; *Chamber of Secrets* as *CoS*; *Prisoner of Azkaban* as *PoA*; *Goblet of Fire* as *GoF*; *Order of the Phoenix* as *OotP*; *Half Blood Prince* as *HBP*; and *Deathly Hallows* as *DH*.

Prologue

Reading Harry Potter
in Context

EMILY LAUER *and* BALAKA BASU

J.K. Rowling's Harry Potter series, groundbreaking in a number of ways, is notable for the way it fits into a number of existing literary traditions. The debt that she owes to the forms and genres that inspired her world-changing work: the fairy tale, the school story, the portal fantasy, children's nonsense prose, the nineteenth century novel, and the golden age mystery; is worthy of extensive analysis. Living in the age of remix and sampling, Rowling recombines these generic forms to make something extraordinary, a narrative that is at once familiar and new. Her series can be read as the culmination of one era of writing bleeding into the next and in fact, the Harry Potter series now often serves as the template for the newly independent reader's introduction and journey through a variety of genres that ought to be understood in order to fully grasp what led to the creation of the Harry Potter phenomenon. In this essay we discuss the tradition of British children's literature as a context and foundation for Rowling's success, addressing how the Harry Potter generation grew up in a world saturated with the series and considering how these stories have shaped and are continuing to shape this generation's interactions with each other and with the world.

Harry and Alice: Selling Stories to Children and Adults

Not since *Alice's Adventures in Wonderland* has there been a narrative that has so clearly shaped both the adult perception of childhood as well as the child's lived experience. Harry's meteoric rise to fame has much in common with the surprising, genre-changing popularity of Lewis Carroll's Alice books, over a century before. *Alice's Adventures in Wonderland* was first printed in 1865 and officially published in 1866 by an Oxford don, Charles Lutwidge Dodgson, writing under the pseudonym Lewis Carroll. The small children's book had 42 illustrations by Sir John Tenniel, a preeminent illustrator of the day, which probably helped the book garner critical attention. It was lauded and loved by many, and along with its sequel in 1871, *Through the Looking Glass and what Alice Found There*, it has been credited with establishing children's literature as it exists today. Each of these books tell the story of Alice, a young girl who alone journeys to a fantasy landscape where it seems neither the laws of physics nor the laws of polite society are to be obeyed. In both Wonderland and Looking-Glass Land, she encounters a number of strange people and creatures, and then wakes up, revealing both lands to be manifestations of her own slumbering mind.

Both Carroll and Rowling introduce the reader to engaging child protagonists and use free indirect discourse to keep the reader in Harry's or Alice's perspective while also providing an authoritative narrative voice. Of course, to be successful, each author had to ensure that readers would want to stay in the mind of the protagonist as they explored the fantastic lands on offer. For Carroll, it was innovative to have Alice be so normal. Neither a purely angelic child who is rewarded for goodness nor a wicked child who is punished for badness, Alice is instead psychologically realistic. She is by turns frustrated, kind, practical and curious, as the events of her adventures warrant. Rowling, too, presents a psychologically realistic child protagonist; despite the abuse and neglect Harry has suffered, he—like Alice—is neither wholly good nor bad. As we read, we are able to identify with Alice's imperfections as she discovers her Wonderland; we want to follow along with Harry as he discovers his wizarding world.

The discoveries they make differ: Alice's stories are those of a wanderer in her own mind, while Harry is on a more linear hero's journey, at the end of which he will represent good as he engages in a showdown against evil. Despite these differences, Alice and Harry each bring something necessary to the field of children's literature and enjoy similar cultural permeation in a variety of ways both official and unofficial, for adults and for children, in versioning and in merchandizing. Both Harry's stories and Alice's exist in multiple versions. For both Carroll and Rowling, different editions abound: in translation into other languages, with academic or childlike covers and illustrations, and parodies proliferate. Carroll and Tenniel together created a *Nursery Alice* book for even younger children, and famous, popular movies of both Alice's and Harry's series brought Carroll's and Rowling's inventions to even wider audiences. In fact, both have acquired an additional level of institutionalized authority through the movies and associated rigorously policed branding made by Walt Disney and Warner Brothers, respectively.

In addition to adaptations and versions, for both Harry's and Alice's worlds there are pirated and fan-produced wares as well as sanctioned, authorized products. A Victorian child fan of Alice might have delighted in the Cheshire cat stamp case designed by Carroll himself, even as an academic adult fan of the same book was publishing a mathematical treatise on the logic puzzles therein. Meanwhile a child fan of Harry Potter might save up to purchase an official replica of the Timeturner necklace worn by Hermione in the film version of *Harry Potter and the Prisoner of Azkaban*, while an adult fan of the same text might commission custom unofficial Slytherin lingerie from an Etsy seller. Fan interaction with the series can combine commodification—the urge to collect and consume being ever present—with an equal creative impulse that must exist, especially in order to satisfy needs for non-official merchandising. While it is true that an Etsy seller or fan fiction author is creating a "product," it is generally also true that the creation of that product is a labor of love—one that extends the story world even further into our own.

The breadth of merchandising for Carroll's and Rowling's worlds is possible in part because the books did not stay mere "children's properties." Rowling, for instance, managed to reignite adult interest in "crossover" novels—children's novels that garner an adult following (Falconer 2008). The first "adult" edition of *Philosopher's Stone*, with a more conventionally grown-up cover, was issued a year after the children's version, and by the time *Half Blood Prince* was released in 2005, adult interest in the series allowed publishers to release the "adult" edition concurrently. Meanwhile, "adult" sales of the last book of the series were equaling if not overtaking the children's edition. The *Telegraph*, for instance, reported that

> Orders from the public for the adult edition of *Harry Potter and the Deathly Hallows* [...] are outstripping demand for the children's edition in many of its stores, the company [Waterstones] said. [...] The editions, published simultaneously, only differ in their covers but pre-orders for the adult version already stand at 45 per cent of the total and are rising faster than demand for the children's version. [...] Wayne Winston, Waterstone's children's manager, said yesterday: "We estimate that 60 per cent of the Harry Potter fan base is now made up of teenagers and young adults, which makes the continuing rise in demand for the adult cover perhaps inevitable" [Reynolds 2007].

While Alice and Harry both find steadfast fans in both adults and children, this manifests differently for the two series. The nonlinear structure of Alice's journey has allowed many different interpretations over the years: as an academic exercise in logic, as a goth rejection of a mad world, as an allegory for puberty, politics, or drug use, as well as a story of a little girl exploring. Notably, Alice's child readers and adult readers are often reading at cross purposes from one another, and might not come into contact with each other. Conversely, Harry's adult and child readers are often reading the books in the same way as each other and interacting with one another in the same fandoms and forums. In Victorian England, adult readers, while glorifying childhood, were also condescending about the innocence of a child reader who would not "get" the academic and political allusions in the layered text.

Through the Wardrobe at Platform 9¾: Escape and Refuge in the Postmodern Era

Along with Lewis Carroll's novels, Rowling's series—published during a time of global upheaval at the turn of the last century—likewise parallels the ways in which the children's fantasist, C.S. Lewis addresses the profound world-changing effects of global war in the mid-twentieth century in his Chronicles of Narnia. While many authors of the time turned to nihilism and despair in the postwar era of the 1950s and 1960s, Lewis took refuge in the mixture of Christian allegory, fairy tale, and myth, a combination that had a profound influence on the children's literature that was to follow. Like Rowling, Lewis allows magic to travel and leak between our reality and the fantastic world he creates. Lewis writes, in his dedication to the first book in the Narnia series, *The Lion, the Witch, and the Wardrobe*: "I wrote this story for you [his goddaughter, Lucy], but when I began it I had not realized that girls grow quicker than books. As a result you are already too old for fairy tales, and by the time it is printed and bound you will be older still. But some day you will be old enough to start reading fairy tales again" (Lewis 2000, front matter). Lewis suggests that one can only appreciate fantasy when one is either very young or very mature. While it is clearly documented that Lewis's contemporary J.R.R. Tolkien thoroughly disapproved of his Narnian remix of Christian iconography, classical mythology, and talking animals, the postmodern era has come to embrace bricolage as a form, as well as the way it incorporates geopolitical issues that affect both adults and children.

In the hungry world of post World War II Britain, sugar-rationed children longed for Turkish Delight and hobbit meals. Similarly, in our own era, the generation reaching adulthood now longs for tools to cope with their adult lives. And as C.S. Lewis commiserated with readers who wanted sweets, Rowling's creation offers an avenue through which therapists can reach their clients of this generation who are now reaching adulthood, who need hope for the future and the tools to manage and cope with their adult lives. For instance, Dr. Brooke Kramer, a psychotherapist and counseling center coordinator at a law school in Chicago, often uses Harry Potter therapeutically to connect with her young clients. Thanks to a number of factors, including the decrease in stigma related to seeking mental health treatment, the greater understanding of children's mental health, and the improved training available for their clinicians and teachers, early diagnoses are more common and the number of students seeking help is on the rise. Dr. Kramer finds that for the Harry Potter generation, the recognition of a shared fan identity is welcome and comforting. When she uses her own lived experience as a Harry Potter fan to model this identity for her patients, they are empowered, which "opens the door to a richer work" (Interview). Dr. Kramer offers her fan clients basic worksheets themed on Harry Potter, such as developing a "time turner" themed schedule or meditating on the form their protective Patronus charm would take. Beyond these invitations to apply the magical metaphors for problem-solving to their own lives, there is often also a deeper resonance with the series. Many of Dr. Kramer's college age patients, for instance, bring up the scene in *Harry Potter and the Prisoner of Azkaban* when Harry has used the time turner, and witnessed an event he does not interpret correctly. Later, waiting for a glimpse of his father, he has the profound realization that his father isn't coming. Rather, he has to save himself by conjuring his own Patronus charm. Dr. Kramer notes that clients of the Harry Potter generation are enabled to recognize this as happening in their own lives by seeing it metaphorically in Harry's. Like the folk and fairy tales of post-war British fantasists like C.S. Lewis and J.R.R. Tolkien, Harry Potter teaches us both that monsters are real and that we can vanquish them.

In Lewis's tradition of genre pastiche, Rowling merges genres together so successfully that readers are able to select whether they read each book in the series as a mystery, a school story, a sports story, a coming of age story, a coming out allegory or something else entirely. Those choices are not bound by the age of the reader. Adult fans of Harry Potter, unlike the Victorian adult readers of *Alice* and unlike Lewis himself, have come to recognize that there are many different ways to read and appreciate a given text, and find fellow fans based on shared interest and focus rather than on level of cultural knowledge.

Growing Up with Harry Potter

The Harry Potter series has thus created a world in which the boundaries between children and adults are not clearly defined in fan spaces. In some ways, this is a development modeled in the novels themselves: Harry and his friends begin by thinking of the people of their parents' generation as entirely other—bounded by professional barriers as with teachers and students, or by personal ones, where children never think of their parents as entities in and of themselves. As the books progress, however, and Harry matures, he learns to see Professor Lupin as "Remus"—and eventually even feels free to judge his love-life; he also learns to see his parents (literally, through occulumency) as "James" and "Lily" rather than as "Mum" and "Dad." This trajectory illuminates the ways Harry's character arc is like that of a bildungsroman even though he does not technically come of age before he joins the adult world. By picking sides, either enlisting in Dumbledore's Army or as Death-Eaters, the children of Hogwarts take on adult roles, while they are still technically children, as Julia D. Morris points out in the essay of this volume titled, *Harry Potter and the Male Student Athlete*. Meanwhile, adults in the series often behave in childish ways, translating arguments on the playground and Quidditch pitch into life-and-death struggles for power with troubling ease.

Harry's maturation over the course of seven books naturally invites readers of his age, who read the books as they were published, to see their own growth in terms of Harry's. We see the Harry Potter generation as a subset of Millennials, who face a challenging economy that often keeps young people from leaving home to start families of their own, and they may see their own second and third comings-of-age modeled within the text as well. Adult fans of the series who identified with some of the characters that Harry measures himself against (Severus Snape, Remus Lupin, and Sirius Black being some of the most common choices) were able to find resonance between their character arcs and the readers' own journeys of maturation, despite the fact that for these particular characters, the journey ends in death. Fans also found common ground with supporting characters, including Neville Longbottom and Luna Lovegood, as Dion McLeod and Elise Payne show in their essay, *Loony Lovegood and the Almost Chosen One: Harry Potter, Supporting Characters, and Fan Reception*. Many of the fan texts about all of these characters discard the endings Rowling has chosen for them, indicating that tertiary characters have been more important to some fans than to Rowling herself.

Immersive Fandom

Like C.S. Lewis's Chronicles of Narnia, the Harry Potter series is predicated on the reader's point of ingress into the text; thus, like Narnia, the wizarding world begs for immersion and participation. As fans of Narnia yearn to escape to it through their closets, cupboards, and wardrobes, so too, fans of Rowling's universe long to receive their own Hogwarts letter, offering them the opportunity to slip into the wizarding world. A group of fans at Brigham Young University, for instance, describe this phenomenon in a parody song they call "Firebolt," set to the tune of Katy Perry's "Firework." The lyrics of

"Firebolt" describe these fans' reactions to the end of the Harry Potter series, and show how their reading of the narrative was colored by their desire to receive Hogwarts letters of their own:

> Did you ever feel so disappointed when /
> You closed the book and realized that the story had to end /
> But maybe you were wrong and you are chosen too /
> So come and ride the floo [BYU Divine Comedy 2011].

There are two possible avenues for those who are disappointed that the story had to end: the sanctioned consumption of the official website Pottermore and the Wizarding World theme parks on one hand, and the unsanctioned/ unauthorized creation and consumption of self and fan-made texts on the other.

As the authorized, digital extension to the Harry Potter universe, Pottermore is meant to accompany the novels; the website offers a series of scenes, quizzes, and click-throughs, with an ever-increasing amount of extra information that J.K. Rowling didn't include within the seven novel series, but has authorized for inclusion on the site. Here, one can be sorted into a particular house, play games to gain house points, and learn extratextual trivia about the Potterverse. The growth of Rowling's writing in the Harry Potter universe is ongoing. In September of 2016, the Pottermore Presents series made its debut, selling e-books that packaged together previously published writing from the Pottermore archives as well as new short stories by Rowling included in two of the volumes, *Short Stories from Hogwarts of Power, Politics and Pesky Poltergeists* and *Short Stories from Hogwarts of Heroism, Hardship and Dangerous Hobbies*, extending the reach of Pottermore even farther than its domain name. Simultaneously, there is the literal reality of the Wizarding World theme park(s) and what Dennis J. Siler calls in his essay the potentially numinous experiences that they can provide for the right kind of visitor. Hugely popular with fans, the theme park provides guided, limited choice, and monetized ways of interacting with the "property" of Harry Potter as a consumer—for example shopping at Diagon Alley, or being selected by a wand at Ollivander's shop. Because commerce is so central to the books themselves, merchandizing for the Harry Potter series can be real world versions of merchandise as it exists in the Wizarding World and immersion in real world commerce can help a fan become immersed in the story world as well.

Due to the ubiquity of the series, it's possible for tourist-readers to visit not only the theme parks, but also Platform 9¾ at King's Cross station in London physically as well as visit what Emily Lohorn calls the "magical heritage sites" in their imagination. Because of the limitless possibilities for such imaginings, fan immersion into the Potterverse often happens through less official channels than those produced and guarded by publishers, studios, and producers. Unsanctioned fan labor and production often include cosplay (short for "costume play" or fans dressing as characters), vids (fan-edited videos), fic (fan fiction), and fan art, all of which illustrate characters and situations both in and out of the text. Digitally disseminated on the internet, fan work provides a space where readers can persist in their efforts to more fully realize Rowling's world. Her less-than-satisfactory elements actually turn out to offer exciting opportunities for fan authors, who can interject their own perspectives to add nuance to the narrative.

While fan-posed questions regarding the series are often asked and answered by fan fiction, "official" new material is often viewed skeptically by fans. Intriguingly, however, occasionally *unofficial* additions to the text find themselves reflected within Rowling's new material. For example, readers who found the all-white main cast of the official illustrations and films lacking in diversity, can choose to imagine Hermione—described in text as having "brown eyes and frizzy hair" (https://twitter.com/jk_rowling/status/6788880 94339366914)—as a black person. In the new play, *Harry Potter and the Cursed Child*, adult Hermione is depicted by a black actress. Rowling accepted this casting graciously, pointing out that Hermione's skin color had never been explicitly described as white. This trajectory of canon creation—where fans might specify changes and authors might accept them—suggests that the Harry Potter generation has re-envisioned the way in which writers and readers create narratives together: fans can become so immersed within the text that they are actually collaborating on its creation.

Politics and the Potterverse

Much as Charles Dickens wrote to inspire empathy regarding adverse social conditions, the Harry Potter series grapples with civil and political issues in an effort to offer children moral guidance. Rowling often asserts that her dominant message in the series is to tolerate difference. Thus the participatory possibilities of Harry Potter fandom have changed not just how a generation expects to be immersed in fiction, but also how it writes and shops, and also, perhaps, how it votes. Andrew Gierzynski, a political scientist at the University of Vermont, studied the differences in political leanings between Millennial Harry Potter fans and nonfans. He and his co-author, Kathryn Eddy, published their findings in 2013 in *Harry Potter and the Millennials: Research Methods and the Politics of the Muggle Generation* (Johns Hopkins Press). Proposing that "the Harry Potter Phenomenon happened in a way that made it an important agent of political socialization for Millennials" (Gierzynski and Eddy 39), he discovered that Harry Potter fans were likely to "be less cynical and more skeptical than nonfans; they are also more likely to participate in politics and were more likely to vote for Obama in 2008" (71) which may have been the first presidential election many of them voted in at all. While his work focused on the attitudes of self-professed fans, he does note that "cultivation theory hypothesizes that repeated exposure to a media source leads audiences to internalize the perspectives of that source and to see the world as similar to the world portrayed in that media" which indicates that fans of the series, through repeated and extensive exposure to the Harry Potter world, have probably internalized it enough to affect their interaction with the real world and thus, their peers (29). However, as Gierzynski and Eddy make clear in their Appendix A, all their study participants were American college students, around fifty percent of whom were enrolled at the University of Vermont, and eighty-four percent of whom were white (84). Therefore, it would be problematic to assume the study results from these white college students in the liberal U.S. Northeast are representative of Millennials overall, or even the subset of Millennials we are calling the Harry Potter generation.

However, other studies on the same topic have yielded similar results in different populations. A later European study published in the *Journal of Applied Social Psychology*, "The Greatest Magic of Harry Potter: Reducing Prejudice" (July 2014), bears out Gierzynski's findings, suggesting that children and university students exposed to relevant passages in the Harry Potter books are less likely to be prejudiced against stigmatized groups. Through identification with Harry, Hermione, and Ron—all of whom are marginalized for various reasons—readers of the series are being encouraged to learn and practice empathy for others who may be likewise marginalized in their own world.

Studies of the political impact of Harry Potter suggest that for many readers, Rowling's series is not just the story of a boy wizard learning to use his powers so that he may defeat the forces of evil. Instead, it is a source of "life lessons" that may be applied to every facet of their lives. Gierzynski and Eddy even suggest that fantasy novels like the Harry Potter series may in fact be more efficacious than more overtly political texts in altering political attitudes, saying:

> the acquisition of the political perspectives that exist in the series was a by-product of reading it for fun. Because this is a case of passive learning, the Harry Potter series is likely to have had an effect on fans even if those fans already had the political values and information to counter-argue the political lessons it contained [29].

Aficionados of the series appreciate that it advocates self-reliance, physical and moral bravery—and it lauds characters for breaking rules when morally obligated to do so. Furthermore, high value is placed upon the social unit of the nuclear family, with maternal bonds portrayed as the most powerful force.

There are distinct political implications to all of these "lessons," however, not all of which are progressive. As Henry Jenkins notes in his 2012 article "Cultural Acupuncture," "like many other popular texts, the Harry Potter franchise is a contradictory blend of progressive impulses and retrograde elements." In fact, the series' portrayals of race, gender and class all tend to be fairly conservative. The Weasley family, clearly invoked as an ideal wizarding family, illustrates many of the conservative assumptions of the series. For instance, the Wizarding world is a fairly gender normative one, which despite its modern, co-educational setting, seeks to uphold the most traditional principles of the British public school. As Balaka Basu mentions in her essay *Magic from the Margins: Harry Potter and the Postcolonial Experience*, this progressive effect of growing up in the Harry Potter generation may be less widespread than previously assumed.

There are far more important male characters than there are female, for one thing, and we know far less about the girls than we do the boys. Harry's orphanhood and longing for his dead parents inflects the whole series, and as a result, we hear all sorts of things about his father James's school life and personality. Although his mother, Lily, has given her life to save him—a sacrifice that is an enormously important plot point—we hear only one specific fact regarding her character (i.e., that she was exceptionally good at Charms) that is independent of her relationships with the people in her life, such as Severus Snape, Remus Lupin, James Potter, her sister, Petunia, and of course, Harry himself. She is defined almost entirely in terms of relationships with men, to whom she appears adjunct. Her other explored relationship is a fraught one with her biological sister, situating her importance in family, rather than in the realm of female friendships, supporting a distinctly Victorian correlation between family, especially motherhood, and moral alignment in the series.

Ruth Jenkins explains how for the Victorians, "in the role of mothers, women became the cultural mediators for men's salvation [… and] so, too, the patriarchally informed role of motherhood, with its appropriated, sacred association, invests women with a meaningless power" (Jenkins 1995, 22). While there are stay-at-home mothers, for instance Mrs. Weasley, there are no stay-at-home fathers. Of the "good" significant female characters in the Potterverse, namely: Lily Potter, Hermione Granger, Molly Weasley, Minerva McGonagall, Ginny Weasley, Nymphadora Tonks and Luna Lovegood—all but one are, or end up as, mothers. Female characters who begin as antagonistic and are redeemed to some degree, however slight, (i.e., Narcissa Malfoy and Petunia Dursley)—are also mothers. Significant evil or primarily antagonistic women—Dolores Umbridge, Rita Skeeter, Bellatrix Lestrange, Alecto

Carrow—are not discussed in terms of motherhood and readers are led to assume they are not mothers. There seems to be a direct link between motherhood and one's ability to do the right thing since childless women on their own are often evil. When they're not evil, they are frequently impotent. Professor McGonagall, for instance, though remarkably efficient in many ways, is unable to lead the professors of Hogwarts alone as we see Dumbledore do, and must be joined by Kingsley Shacklebolt to lead the defense of the school during the Battle of Hogwarts in *Harry Potter and the Deathly Hallows*. Madame Bones, the head of Magical Law Enforcement, is defeated and killed by Voldemort off page. In contrast, there is a vast panoply of male characters that significantly outnumber the female characters and, as well, provide no such template for determining moral alignment with their parenthood.

The retrograde gender politics are joined by retrograde class politics. In terms of class, as Bethany Barratt points out in her 2012 book *The Politics of Harry Potter*, a common panacea is applied to the Weasley family's poverty in the series. She writes that the Weasleys are "more than compensated for their relative poverty by love, laughter, and loyalty" (151), Rowling also makes clear that the Weasleys have made a conscious choice in this matter; as Barratt points out, "Arthur has foregone chances for advancement because he will not compromise his principles" (151). Painting poverty as ennobling, and in fact, a principled choice, is a fine Dickensian tradition, but also serves to reinforce the status quo.

Overall, while the series does insist on tolerance of many kinds, it is essentially conservative not only for its traditional portrayals of gender, class and, as we will shortly address, race, but also in that it elides defeating evil with the preservation of the existing political system. Throughout the series, Voldemort is seen as a threat to the existing order, and in vanquishing him, Harry is the savior of that order. In fact, as Rowling has said in interviews and made explicit in the 2016 play, *Harry Potter and the Cursed Child*, our hero even goes on to work for the ministry in his adulthood, upholding the order he has restored. Even the allegorical racial tolerance, which Rowling so often mentions in interviews as her main moral for the series (Barrett 4), is itself sometimes troubling. Wizards who are "pro-muggle" are generally paternalistic to the point of fetishizing, like Arthur Weasley and his collection of plugs, and many of the non-human races in the series are seen as either potentially dangerous (goblins, veela, werewolves) or laughable (gnomes, house elves).

Connectedly, despite the theoretically diverse student body, Rowling's novels are so steeped in Anglocentrism that they appear culturally homogenous and monolithic. As Basu discusses in her essay, *Magic from the Margins: Harry Potter and the Postcolonial Experience*, the Harry Potter series markets a particular version of Anglophilia to the world: it communicates at once a reassuring sense of imperialist nostalgia and a distrust of the "foreign" other. The international wizarding schools introduced in the middle of the series, Beauxbatons and Durmstrang, are filled with stereotypical versions of the French and the Slavic or Eastern European. Such Anglocentrism is not always embraced with ease by global readers: in 2012, the Chinese President, Hu Jintao accused Harry Potter of being part of the Western arsenal that threatens to dismantle Chinese culture. An official condemnation like this is in tension with the economic fact that nevertheless, Harry Potter has been translated into 67 languages besides English; it is one of the most translated texts of all time. Clearly, while official governmental responses and postcolonial criticism of the series' themes may be negative, the books have still been read and received positively throughout the world.

Readers and Writers

While the Harry Potter series is largely set at a school, the novels suggest that school is at its best a place of social development, where academics are less important than the inculcation of virtue and the playing of sport. And while Hermione famously spends a lot of her time and attention reading books, there is still an implied contradiction in any reader identifying with the child characters in the series: the Harry Potter series, which has clearly contributed to the current "golden age" of children's literature, and which has fostered a love of novels in so many children, does not itself model fiction reading within the text. In this essay we have addressed various ways that the Harry Potter generation has been able to see Rowling's series as a model, but this is not one of them.

Even though it doesn't model reading fiction, however, the series can still be utilized as a model *of* fiction. Susanne Keen, a professor of English at Washington and Lee University, who has been teaching Victorian literature for many years, suggests that her freshman students, who had in the past been resistant to long, intricate novels like those by Dickens, were now primed to enjoy them: "Reading Harry Potter," Keen argues, "is like taking a crash course in reading Dickens because it's got the humor, it's got the caricatured names, it's got the multi-plots, it's got the really long stories that you read for hours and hours and hours, and you enjoy the fact that they're long" (qtd in Hanna 2012). Similarly, Christina A. Valeo argues in her essay of this volume, *Lumens and Literature: Teaching Harry Potter in the College English Classroom*, that the series is a good pedagogical choice for introducing literary ideas at the college level.

Rowling's series functions as this kind of gateway to an appreciation and enjoyment of other literature only when it is read and internalized to the point where students perceive reading the Harry Potter novels and other books like them as natural, necessary activities. Thus, while the Harry Potter series may prepare readers to enjoy other long elaborate texts in the future, it has also necessarily created a world in which reading books *like* Harry Potter must figure into a realistic portrayal of the world we actually live in—even if it doesn't figure into the books that Harry and his friends read.

The Harry Potter Phenomenon Changes Realism

It is indicative of how the Harry Potter series has changed our cultural landscape that there are not just more middle grade book series set at magic schools being published now, but also that there are books like *Fangirl* (2013), and comic book series like *The Unwritten* (2009–2015), which are based on the Harry Potter phenomenon even more than on the content of the series itself. If the Harry Potter series indeed "saved reading," it has created a cultural climate where avid readers are acceptable, making stories about readers acceptable, too, making these readers welcomed into the pages of the text. Thus, we see novels and comics where metafiction—fiction about fiction itself—has become increasingly popular, and notably, in both *The Unwritten* and *Fangirl*, the effect of fiction on the lives of the "real" people in the stories is not just part of the backdrop of world creation, but rather is serious and significant.

The Unwritten, written by Mike Carey and illustrated by Peter Gross, was published by DC Comics' Vertigo imprint, which has historically tended toward adult and experimental titles. The series began in 2009 and was collected into ten graphic novel volumes. In it, a young man named Tom Taylor finds his life beginning to mirror that of his namesake from a series of children's fantasy novels written by his father. In the comic, adult Tom is doing a celebrity appearance circuit, trading on the popularity of his father's Tommy Taylor books. In the novels, Tommy, with his pals Peter and Sue, battle the evil Count Ambrosio. In the comic, as Tom begins to suffer a variety of strange mishaps, he uncovers a metaphysical conspiracy that uses the nature of story to shape reality. In so doing, he joins forces with adult versions of Tommy's two best friends (one boy and one girl) from his father's novels. While the Tommy Taylor books are clearly a reference to the Harry Potter books, the audience for *The Unwritten* is likely to include not children who enjoy Harry Potter and want more of it, but rather adults who are interested in the philosophical ramifications of the Harry Potter phenomenon itself.

Likewise, the 2013 young adult novel *Fangirl* by Rainbow Rowell is not simply like the Harry Potter series, but rather seems to have been written for a readership who welcome a realistic world with characters shaped by something like Harry Potter. In *Fangirl*, the protagonist Cath is starting college with a long list of family problems dogging her. She has a built-in escape from personal issues, however, because she is internet-famous: she writes popular fan fiction based on the Simon Snow books. Simon Snow, like Tommy Taylor, is a clear stand-in for Harry Potter, and Cath's fandom is part of her character. Both *The Unwritten* and *Fangirl* incorporate passages from their fictional Harry Potter series surrogates, with the effect that these fragments seem interwoven with the "real" world of the dominant narrative. Rather than embedding complete stories, the scenes we see of Tommy Taylor or Simon Snow hint at the larger stories that are currently shaping Carey's and Rowell's protagonists. The interplay between scenes presents a simulacrum of intertextuality, not actually created by different authors. By simulating "excerpts" from in-universe fantasy novels, *The Unwritten* and *Fangirl* indicate that their intended readership expects the world to interweave popular fantasy stories with their own lived narratives. Rowell has since published *Carry On* in 2015, a full-length Simon Snow novel.

These examples of post–Potter texts indicate a lot about the Harry Potter generation that embraced them. If we go back to the days of Alice and Narnia, we see that each presents a different kind of invented world. In the Alice books, we find dreamscapes that exist in the protagonist's own mind. With the adventures of Peter, Susan, Edmund, and Lucy in The Chronicles of Narnia, we are presented with portals to a fantasy world that purports to be *more* real than our own. With Harry Potter, however, reality and fantasy are brought together. The series encourages us to feel that a vibrant community is waiting in our own world to be discovered, embraced, enhanced, and extended. For the Harry Potter generation, the books become a moral, civic, and aesthetic guide for interactions in classrooms and political campaigns, on social media and public transportation. Comfortable with ever-expanding fictional worlds and with seeing many sources of valid creation in a shared universe, the Harry Potter generation recognizes its right alongside Rowling and other figures of authority to extend these stories both textually and in their own lives.

REFERENCES

Barratt, Bethany. 2012. *The Politics of Harry Potter*. New York: Palgrave Macmillan.
BYU Divine Comedy. 2011. "Firebolt." *YouTube.com*. Accessed March 1 2017. http://www.youtube.com/watch?v=ySN8Q4U6wys.
Carey, Mike. 2009–2015. *The Unwritten*. New York: Vertigo.
Falconer, Rachel. 2008. *The Crossover Novel: Contemporary Children's Fiction and Its Adult Readership*. London: Routledge.
Gierzynski, Andrew, and Kathryn Eddy. 2013. *Harry Potter and the Millennials: Research Methods and the Politics of the Muggle Generation*. Baltimore: Johns Hopkins University Press.
Hanna, Jeff. 2012. "W&L English Professor Thanks Rowling for Students' Appreciation of Dickens." The Columns. February 1. https://columns.wlu.edu/wl-english-professor-thanks-rowling-for-students-appreciation-of-dickens/+&cd=1&hl=en&ct=clnk&gl=us.

Jenkins, Henry. 2012. "'Cultural Acupuncture': Fan Activism and the Harry Potter Alliance." *Transformative Works & Cultures* 10. http://journal.transformativeworks.org/index.php/twc/article/view/305/259.

Jenkins, Ruth. 1995. *Reclaiming Myths of Power: Women Writers and the Victorian Spiritual Crisis.* Lewisburg, PA: Bucknell University Press.

Kramer, Brooke. 2017. Interview with authors. Email and phone. November 17–28.

Lebrecht, Norman. 2011. "How Harry Saved Reading." *Wall Street Journal.* July 9. Accessed March 1, 2017. https://www.wsj.com/articles/SB10001424052702304584004576419742308635716.

Lewis, C.S. 2000. *The Lion, the Witch and the Wardrobe.* New York: HarperCollins.

_____. 2002. *The Last Battle.* New York: HarperCollins.

Reynolds, Nigel. 2007. "Adult Fans Taking Over Harry Potter." *The Telegraph.* 22 June. http://www.telegraph.co.uk/culture/books/3666031/Adult-fans-taking-over-Harry-Potter.html.

Rowell, Rainbow. 2013. *Fangirl.* New York: St. Martin's Press.

Rowling, J.K. 2015. Tweet. 5:41 AM, 21 Dec 2015 https://twitter.com/jk_rowling/status/678888094339366914.

Rowling, J.K., Jack Thorne and John Tiffany. 2016. *Harry Potter and the Cursed Child.* New York: Scholastic.

Vezzali, L., Stathi, S., Giovannini, D., Capozza, D. and Trifiletti, E. 2015. "The Greatest Magic of Harry Potter: Reducing Prejudice." *Journal of Applied Social Psychology* 45: 105–121.

Yours to Keep

Owning Harry and Hermione

ISAAC VAYO

As two of the central characters around which the universe of Harry Potter pivots, Harry Potter, played by Daniel Radcliffe, and Hermione Granger, played by Emma Watson, garner the most attention from fans both young and old (but especially young), who in turn develop deep attachments to those characters and the actors who become inexorably associated with them.[1] Within that universe, dual timelines emerge: those of the fans, who may linger there long beyond the debut of the final film of the series, and those of Radcliffe and Watson who, though to some degree always connected with those roles, must necessarily move onto other projects as a means of growing as actors and furthering their careers. When these two timelines collide, tensions emerge, with fans desiring that Radcliffe and Watson remain Potter and Granger forever, while the actors hope that those same fans will follow them into their new roles, or that others will take their place.

When examining the nature of that tension more closely, a three stage progression is evident, where Radcliffe and Watson exist solely as part of the Potter universe (up to at least the later films in the series, if not the conclusion of the series), where they begin to bridle against the confines of the series itself (during the later films), and where they go next, the terrifying and exhilarating "after" that appears once the series has come to a close. For Radcliffe and Watson, these experiences are somewhat unique, and each confronts them in a different manner, Radcliffe enduring a purgatory of drink before attempting a physical transformation of sorts, and Watson carefully managing her private life and public image while pursuing more broad-reaching and impactful work with the UN. Perhaps the ideal site for locating these stages in process is press interviews with Radcliffe and Watson during and after the Potter years, where their respective efforts at self-creation, self-definition, and self-realization are on display in all their relative messiness. Though both Radcliffe and Watson make strides in the direction of post–Potter careers, their efforts are imperfect and incomplete to date, making them fitting icons for a generation plagued by the same issues of self-creation, self-definition, and the process of moving beyond one's origins, however comfortable and rewarding.

To the extent that their respective time in the Harry Potter universe proves rewarding, it is in the later, darker films of the series that Radcliffe and Watson begin to come into their own, hitting their stride as actors and developing the tools they will call upon to a greater degree in the post–Potter landscape. For Radcliffe, this process begins as early as the third book and film, *Harry Potter and the Prisoner of Azkaban*, which Radcliffe posits as being "focused a lot more on the emotional contents. It's a more emotionally intense journey in terms of Harry's character" (quoted in Morreale 2016). This emotional focus at once allows Radcliffe a deeper engagement with the role beyond the younger audience orientation of the first two films, one that challenges him as a budding actor, while also preparing him for the turmoil that will greet him upon his move away from the Potter universe. Though this move is in the back of Radcliffe's mind throughout, he also understands the unique impact of his role as Harry, saying that "[t]he most wonderful thing I hear is people coming up and saying 'Thank you for my childhood'" (quoted in Cavendish 2013), though the childhood that he grants others may in some ways come at the expense of his own. Similarly, Radcliffe understands his Potter experience as rewarding not only for the fans who take inspiration from him, but also as a gateway to what follows, noting that "every opportunity I will get for the rest of my life, I would not have got if it wasn't for *Harry Potter*. And it would be the height of ingratitude if I was ever anything but proud to be associated with these films" (quoted in Weintraub 2010). It is difficult not to find a hint of forced manners in Radcliffe's phrasing here, a sense of perfunctory gratefulness rather than the genuine sort, but potential cynicism aside, he does evince a sense of Potter's importance, if only as a starting point. In Radcliffe's case, though he does seem to plot an exit strategy from relatively early in the Potter series, that foresight does not prevent him from smelling the roses along the way, a quality shared for the most part with Watson, though her experience ends up being somewhat more limiting.

For Watson, the more sinister turn in the mid-to-late Potter films provides a similar opportunity for development and post–Potter preparation, though one colored by gender politics in her case. Dating back to her reflections on the second Potter film, *Harry Potter and the Chamber of Secrets*, Watson suggests that "all of the characters have matured" (quoted in "Emma Watson" 2016), a maturity mirrored in that developing amongst the actors more generally, and in Watson more specifically. The more serious turn in the films allows Watson to act likewise, moving beyond the child actor framing and dropping the limiting descriptor. This darkness deepens through the balance of the Potter series, and with it comes Watson's preparatory turn, as observed by Amanda Foreman in *Vogue*: "*The Deathly Hallows* parts one and two are the darkest of all the Potter movies, the innocence of the previous films replaced by a grim meditation on the nature of terror. The more complex material in the finale allowed Emma to stretch her wings" (Foreman 2011). While Foreman overstates the potentially saccharine content of the earlier films (darkness appears long before the two-part finale), her avian metaphor is apt, Watson in this case rising phoenix-like from the fiery ashes of the collapsing Pottersphere and rebirthing herself as an actor sans modifier. That said, Watson's position as a girl, then woman, complicates her transition, a complexity borne out in the series itself, where Watson concludes that "Hermione's always there for Harry" (quoted in Sims 2014), and though "it was Hermione's journey as much as Harry's at the end … her sacrifice was massive, completely" (quoted in Sims 2014). As per persistent gender stereotypes, Watson is paradoxically lesser, supporting Harry and making a grand sacrifice, while also having more expected of her, being given a much shorter leash than the one given Radcliffe as he sorts out his early career somewhat imperfectly.

This shorter leash manifests itself for Watson in the archetypal smart girl role of Hermione, a role that is as much opportunity as trap, albeit a less painful trap than others in which she may have found herself. Will Self neatly encapsulates the nature of this trap in *The New York Times Magazine*: "Watson will always be, for me, a nice middle-class English girl pretending to be another nice middle-class English girl who's lucky enough to have magical powers for which she's extremely grateful" (Self 2012). Self is not alone in this appraisal, and one may easily imagine large swaths of the Potter audience thinking likewise: Watson is forever unassuming, a bit awkward, and gushingly happy for what providence has bestowed upon her, without a hint of a more unseemly forceful presence and sense of having earned what has come to her. So classified, Watson may easily be placed in the Anne Hathaway box, typecast as a generally harmless but not particularly gifted actor whom people think little of when they think about her at all, that little being primarily reflection on earlier roles that bear out comforting gender stereotypes (*The Princess Diaries* for Hathaway). Any moves meant to push the boundaries of that classification are met with mild opprobrium at best, and mean-spirited scoffing at worst. Still, Watson finds a silver lining in Hermione, describing her as "a role model.… I think she rocks. I don't think there's anyone on screen who can compete with her really, female action-hero-wise" (quoted in IGN AU 2016). Whether this is indeed true, that Hermione is the thinking woman's action hero, or whether the statement is instead a reflection of the relative paucity of strong female roles in film, Watson does take away positives from the Potter trap in much the same manner as Radcliffe, though in her case less as a door opener for other roles for herself than as a broadening of roles for female actors more generally. Both Radcliffe and Watson are able to take enlightened perspectives on their respective Potter experiences, though that does not mean that either wishes to tarry in that universe unduly long, and the process of loosing those particular shackles is a vexing one for both.

Radcliffe's efforts to free himself from the world of wizards take on a particularly physical bent, a movement from claustrophobic comfort to a discomfort with his own body and its associations with Harry, choosing to exorcise that association via drink. As is true earlier in his experience, Radcliffe is careful to give credit where credit is due, asserting that "[y]ou have to embrace the fact that you were involved in this incredibly cool thing … and though you might not always be happy with the work you did on it, the opportunity it has given you to forge a career for yourself is amazing" (quoted in Hattenstone 2013). Digs at his own performance aside, Radcliffe is at once grateful for and grated upon by the Potter world, ready to try his hand at something, anything, else. This urge is apparent even during the series itself, and Radcliffe is given pause by the thought of even participating in the full run: "I thought, if I do all of them, will I be able to move on to other stuff or should I start doing other stuff now?" (quoted in Hattenstone 2013), lending further urgency to the prospect of moving on once the series is complete. However, Radcliffe is once more tactful in his treatment of his Potter legacy, "describ[ing] it as his comfort zone, a place where he evolved into who he is, where he learned to love working in film, for better or worse" (Dominus 2013). For Radcliffe, his work on Potter is not an altogether unpleasant experience, and indeed provides him with a starting point in the film industry, though the key phrase there is "starting point." Potter is the beginning, hopefully, of a more enduring career, though Radcliffe's first steps in that direction are shadowed by specters of Harry.

Perhaps due to his relatively short stature, Radcliffe finds it difficult to physically distance himself from his role as Harry, gaining geographical remove from those sets, but finding that the role lingers in his very body, provoking mistreatment of the same. An interviewer for *The Guardian*, Simon Hattenstone, outlines the conundrum neatly: "The funny thing is, apart from the fags and the facial hair, he doesn't really look any different from the speccy schoolboy wizard who made his screen debut in 2001" (Hattenstone 2013). It is as if Harry is still there, just a shave or a round of Chantix away, moored to Radcliffe's own physicality, an inhabitation inescapable in any form short of death. Radcliffe's attempted erasure through markers of masculinity, cavalier lung destruction and rugged stubble in this instance, finds a mate in his treatment of the name that haunts him so, a semantic move that fails to escape Hattenstone's notice: "'there's no master plan to distance myself from Potter with every role.' But it's telling that he uses just the surname, which has exactly that distancing effect" (Hattenstone 2013). Indeed, using the surname demonstrates Radcliffe's efforts to put away childish things, to firmly place Potter behind him, in his youth, in a space long passed and long outgrown in favor of more serious roles. Whether a master plan is evident or not is an open question; that Radcliffe is attempting to distance himself from Potter is beyond question. Susan Dominus observes that this distancing manifests itself in reckless alcohol abuse, "every-night drinking, heavy drinking, drinking to the point of making a scene and then blacking out … [h]aving spent so many years protecting the image of Harry Potter, he felt unknown by the same public that considered him an intimate part of their childhoods" (Dominus 2013). Through alcohol, Radcliffe is able to create psychological distance between himself and Potter and, by acting in a very un–Harrylike fashion, cultural distance as well, though his body betrays him once more.

If physicality is something of a trap for Radcliffe, forever holding him back in school, perpetually matriculating at Hogwarts, it may eventually provide an avenue out of the selfsame trap, though not at this point in Radcliffe's struggle. For the moment, he is doomed merely to describe the contours of his confinement: "It's just my face. I have to accept the fact that my face is going to remind people of Harry because I played that character. If I try to avoid being expressive in that same way, all I'll do is stop being expressive, and I won't be any farther away from that character" (quoted in Dominus 2013). Radcliffe's face, his most legible form of identity, is not his own, belonging instead to Harry and merely on loan to Daniel, provoking an interesting rhetorical move on Radcliffe's part. Putting himself in the shoes of potential critics, Radcliffe anticipates them saying that "[h]e got there because he fell into it; he's not really an actor" (quoted in Dominus 2013), an accusation that both plays on Radcliffe's deepest doubts and into his hands. If he is indeed a non-actor, then his previous performances must have been execrable, meaning that the bar is set low for anything that follows, increasing the likelihood for a friendly reception of his later work. Radcliffe literalizes this move in his own words, thinking back on "moments I'm not proud of, mistakes other actors get to make in rehearsal rooms or at drama school, [that] are all on film for everyone to see" (quoted in Reed 2014). In the process, he rejects the physical limitations of Potter by designating Potter as a period of limitation, a moment when his acting was admittedly subpar, a moment from which he has moved on to bigger (somewhat unlikely given the breadth of Potter) and better (at least in terms of "serious" acting) things, an aspiration shared by Watson.

Watson finds herself at a similar fork in the road to that confronted by

Radcliffe, suffering from the same sense of unwelcome enclosure in the Potter world, though her efforts at self-(re)definition are more psychological than physical, taking the form of a tightly managed privacy. In conversation with *Rookie*'s Tavi Gevinson, Watson concedes that "there's a definition of me out there that feels kind of stuck in the moment when it was formed ... sometimes I've felt a little constrained by that idea of who I'm meant to be" (quoted in Gevinson 2013), pointing to the limitations imposed by a world viewing her solely through the lens of Hermione. As Potter ends, following the release of *Harry Potter and the Deathly Hallows Part 2*, Watson asserts that "I have to really enjoy the good things because it makes the bad things OK" (quoted in Foreman 2011), suggesting that all is not well in Potterville, that the bad things substantially outnumber the good, and that the former must be appreciated if she is to survive the gilded cage that Potter hath wrought. Watson is, at this point, coping, with mechanisms in place to make the balance of her tenure as Hermione bearable, but only with the prospect of other roles, other identities, in the near offing. Without that prospect, the bad might overwhelm the good, pushing Watson in the same self-destructive direction as Radcliffe. Her ambition at this point is modest, but paradoxically specific: to make audiences think "'[o]h, she is not just Hermione, she is an actress and she can go and do these other parts and roles'" (quoted in Self 2012), that she can do other things (a fairly general goal), but also that she can do *other* things, as in things other than Hermione, a specific denial of that role, though not wholesale rejection of all that it entails.

To say that Hermione is an outright curse for Watson is an overstatement, and there are some advantages to having that role on her resume, though it does have an insidious staying power that exceeds its welcome. In an article for *Vanity Fair*, Eduardo Munoz Alvarez posits that "[Watson's] role as Hermione Granger, the universally adored heroine of the Harry Potter series, gives her an automatic in with male and female millennials. This is a rare case where an actor being conflated with her role might be a good thing" (Alvarez 2014). There are worse fates than having people perceive you as a smart, resourceful, wildly competent woman, and having a built in audience might make future roles easier to both attain and retain. Still, Hermione as a role may not be all that it is cracked up to be, as evidenced by UN Secretary-General Ban Ki-Moon's comments following Watson's speech to the UN: "She's been waving a magic wand. I hope you use your magic wand to end violence against women!" (quoted in Alvarez 2014). In a venue not generally given to lighthearted talk, in the wake of a speech about a quite important issue (gender equality), Ki-Moon is moved not to address the gravity of Watson's message, but rather her past role as Hermione, diminishing the seriousness given to her post–Potter work. In another piece for *Elle UK*, interviewer Lorraine Candy expresses her concern that "I'd have to put the cloak of authenticity over Emma when I wrote up this cover interview. Before meeting her, it wouldn't have been unreasonable to assume this actress, famous for her role as witch Hermione, was simply lending her name to a project in the way many celebrities do" (Candy 2014). Though Candy may be gesturing toward the fairly regular superficial association of celebrity with cause, it is difficult to avoid reading a special incredulity in her words, as if a child actor could give any weight to a profound issue like gender inequality, as if Hermione, beloved though she may be, could do anything other than wave a wand, much as Ki-Moon suggests. It is better for Watson to hide under a cloak of invisibility, it seems, than to step outside the bounds set by Hermione, and she seeks a form of that cloaking in her careful protection of her private life.

With the world seeming dead-set on compartmentalizing Watson-as-Hermione, Watson answers that framing with one of her own, establishing her own private space free from those limitations, where she may construct alternate presents and futures as ways of being and ways of moving forward. Gevinson praises Watson's artful management of her inner world and the opportunities that that management provides: "She's managed to protect her private life while using her work to reveal the kinds of vulnerabilities that feel the *most* private" (Gevinson 2013), a deft inversion of the tightly constricted Hermione role. Where audiences assume a fallacious private knowledge of Watson on the basis of the public Hermione, she instead offers a more realistic private version of herself in her ensuing roles, one that makes up in accuracy what it loses in rabid fandom. This Watson is not a finished product, but rather a work in progress, as perceived by Will Self: "There are inchoate glints here of a future Hollywood mover and shaker, but, speaking to Watson, they were offset by an impression of someone still looking for nurture in each new temporary family she encounters" (Self 2012). While potentially problematic in its doubly stereotypical association of a young woman with the concept of nurture, Self does hit the mark in underlining Watson's relative youth and associated potential, putting her at the threshold of the aforementioned bigger and better without having stepped out into that space just yet. Halting though Watson's steps may be at this point, she has yet to put a foot particularly wrong, a path which could easily have gone awry, as noted in *W* by Lynn Hirschberg in relation to one of Watson's post–Potter roles: "*The Bling Ring*, which is based on a true story about a group of teenagers who broke into the homes of celebrities like Lindsay Lohan and Paris Hilton, could be read as the chronicle of Watson's road not taken" (Hirschberg 2013). Unlike Radcliffe, Watson is able to avoid that pratfall, though both run into other issues in the dreaded "after-" that soon precedes "Potter" in their chronologies.

After battling through a bout with drink and an unnerving sense of being possessed by a former role, Radcliffe seizes upon that physical locus as a means of redefining not only himself, but also the child actor more broadly, offering a curt rejoinder to those expecting him to follow the path to ruin well-trod by others of his ilk. Speaking of his role in 2013's *What If*, Radcliffe demonstrates an awareness of his reception by audiences raised on Potter, who say things like "[y]ou're a really unconventional romantic lead … it's probably the fact that you know, we associated you with playing Harry, the young boy wizard" (quoted in Essert 2014). Radcliffe responds sharply to the thought that Potter makes it difficult to think of him as a sex symbol, noting that "the male population had no problem sexualising Emma Watson immediately" (quoted in Essert 2014), cannily identifying the double standard at work and also rendering himself just as plausible a sex symbol as Watson. If that sexuality was not already apparent, or not convincingly so, in *What If*, Radcliffe's earlier turn as Alan in *Equus*, a role which includes full frontal nudity, literalizes Radcliffe-as-object, stripping away the trappings of Potter, positing an alternate use of his heretofore Potterized body, and shocking audiences more accustomed to seeing him in robes than out: "some of the audience may be shocked. People may even possibly think that I shouldn't be doing it because of the Potter fans" (quoted in McLean 2007). As a means of presenting a new Radcliffe, warts and all, the decision to go nude removes nearly all pretense; in Radcliffe's words, "[w]hen you take your clothes off—whoever you are—there is very little acting going on" (quoted in Reed 2014), making it quite difficult indeed to see Radcliffe as the young Potter in that moment. Of course, Radcliffe's bold move does not fully preclude the odd "'Harry Gets His Wand Out' headlines" (McLean 2011), suggesting that while Potter might be inescapable, he still might escape the fate of so many child stars before him.

As an international phenomenon provoking no small amount of hysteria at Potter's peak, Radcliffe is situated firmly within the world of child stars, though he makes it a particular goal to not only avoid the mistakes of those who have gone before, but to rehabilitate the Child Star-as-type. Radcliffe contends that "'child star prick' is the image many people have of actors who started young; that's the stereotype you're coming up against" (quoted in Cavendish 2013) and, *Equus*'s dual presentation of the child star prick in its very adult iteration notwithstanding, Radcliffe does his best to diffuse the hubris associated with those who find fame so young. To his credit, Radcliffe is also keenly aware that this shift is not one that can happen overnight; rather, as Sarah Lyall puts it in *The New York Times*, "Mr. Radcliffe appears to be negotiating the tricky transition from child star to adult actor without falling prey to drug-addled delusion, insufferable narcissism or late-night reality television" (Lyall 2008). While engaging in a brief dalliance with the bottle, Radcliffe otherwise steers clear of the stereotypical downfalls associated with child stars, and quite deliberately sets his sights on dispelling those stereotypes altogether: "If I can make a career for myself after Potter, and it goes well, and is varied and with longevity, then that puts to bed the Child Actors Argument" (quoted in McLean 2011). With this mission in mind, Radcliffe is out not only to carve a path in the wake of and free from Potter, but also to serve as a vanguard for others looking to move beyond their earlier work, and the trail that Radcliffe clears is carefully hewn from the wilds where fame dwells.

Radcliffe is, in a word, driven, pushed from behind by the enormity of Potter and pulled towards a different future by his own desire to escape that past, though not so urgently that he is unable to dodge the obstacles that appear before him. Dominic Cavendish expresses concern for the near-breakneck pace at which Radcliffe moves, thinking "[p]erhaps he will drive himself to some kind of breakdown, pushing away at proving himself to the exclusion of anything one could call a normal life," though he concludes that "[h]e won't be hobbled by Harry Potter" (Cavendish 2013). Though Radcliffe's trouble with drink may hint at the potential for a breakdown, his self-awareness brings him back from that precipice, and though he is not as cagily protective of his private life as Watson, he still manages to keep that world separate from his professional life. *Equus* is something of a turning point for Radcliffe, not only as it facilitates his repossession of his physical being, but also as a means to "establish that I can do other things. And I'm not afraid to do very, very different things from Harry. Harry is an incredibly challenging part. But Alan is just so different" (quoted in McLean 2007). Potter lingers in the background here, but only as a point of comparison, not as a point of definition/identity, more as a sense of who Radcliffe once was than of who he will always be. Craig McLean aptly characterizes Radcliffe's subtle transformation, stating "[f]or all his youthful enthusiasm there's a serious, calculating and ferocious ambition under all that kiddie fluff and franchise candyfloss" (McLean 2011), and locating Radcliffe at some distance from Potter, using it as a smokescreen perhaps, but only to conceal a new identity yet under construction, one that reveals itself in increasingly daring roles.

If seeking out roles different from Potter is one of Radcliffe's key methods of moving forward, then he is especially successful in the case of 2013's *Kill Your Darlings* and *Horns*, which allow him to stake out new ground in the wake of his participation in an epochal series. Taking on the role of poet Allen Ginsberg in the former film, "Radcliffe considers *Kill Your Darlings* the high-water mark of his career to date, and the project of which he is the proudest" (Hicklin 2013), and the role notably stretches his acting chops to their limits, as Radcliffe concedes: "I don't look like him, and I'm English and middle-class and not from New Jersey. But that's what I think is so exciting about it, because people have no idea" (quoted in Hicklin 2013). *Horns*, where Radcliffe plays Ig Perrish, who wakes one day to find himself sprouting a pair of horns, offers another sort of physical distancing in the form of a (temporary) body modification that doubles as a reputation modification, as seen in fan reactions: "I was told that *Horns* is kind of the 'Anti-*Harry Potter!*'" (quoted in Burkart 2014). Both roles at once challenge Radcliffe while also challenging his Potter-centric reputation, suggesting that he has greater breadth and depth than the wizarding world might allow, while also marking out the post–Potter period as one of nerve-making uncertainty. Aaron Hicklin draws an intriguing parallel with 9/11 and its aftermath, noting that audiences "watched him—or a version of him—grow up before our eyes at the very time when many of us needed cinema's charms and potions the most" (Hicklin 2013), with the Potter series "climax[ing] 10 years later, in July 2011, with a self-aware, determined young man finally vanquishing Ralph Fiennes's Lord Voldemort, coincidentally a few months after Navy SEALS dispatched Osama bin Laden" (Hicklin 2013). While putting Potter on par with the War on Terror may be slightly ambitious (though both often battle unseen forces in a form of asymmetrical conflict), the parallel between post–OBL and post–Potter holds: after the demise of an iconic figure, a vacuum emerges, and determining what comes next is paramount, a primary matter for Watson as well.

Watson, with her attentions focused on maintaining a firm divide between her private and professional lives, is in a somewhat better position than Radcliffe to make a smooth transition to her post–Potter career, though her engagement with the personal-as-political issue of gender inequality reveals the limits that Hermione still places upon her. In her interview with Lynn Hirschberg, Hirschberg notes Watson's "keen interest in image control. At our shoot, Watson was meticulous about her hair and makeup, and aware of every frame" (Hirschberg 2013), demonstrating Watson's awareness not only of how she may be perceived, but of the fact that, as a woman, her appearance will have much to do with that perception. A similar effort towards image control is apparent later in that same interview, when Watson remarks "I've never wanted to grow up too fast: I wanted to wear a sports bra until I was 22!" (quoted in Hirschberg 2013), again displaying an understanding of the physical not as a place of potential redefinition (as for Radcliffe), but as one that is defined from without. By wearing a sports bra, Watson is minimizing a marker of femininity both materially (reducing the dimensions of her bust) and ideologically (associating with unladylike sports), putting her at a distance from, though not out of reach of, the ongoing sexualization observed by Radcliffe. Indeed, the *Elle UK* profile of Watson's speech before the UN describes her appearance in some detail, calling Watson "this mesmerising woman in her Dior dress, dark lipstick and neat ponytail" (Candy 2014), the type of rundown more common on the red carpet than in political circles (though not, unfortunately, altogether absent in the latter). For Watson, the physical is less a space of transformation than of information, her carefully managed image signaling her growing sophistication of style and mind.

That sophistication is abundantly apparent in Watson's role as UN Women Goodwill Ambassador, particularly her work on the HeForShe project, and through that role she is able to largely transcend not only Potter, but film more broadly. When speaking before the UN on 20 September 2014, Watson identifies herself as being "among the ranks of women whose expressions are seen as too strong, too aggressive, isolating, anti-men and unattractive" ("Emma Watson: Gender equality" 2014), feedback received as much by the Hermione of her past as by the Emma of her present. In making the personal political, or in bringing her personal to bear on the larger political sphere, Watson is taking control of her image in a more effective way than Radcliffe takes his, less avoiding a hard fall than preparing herself for a leap to the next level. Watson also points to some of the problems faced by Radcliffe later in the speech, noting that "[w]e don't often talk about men being imprisoned by gender stereotypes but I can see that they are and that when they are free, things will change for women as a natural consequence" ("Emma Watson: Gender equality" 2014), in Radcliffe's case the lessened masculinity associated with his height. By casting a broader net and showing how gender stereotyping negatively affects everyone, Watson aims to create a successful coalition to challenge deeply entrenched gender roles, an aim furthered by the HeForShe project in which she participates. Rooted in "a simple affirmation that gender equality is not only a women's issue, but a human rights issue that requires the participation and commitment of men … asking men to define what matters to them, and what they will do to make a difference" ("In Brief" 2016), HeForShe looks to create alliances where animosity may have existed previously, ultimately aiming to free both women and men from the structures that confine them, though Watson is haunted by Hermione even in this venture.

Through her efforts to spur the movement towards gender equality, Watson is taking significant strides to make a name for herself beyond Potter, though her name from that past life lingers even in this new setting. In her biographical page for the UN Women Goodwill Ambassador position, Watson is first described in terms of her work for the UN; however, in the subsection "About Emma Watson," the first line concedes that "Emma is best known for her role as the iconic character of Hermione Granger in the globally successful 'Harry Potter' films" ("UN Women" 2016), returning Watson to her origins. The familiar "Emma," while making her more approachable, also recalls the ubiquitous "Harry" hung on Radcliffe, pointing to Watson's own ubiquity as Hermione (no last name required) and perhaps suggesting that she may herself attain such mononomial acclaim. Watson herself incorporates this association into her comments before the UN, saying "[y]ou might be thinking who is this Harry Potter girl? … I don't know if I am qualified to be here. All I know is that I care about this problem. And I want to make it better" ("Emma Watson: Gender equality" 2014), understanding that many in attendance will view her either through the Potter lens, as an interloper, or both. Despite her best efforts, Watson is unable to escape Hermione; however, Hermione is now relegated to subsections of her biography, to use as a disarming device of self-effacement, less a trap to be endured than a tool to be used, a way to open doors that, once open, may be firmly closed behind.

As generational touchstones for so many young boys and girls turned women and men, the paths that Radcliffe and Watson take are of particular interest not only as a means of maintaining a connection to the beloved Harry and Hermione, however indirect, but also as both models for and kindred spirits within the uncertain work of adulthood. Growing up is messy business: one must move beyond perceptions of who they are (or were), develop one's own ideas outside of the hothouse environment of the parental nest, and emerge into the world half-formed, unsteady, making as many mistakes as good decisions, and learning all the while. Between them, Radcliffe and Watson provide an object lesson in self-creation for the Harry Potter generation, showing the missteps that one may take (being haunted by reputations deserved or otherwise, indulging a bit too much in adult beverages, engaging in some potentially embarrassing public nudity, taking serious steps at sophistication and having them undermined by images of childhood) and the successes that may result (more numerous career options, the wisdom that may only come from failure, broadening one's horizons into issues of global import). As Harry and Hermione, Radcliffe and Watson offer lessons on how to navigate childhood, through lessons that must be transposed from Hogwarts to the Muggle world; as themselves, they are still teaching, still opening doors, giving a master course in the perils and rewards of becoming your own person. After the final credits, the audience must go home, and Radcliffe and Watson give them much to discuss when they get there.

NOTE

1. Editorial Note: Since the time of writing, Emma Watson has also played the iconic role of girl reader, "Belle" in *Beauty and the Beast* (2017). Clearly, situating Watson at the nexus of the Potterverse, feminist discourse, and the fairy tale as this casting does will have important future implications on the way she is and continues to be perceived by the Harry Potter generation. We hope that others working on children's literature and celebrity culture will address these in some future work.

REFERENCES

Alvarez, Eduardo Munoz. 2014. "Watch Emma Watson Deliver a Game-Changing Speech on Feminism for the U.N. (Updated)." *Vanity Fair*. Last modified September 21. http://www.vanityfair.com/hollywood/2014/09/emma-watson-un-speech-feminism.
Burkart, Gregory S. 2014. "[Interview] Daniel Radcliffe on 'Horns,' 'Frankenstein,' and More."

Bloody Disgusting. Last modified November 3. http://bloody-disgusting.com/news/3320144/interview-daniel-radcliffe-talks-horns-frankenstein/.

Candy, Lorraine. 2014. "Emma Watson, the December 2014 *ELLE* Cover Interview." *Elle UK.* Last modified December. http://www.elleuk.com/now-trending/emma-watson-december-2014-elle-magazine-feminism-issue-cover-interview-in-full.

Cavendish, Dominic. 2013. "Daniel Radcliffe interview: 'I've never done something nasty … until now.'" *The Telegraph.* Last modified May 23. http://www.telegraph.co.uk/culture/theatre/10061864/Daniel-Radcliffe-interview-Ive-never-done-something-nasty...-until-now.html.

Dominus, Susan. 2013. "Daniel Radcliffe's Next Trick Is to Make Harry Potter Disappear." *The New York Times Magazine.* Last modified October 2. http://www.nytimes.com/2013/10/06/magazine/daniel-radcliffe.html?_r=1.

"Emma Watson." 2016. *Scholastic.* http://teacher.scholastic.com/scholasticnews/indepth/harry_potter/emma_watson.htm.

"Emma Watson: Gender equality is your issue too." 2014. *UN Women.* Last modified September 20. http://www.unwomen.org/en/news/stories/2014/9/emma-watson-gender-equality-is-your-issue-too.

Essert, Matt. 2014. "Daniel Radcliffe's Table-Turning Interview Answer Reveals How We Sexualize Young Women." *Mic.* Last modified October 26. http://mic.com/articles/102374/daniel-radcliffe-s-table-turning-interview-answer-reveals-how-we-sexualize-young-women#.36ZO0VFfR.

Foreman, Amanda. 2011. "Emma Watson's New Day." *Vogue.* Last modified June 13. http://www.vogue.com/865432/emma-watsons-new-day/.

Gevinson, Tavi. 2013. "I Want It to Be Worth It: An Interview With Emma Watson." *Rookie.* Last modified May 27.http://www.rookiemag.com/2013/05/emma-watson-interview/.

Hattenstone, Simon. 2013. "Daniel Radcliffe: 'There's No Master Plan to Distance Myself from Harry Potter.'" *The Guardian.* Last modified November 23. http://www.theguardian.com/film/2013/nov/23/daniel-radcliffe-interview-no-plan-distance-harry-potter.

Hicklin, Aaron. 2013 "The Long Education of Daniel Radcliffe." *Out.* Last modified February 11. http://www.out.com/entertainment/movies/2013/02/11/long-education-daniel-radcliffe.

Hirschberg, Lynn. 2013. "The Prime of Miss Emma Watson." *W.* Last modified June. http://www.wmagazine.com/people/celebrities/2013/06/emma-watson-the-bling-ring-harry-potter-actress-cover-story/.

IGN AU. 2016. "18 Questions With Emma Watson." *AskMen.* http://www.askmen.com/celebs/interview_200/247_emma_watson_interview.html.

"In Brief." 2016. *HeForShe.* http://www.heforshe.org/~/media/heforshe/files/our%20mission/heforshe_overview_brief.pdf.

Lyall, Sarah. 2008. "Onstage, Stripped of That Wizardry." *The New York Times.* Last modified September 11. http://www.nytimes.com/2008/09/14/theater/14lyal.html?pagewanted=all.

McLean, Craig. 2007. "Dirty Harry." *The Guardian.* Last modified February 10. http://www.theguardian.com/film/2007/feb/11/harrypotter.

_____. 2012. "The Exorcism of Harry Potter." *GQ.* Last modified March 29. http://www.gq-magazine.co.uk/article/gq-film-daniel-radcliffe-harry-potter-interview-drinking.

Morreale, Marie. 2016. "Daniel Radcliffe Talks About the Changes in Harry's Life." *Scholastic.* http://teacher.scholastic.com/scholasticnews/indepth/harry_potter_movie/interviews/index.asp?article=danielradcliffe&topic=1.

Reed, Ryan. 2014. "Daniel Radcliffe Blasts Own 'Harry Potter' Acting." *Rolling Stone.* Last modified August 11. http://www.rollingstone.com/movies/news/daniel-radcliffe-blasts-own-harry-potter-acting-20140811.

Self, Will. 2012. "The Graduate." *The New York Times Style Magazine.* Last modified August 17. http://www.nytimes.com/2012/08/17/t-magazine/emma-watson-the-graduate.html.

Sims, Andrew. 2014. "J.K. Rowling and Emma Watson Discuss Ron, Hermione, and Harry: The Full Interview." *Hypable.* Last modified February 7. http://www.hypable.com/jk-rowling-ron-hermione-interview/.

34   Part I: The Phenomenon

"UN Women Goodwill Ambassador Emma Watson." 2016. *UN Women.* http://www.unwomen.
org/en/partnerships/goodwill-ambassadors/emma-watson.
Weintraub, Steve "Frosty." 2010. "Daniel Radcliffe On Set Interview *Harry Potter and the
Deathly Hallows." Collider.* Last modified October 5. http://collider.com/daniel-radcliffe-
on-set-interview-harry-potter-and-the-deathly-hallows/.

Loony Lovegood and the Almost Chosen One

Harry Potter, Supporting Characters and Fan Reception

DION MCLEOD *and* ELISE PAYNE

"Neville is not an idiot and Luna is not an oddity!"
—Hermione Granger

"'Look [...] it's always you who gets all the attention, you know it is'" (*GoF* 318). This line, spoken by Hermione to Harry, encapsulates both the canonical and scholarly critiques of Harry Potter. When one hears or thinks of the Harry Potter franchise, Harry—along with Ron, Hermione, Dumbledore, and Voldemort—are likely the first characters that come to mind. Harry's characterization, his friendship with Ron and Hermione, and the multitude of thematic concerns of the story have been the focus of numerous critical approaches to Rowling's series (See: Anatol 2003; Heilman 2009; Whited 2002). This focus on central, or main, characters reflects the belief that it is these characters who are most valuable to narratives and that it is these characters with whom readers establish the strongest connections. While "main" characters are pivotal in shaping the ways that readers respond to texts, they are not the only characters worthy of scholarly examination.

It should be noted that the plethora of scholarship surrounding the primary characters of the series is fruitful and engaging. Vayo's essay of this collection explores Harry and Hermione and the way that Radcliff and Watson have become synonymous with their characters and how that can raise further questions about what it is about primary characters that leads to this blending of actor/character. However, in this essay, we want to shift the focus from the "main" characters towards two characters who have not received the academic attention they deserve: Neville Longbottom and Luna Lovegood. Neville and Luna play significant roles in the Harry Potter narrative, but in the transition from book to film the importance of their roles is minimized. Despite these changes, however, both Neville and Luna have significant presence in fanfiction and art produced by fans of the Harry Potter series. Our primary points of analysis for this essay are, therefore, Neville and Luna's canonical representation in the seven books and eight films, as well as fan responses to these characters on social media sites, including Tumblr and DeviantART.

This essay has four main components: an examination of what makes Harry Potter unique in regards to supporting characters; an overview of the way fans are enrolled into the Harry Potter narrative as "(pseudo)supporting" characters, drawing on recent character and narrative theory; an exploration of Neville and Luna's novelistic representations and how these representations lead one to understand these characters' identities; and finally, by moving into the world of the Harry Potter fandom, an exploration of what fans think, say, and produce in relation to their readings and experiences of Neville and Luna. This analysis demonstrates that the significance of these "minor" characters to the Harry Potter generation is not so minor. Furthermore, we suggest that a reading that shifts the critical focus from Harry onto Neville and Luna transfigures the perception of all three characters' narrative significance— that is, without Neville or Luna, the series' journey on the way to narrative resolution (the defeat of Voldemort) would have been prolonged. Without Neville's and Luna's contributions, Harry would have had to overcome many more obstacles alone.

Our Hogwarts Letter Was Lost in the Post. Or Was It?

The concept of supporting characters is, we argue, a key facet of what makes the Harry Potter franchise unique, and of what makes the Harry Potter generation distinct from other modern fandoms. On his blog, Henry Jenkins describes a phenomenon he calls transmedia storytelling. This storytelling, he notes,

> represents a process where integral elements of a fiction get dispersed systematically across multiple delivery channels for the purpose of creating a unified and coordinated entertainment experience.... There is no one single source or ur-text where one can turn to gain all of the information needed to comprehend the [storyworld].... This process of world-building encourages an encyclopedic impulse in both readers and writers. We are drawn to master what can be known about a world which always expands beyond our grasp. This is a very different pleasure than

we associate with the closure found in most classically constructed narratives, where we expect to leave the theatre knowing everything that is required to make sense of a particular story [http://henryjenkins.org/2007/03/transmedia_storytelling_101.html].

It is the encyclopedic impulse we wish to draw upon for our discussion. Jenkins notes that there is no one source that contains all the information needed, and that we *need* to know that which is absent from the books/films/other related media. We suggest that what makes Harry Potter stand apart from other franchises is J.K. Rowling herself, and we propose an adaption of the concept of the "ur-text" to examine Rowling as the "ur-fan."[1]

Fans of many franchises have long submerged themselves in their respective secondary worlds—*Star Trek* fans have learnt the Klingon language; *Lord of the Rings* fans have learnt Elvish; and fans of *A Song of Ice and Fire* have learnt Dothraki. This process of learning fictional languages has blurred the distinction between the storyworlds and real worlds for many years. But Harry Potter fans have been provided with a different way to become immersed in the storyworld, and this immersion begins with Rowling.

Rowling has an active social media presence, particularly since joining Twitter in 2009, and constantly updates fans with information—both that which has been requested by followers and that which she chooses to provide without any prompting. This process of updating fans extends the temporality of fandom; as each novel in the series was written for a slightly older audience, fans "grew up" alongside Harry and his peers. But rather than moving on from the story, the Harry Potter generation continues to reread and remain in the temporality of the storyworld. Fans' dedication to gaining and sharing information from social media platforms is also interesting as the Harry Potter generation not only grew up with Harry Potter, but is also the first generation to grow up with social media.

One instance of Rowling updating fans occurred on Sept. 1, 2015, when she posted two significant tweets to her followers. The first informs us that she is "in Edinburgh, so could somebody at King's Cross wish James S Potter good luck for [her]? He's starting at Hogwarts today. #BackToHogwarts." The second, posted nine hours later, notes that she has "just heard that James S Potter has been Sorted (to nobody's surprise) into Gryffindor." Quite obviously, James S Potter would not have been at Kings Cross, nor would he have been sorted into Gryffindor that day; James is a fictional character, Gryffindor a fictional House, and both exist in a fictional world. But Rowling, through her positioning as ur-fan, is continually feeding the encyclopedic impulse in her fans. Through her strong social media presence, and real-time updates, Rowling begins to blur the line(s) between the fictional storyworld and our world; between fictional storytime and our linear time.

This blurring does not end with her tweets, however. With the creation of both Pottermore and The Wizarding World of Harry Potter, fans are given an even more immersive experience. On Pottermore, fans go through their own Sorting Ceremony and are given a Hogwarts House; they can make potions, allow their wand to choose them, and choose an animal companion. On Sept. 23, 2015, it was announced that "for the first time, there will be reporting and features by the Pottermore Correspondent, a journalist dedicated to reporting on all the latest updates going on in the Wizarding World" (McCrum n.p.). With the creation of this correspondent, the lines between fiction and reality are further collapsed. As is discussed in Dennis J. Siler's essay, The Wizarding World of Harry Potter takes the immersion of Pottermore one step further: fans can buy house robes and a wand (and use this wand throughout the park); they can drink Butterbeer and eat Bertie Botts Every Flavour Beans; and can exchange Muggle dollars for Galleons.

Most recently, Niantic, the company behind the widely successful game Pokémon Go, announced a Potter version to be released in 2018. They explain, "[w]ith *Harry Potter: Wizards Unite*, players that have been dreaming of becoming real life Wizards will finally get the chance to experience J.K. Rowling's Wizarding World. Players will learn spells, explore their real world neighborhoods and cities to discover & fight legendary beasts and team up with others to take down powerful enemies" (https://nianticlabs.com/blog/wizardsunite). After 20 years of dreaming about becoming a wizard, Potter fans will be able to don their house robs, grab their wands, and bring the virtual experience into real life.

These additional levels of immersion, combined with Rowling's frequent wizarding updates, provides Harry Potter fans with something unavailable to all other franchises. Because of the incredible blurring of fiction and reality on many levels, the Harry Potter generation is encouraged to *become* (pseudo)supporting characters in the storyworld. This encouragement is key to the specific nature of the Harry Potter generation's ongoing and intense involvement in the storyworld. Because fans become (pseudo)supporting characters themselves, they are invited to identify with other supporting characters, such as Neville and Luna, as they read and watch the Harry Potter novels and films. This discussion about fans as supporting characters is one that invites deeper examination; however, for the purpose of this essay we use the idea of fan-as-supporting character to examine not only how actual fans are reading the series through Neville and Luna, but also how their encouraged identification with supporting characters is discernible in the fan fiction and art that they produce. To do so, as previously mentioned, we will begin with an analysis of Neville and Luna's novelistic and filmic representations before moving into the Harry Potter fandom and examining some fan responses to the series.

A Muggle's Note on Character Theory

By necessity, specific connotations are ascribed to each of the different terms that can be used to describe the characters we discuss (minor, supporting, non-major, marginal, non-central, secondary, subordinate, and so on). For the purposes of this essay, we refer to Neville and Luna (as well as other non-primary characters) as "supporting" characters. We have chosen this term specifically, following the usage in David Galef's book, because unlike other terms such as "secondary" and "minor," which connote a lack of narrative significance, the term "supporting" suggests those who exist just beyond the central locus of the narrative, but who are structurally necessary to the series. Thus, we seek to demonstrate the significance of these characters in supporting the *narrative*, rather than supporting the *protagonist*.

While scholars have long debated the manner in which character analysis should be approached, more recently Alex Woloch and John Frow have done much to resolve these tensions and inform the way we undertake character analysis in this essay. In his recent book, *Character and Person*, Frow discusses an ongoing conversation in character theory involving a divide between characters as plot devices or as pseudo-persons, and suggests that while there is a "tension between thinking of characters as pieces of writing or imagining and thinking of them as person-like entities" it is possible "to resolve that tension by proposing that fictional characters must ... be seen to be both at once" (Frow 2014, 2). Frow's insistence upon the validity of reading characters as person-like speaks to the approach that we take to characters in this essay: that is, alongside analyzing these characters in terms of their narrative function, we also approach them as sites of audience engagement whom the audience view as individuals with stories to tell.

While Frow and others (for example, Uri Margolin and Mieke Bal) discuss an appreciation of characters as pseudo-persons and of being worthy of study, Woloch argues for the importance of minor characters to the study of texts. Taking this argument as our impetus, we therefore not only approach characters as (fictional) people with their own stories to tell, but do so with a focus on those characters whose stories are not typically championed in either the scholarship or the narratives of which they play a crucial part.

These lesser-represented characters have long been overlooked in the academic sphere. In fan circles, however, supporting characters are some of the most popular. In order to determine who we consider to be supporting characters, we adopt and adapt Woloch's notion of minor characters as those who are "only partially inflected into the narrative universe, reduced to a 'function reference'" (Woloch 2003, 24). For Woloch, the "'minor identities' that ensue produce 'apparitions' which hazily reflect the fullness that has been excluded" (24). Neville and Luna satisfy these conditions. Though Luna attends Hogwarts with Harry from his second year, she is not introduced into the narrative universe until his fifth year. Conversely, Neville is sorted into Gryffindor with Harry in the same ceremony, but for much of the series he is reduced to a punch line. Ironically, with the revelation of the prophecy in *Order of the Phoenix*, we learn that Neville is, metaphorically, a shadowy reflection of Harry—he is, essentially, the "Almost Chosen One." Thus, while Neville and Luna both perform a supporting rather than primary character function, this essay shows how this support is crucial for the completion of the Harry Potter narrative, and that fans of the story are determined to ensure that Neville and Luna's significance for the narrative be acknowledged and appreciated.

Neville and Luna's Transfiguration

We first meet 11-year-old Neville as he stands with his Gran on platform 9¾, preparing to leave for his first year at Hogwarts. While he waits for the train, we learn that he has lost his toad—again (*PS* 105). This first mention of Neville in *Philosopher's Stone*, albeit brief, is a clear snapshot of the way in which readers will come to understand his character. How does one begin to describe the Neville Longbottom to whom Rowling introduces us? Or, as Chantel Lavoie asks, "What of Neville Longbottom, over whom the Sorting Hat also lingers in the first book? Is he merely Gryffindor by default, because he is neither clever, notably hard working, nor ambitious? The reasons for Neville's position in this house are not apparent even to him" (Lavoie 2003, 43). From the outset of the series, Neville is used both for comedic effect and as a comparison to show that things could always be worse for Harry, Ron, and Hermione (hereafter, "the trio"). He is shy and clumsy, with little self-confidence and an apparently low level of magical ability and skill. In *Philosopher's Stone* (1997), it is revealed that his family had believed him to be "all Muggle for ages," (137) and in *Chamber of Secrets* (1998), Neville's internalization of this belief is demonstrated when he notes, "everyone knows I'm almost a Squib" (201). As the series progresses, however, Neville develops from the "round-faced and accident-prone boy with the worst memory of anyone Harry had ever met" (*CoS* 96) to a hero who vocally rejects Voldemort, destroying his final horcrux using Gryffindor's sword.

Luna "Loony" Lovegood, on the other hand, is only introduced to readers in her fourth year (the trio's fifth year) at Hogwarts. With Ginny Weasley, she is one of only two female supporting characters who are shown to have a close involvement with the trio and the significant events of the series' narrative. A vital supporting character, Luna is repeatedly mocked throughout the series, and like Neville, she is often the butt of a joke. An eccentric teenager, whose belief in (assumedly non-existent) creatures such as the Crumple-Horned Snorkack sees her isolated from her peers, Luna is better known at Hogwarts as "Loony." Maria Harris suggests that in the series "'mad' … is a derogatory label for those who look different and/or look at things differently from most people" (*OotP* 87). Upon Luna's introduction to the series in *Order of the Phoenix*, the reader is immediately aware of her uniqueness, and a reading of the books could see her immediately set up in opposition to Harry. As Harris notes, "Harry's first meeting with Luna on the train gives little hint that the two of them will become friends" (Harris 2004, 88). However, as with Neville, Luna's character development as the series progresses is substantial, and her willful eccentricity comes to be an accepted asset.

Of all the characters in the book series, it is arguably Neville who undergoes the most substantial narrative transformation. Neville is established as clumsy, unintelligent, hopeless, and a joke. He loses the Gryffindor passwords allowing Sirius, who is at this point believed to be a dangerous escaped criminal, entry to the Gryffindor common room (*PoA* 291), is repeatedly mocked and belittled by teachers including Snape and McGonagall (*PoA* 144; *GoF* 260), and appears to succeed only in Herbology (*HBP* 207). For well over half of the book series, the narrative does not overtly suggest that Neville will play a great role in the defeat of Voldemort; rather, he is more aligned with Dean and Seamus, two students who share a dormitory with Harry and Ron, but who exist only to further highlight Harry's heroism.

If one reads the series through Harry, Neville's personal narrative is almost completely overshadowed by Harry's. This is in part due to the narrative's focalization. In the Harry Potter novels, the narrator's voice is combined with—or focalized through—Harry's perspective. Reading the narrative through Harry is, therefore, the expected and invited reading, given that any information we receive from the narrator is influenced by Harry's judgment. This information, filtered through Harry, includes what knowledge readers receive about not only Harry, but all other characters in the narrative as well.

Neville's story is also at other times overshadowed by those of his parents. Perhaps the most overt instance of Neville's personal narrative being undermined occurs in *Order of the Phoenix* when Draco Malfoy makes a joke about people who end up in the wizard hospital St. Mungo's as a result of magical damage. After Neville attacks Malfoy, Ron wonders aloud why Neville has done so. In this moment, the narrator informs the reader that, "Harry … knew exactly why the subject of people who were in St. Mungo's because of magical damage to their brains was highly distressing to Neville, but he had sworn to Dumbledore that he would not tell anyone Neville's secret [that his parents are permanently hospitalized]. *Even Neville did not know that Harry knew*" (401, our emphasis). In this way, as the series is primarily Harry's story, and because he is the eponymous hero, other characters are necessarily pushed to the narrative margins. In this scene it becomes apparent that Neville is not even in control of his own narrative; Harry knows Neville's story, even though Neville does not know that Harry knows.

The above scene illustrates how the books themselves reinforce Neville's narrative subordination to Harry. However, a shift in the characterization of Neville occurs in *Order of the Phoenix*. Once Neville learns that Bellatrix Lestrange, the witch who attacked his parents, has escaped from Azkaban, he is portrayed as a new wizard. Though he is still at times mocked, he is much more aligned with Harry. Since, as Margolin explains, "any two coexisting characters must differ in at least one property" (Margolin 2007, 74), the major distinction between Harry and Neville is that Harry receives much greater respect from both his peers and teachers than Neville does. However, one of the more important moments of Neville's increasing competence comes during a meeting of Dumbledore's Army when the narrator notes that "Harry would have given a great deal to be making as much progress at Occlumency as Neville was during D.A. meetings" (*OotP* 610). From this moment Neville becomes a hero in his own right. The need to defend his parents' names and protect others from Bellatrix urges Neville forward.

The most significant moment for Neville's narrative shift from fool to potential hero occurs when Dumbledore tells Harry about the prophecy that led to Harry's parents being murdered. While Harry Potter is the "Chosen One" (*HBP* 167), it is revealed during a conversation with Dumbledore in *Order of the Phoenix* that Voldemort determined Harry's fate:

> "The odd thing is, Harry," he said softly, "that it may not have meant you at all. Sibyll's prophecy could have applied to two wizard boys, both born at the end of July that year, both of whom had parents in the Order of the Phoenix, both sets of parents having narrowly escaped Voldemort three times. One, of course, was you. The other was Neville Longbottom."
>
> "Then—it might not be me?" said Harry.
>
> "I am afraid," said Dumbledore slowly, looking as though every word cost him a great effort, "that there is no doubt that it is you" [*OotP* 925].

Dumbledore follows this statement with the clarification that "Voldemort himself would *mark him* [The Chosen One] *as his equal*. And so he did, Harry. He chose you, not Neville" (*OotP* 925, emphasis original). *Harry Potter*, therefore, could easily have been *Neville Longbottom*. Dumbledore's words, "He [Voldemort] chose you, not Neville" suggests that it is simply a matter of luck that Harry would become the Chosen One. Reading this line in relation to Neville's own narrative emphasizes that the admiration Harry receives as the Chosen One is not something he has earned by his own efforts. It is not fate that spares Harry from death, but simply a decision by one wizard to attempt to kill one child instead of another. Or, as Jeremy Pierce notes, "the prophecy didn't itself determine whether it was about Harry or Neville. Voldemort's choice of Harry made it true of Harry" (Pierce 2010, 45).

Fans have also taken up the belief that Neville could have done everything Harry does. As Tumblr user Analyze It and Weep notes, "Neville Longbottom: not chosen. Not 'the hero.' But heroic all the same. The Wizarding World would have been just fine, had Voldemort taken the other option. Because they would have had Neville Longbottom. And thankfully, the readers had him too." The role Neville plays in the series' narrative resolution is one that, though diminished in the films, is not overlooked by fans. For instance, an image by Tumblr user daily-harry-potter shows an image of a woman at an anti-abortion protest, holding a sign saying "if Lily Potter had an abortion then who would stop Voldemort?" Superimposed in the bottom left corner of this image is a quote by Tumblr user stalinchristmasspecial that simply notes "neville longbottom jesus christ read the books [sic]." Fans are well aware that Neville could do anything Harry does. As Margolin explains, though two characters may both exist in the same storyworld, the "version" of one of these characters as understood in the mind of the other character is sometimes wrong (Margolin 2007, 72). Thus, not only is it quite easy to overlook supporting characters like Neville and Luna—and especially in narratives with an eponymous hero such as Harry Potter—but it is also important to question the view of a character that another character presents.

In this essay we refer to Book Luna/Neville and Film Luna/Neville as proper nouns, because they are, we suggest, different iterations of the same characters. Book Luna follows a similar narrative trajectory to Book Neville, though she exists for much less time in the narrative. Luna is first mentioned during a chapter in *Order of the Phoenix* titled "Luna Lovegood," reading (what Hermione sees as) an unpopular magazine, *The Quibbler*, upside down. Immediately, Luna is established as an eccentric (or, odd) witch. When the students arrive at Hogwarts and step into the carriages, Harry believes he is going insane, seeing creatures (Thestrals) which Ron and Hermione cannot. Harry's paranoia is confirmed when Luna attempts to comfort him:

> "It's all right," said a dreamy voice from beside Harry as Ron vanished into the coach's dark interior. "You're not going mad or anything. I can see them too."
> "Can you?" said Harry desperately, turning to Luna. He could see the bat-winged horses reflected in her wide, silvery eyes.
> "Oh yes," said Luna, "I've been able to see them ever since my first day here. They've always pulled the carriages. Don't worry. You're just as sane as I am" [*OotP* 222].

This conversation is not only humorous, but establishes Luna's complexity. The line "you're not going mad, I can see them too" is the first spoken by Film Luna (*OotP* 2007). More important is Luna's insistence that Harry is "just as sane" as she is. The narrative, and by extension the reader, rarely questions anything Harry does or says. This scene establishes Luna as willfully eccentric, odd, questionable, and engaging; she *is* an odd character. But in this situation she is also correct. The reader eventually learns that only those who have seen death can see Thestrals. Despite Hermione's staunch opposition to anything she cannot physically see herself, the reader becomes aware that Luna has knowledge that others do not.

Over the course of the final three books of the series, Luna narratively transforms from someone with a "knack for speaking uncomfortable truths" (*HBP* 368) into a strong witch who stuns Alecto Carrow to defend Harry, protects Harry from Dementors, and fights Bellatrix alongside Hermione and Ginny (*DH* 646; 712; 806). As with Neville, small instances in the books show that Luna is capable of more than meets the eye. Book Luna is repeatedly a source of comfort for the trio, but also of bemusement for her other peers at Hogwarts, who refer to her as "Loony." Her capacity to be simultaneously a source of comfort and bemusement becomes most apparent following the Battle of Hogwarts. Luna sees Harry becoming overwhelmed and offers her assistance:

> "I'd want some peace and quiet, if it were me," she said.
> "I'd love some," he replied.
> "I'll distract them all."
> And before he could say a word she had cried, "Oooh, look, a Blibbering Humdinger!" [*DH* 816].

By the end of the series Luna is able to use her "oddness" and belief in the (presumably) non-existent to provide Harry with the opportunity to escape and spend some time alone. J.K. Rowling herself has given fans insight to how important Luna has become in the lives of other characters, especially Harry. Though in the epilogue of *DH*, Luna's post–Hogwarts fate is not revealed, we do learn from an interview with Rowling that she is regarded highly enough by Harry and Ginny to be included in the naming of their daughter: Lily Luna Potter (SlickGenius "'A Year in the Life' Part 5"). Once more, Rowling has used her authority and position as ur-fan to provide to readers (and fans) an important piece of information from the storyworld. As a result, Luna's overall novelistic development from ostracized oddity to embraced eccentric encourages readers to see a different incarnation of the stereotypical hero.

Changes made to the Harry Potter story in its adaptation from seven books into eight films not only serve to alter fans' understandings of characters' identities, but also to alter the number and manner of opportunities available for fans to perceive different characters' significance to the narrative. For Neville and Luna specifically, the changes relating to their characterization and presence in the narrative fall into three main categories: their visibility is reduced through omission and being overshadowed by the trio in the narrative space; their personal (background) stories—a substantial aspect of any character's identity—are not as thoroughly represented in the films as they are in the books; and the nature and importance of their respective involvements in the resolution of the narrative is noticeably altered.

An adapted text is necessarily going to be different from the original. Indeed, with reference to the adaptation of the Harry Potter series, Philip Nel notes that "Fans' devotion to and expertise on Potter make these novels especially challenging to adapt" (Nel 2003, 275). We suggest that it is precisely as a result of an unsatisfying transfer of their narrative significance that fans have taken up the task of transfiguring Neville and Luna in fan spaces to a state that better reflects their novelistic representations than do their film versions. Because Harry Potter fans are encouraged to become (pseudo)supporting characters, their identification with Neville and Luna drives their determination to have others see and respect these characters' worth.

In his transition from book to film, Neville is frequently omitted and also replaced a number of times by members of the trio. His replacement occurs as early as the first film: he is physically replaced by Ron during the forest detention scene, and again during the Dueling Club scene (*PS* 2001; *CoS* 2002). This substitution demonstrates that Film Neville is significantly undervalued as a key figure in the eventual demise of Voldemort. Key opportunities for fans' engagement with his identity and story are also omitted or heavily reduced. The most significant removal of Neville in the firm series is the lack of reference to him in the prophecy.

The other major aspect of the films that may be seen to inhibit fans' engagement with Neville is the removal of his parents' backstory. In *Order of the Phoenix*, during their visit to St Mungo's, the trio run into Neville and his Gran. After learning that Neville has not told the trio about his past, his Gran chastises him:

> "Well, it's nothing to be ashamed of!" said Mrs. Longbottom angrily. "You should be proud, Neville, proud! They didn't give their health and their sanity so their only son would be ashamed of them, you know!"
>
> "I'm not ashamed," said Neville very faintly, still looking anywhere but at Harry and the others. Ron was now standing on tiptoe to look over at the inhabitants of the two beds.
>
> "Well, you've got a funny way of showing it!" said Mrs. Longbottom. "My son and his wife," she said, turning haughtily to Harry, Ron, Hermione, and Ginny, "were tortured into insanity by You-Know-Who's followers" [*OotP* 566].

While in the books this moment is one of empathy for Neville, in the films the creation of empathy does not exist. In the films, we learn this information through snippets that a viewer may easily miss (such as in Dumbledore's memory of Igor Karkaroff's trial in the film *Goblet of Fire*) and eventually through a short exchange between Neville and Harry in the film of *Order of the Phoenix*. A detailed account of his parents' story is never afforded to viewers of the films, nor do film viewers meet the Longbottoms as characters—these are both narrative elements only available through reading the books. Film Neville, as a result of these major omissions, is therefore a less sympathetic character and a character with whom the audience cannot engage as readily or extensively as they can with Book Neville, about whom we know more.

In the book series, we get to know Luna as compassionate, kind, and caring, despite her eccentricities and often blunt nature: these qualities make Luna a source of comfort for other characters. A key omission that serves to limit fans' ability to fully understand and engage with Film Luna occurs in the scene in *Deathly Hallows Part 1* where the trio go to visit her father, Xenophilius. During this scene, the viewer is shown the outside of the Lovegoods' house, as well as the kitchen and living area; however, in the book, readers also see Luna's bedroom. What readers find here is crucial to a fuller understanding of Luna's emotions and identity, and is something that viewers of the film version of the story miss out on completely:

> Luna had decorated her bedroom ceiling with five beautifully painted faces: Harry, Ron, Hermione, Ginny, and Neville.... What appeared to be fine golden chains wove around the pictures, linking them together, but after examining them for a minute or so, Harry realised that the chains were actually one word, repeated a thousand times in golden ink: *friends ... friends ... friends ...* [DH 461].

The omission of this detail of Luna's life means that viewers lose a moment that enables an understanding of Luna as a caring character who longs for inclusion, and for whom friendship is crucial to her happiness and sense of self. This also occludes Luna's ability to present her own narrative—in the film series we get to hear Harry name Luna as his friend (*HBP* 2009), but Luna is not afforded the opportunity to return the gesture.

Perhaps the most noticeable change in Luna from book to film occurs in her contributions to the achievement of narrative completion—specifically, the defeat of Voldemort. In the books, Luna is shown as an active and important participant in the three major battles of the series: the Battle of the Department of Mysteries (*OotP*), the Battle of the Astronomy Tower (*HBP*), and, of course, the Battle of Hogwarts (*DH*). Book Luna is seen in each of these battles fighting alongside the trio and Neville, demonstrating her magical skill and her bravery.

In the film versions, though, these aspects of Luna's significance to the Harry Potter narrative are largely omitted. In *Order of the Phoenix* (2007), her involvement in the Battle of the Department of Mysteries is limited; the Battle of the Astronomy Tower in *Half Blood Prince* (2009)—save the moment of Dumbledore's death—is omitted entirely; and in *Deathly Hallows Part 2* (2011) we do not see Luna in active combat at all. She is shown in the background in various scenes, such as during Neville's courtyard speech to Voldemort, however she is afforded neither *active* screen time nor dialogue (*DH2* 2011). Overall, in the films (as in the books) Luna still develops from ostracized oddity to embraced eccentric. Her significance to the overall narrative, though, is severely diminished, as are opportunities for viewers to see and understand her psychology and identity. As with Neville, therefore, Film Luna is a less sympathetic character than Book Luna, and is a character with whom fans have less opportunity to emotionally engage.

With the near exclusion of Neville and Luna from the films comes the reduction of their roles in defeating Voldemort. The films appear more streamlined and attuned to Harry's own narrative—Film Neville and Luna's narrative presence is significantly less than that of Book Neville and Luna, but the opposite is true for Book and Film Harry. However, fans have taken issue with this aspect of the adaptations. There are hundreds of fan-created and -curated responses to Neville and Luna's narrative changes to demonstrate how the Harry Potter generation transfigure Neville and Luna into characters who are more in line with their novelistic characterization—an "idiot" and an "oddity" who are essential to the narrative's resolution.

The Magic of the Harry Potter Generation

With respect to an audience's engagement with and response to an adaptation, Linda Hutcheon and Siobhan O'Flynn explain that, "it is probably easier for an adapter to forge a relationship with an audience that is not overly burdened with affection or nostalgia for the adapted text. Without foreknowledge, we are more likely to greet a film version simply as a new film, not as an adaptation at all" (Hutcheon and O'Flynn 2013, 121). It is the presence of foreknowledge that has resulted in fans' dissatisfaction with Film Neville and Luna. Because fans are "burdened with affection or nostalgia" (121), any changes to their narrative arcs make it harder to see the film as a "new film."

In a recent BuzzFeed poll created by Jarry Lee, titled "Who Is The Best 'Harry Potter' Character?" users were asked to select their favorite characters of the Harry Potter series. (Un)surprisingly, neither Harry nor Ron were near the top of the list. At the time of writing this essay, Hermione is perceived as the most popular character with 25 percent of the votes, Luna is tied for third place with 8 percent of the votes, Harry and Neville both share 5 percent, and Ron is the best character to only 4 percent of voters. While by no means quantitatively or statistically authoritative, this poll does show that Neville and Luna are just as popular in fan communities as the trio.

It is interesting, then, that Neville and Harry share popularity, because as Shira Wolosky notes, "Neville is more specifically a double for Harry. Neville is with Harry through all seven books. At first, he is almost a clownish figure: the wizard without talent contrasted to Harry's dazzling promise of exceptional fate and power" (Wolosky 2010, 103). It is because of the removal of much of this doubling in the films that fans have taken it upon themselves to move beyond the canon and transform Neville and Luna into strong(er), more important figures than they appear to be in the films.

Neville has received a great deal of attention on social media sites such as Tumblr. Part of this popularity comes from fans' perception of him as the "almost chosen one." As Tumblr user Analyze It and Weep notes,

> I don't really need to argue with anyone that Neville Longbottom is an [sic] stone-cold badass.... One of the most remarkable things about Neville is that when he is first introduced to us, and for a long time after, the audience is led to have little or no faith in him. He is the blundering comic relief. *Oh, poor Neville, messing up in Potions. Oh, poor Neville, forgetting the password. Oh, poor Neville, losing Trevor again.* Then, come the seventh book, it's *Oh, Poor Neville, leadING A REBEL ORGANIZATION AND BEHEADING NAGINI WITH A SINGLE SWIPE? WHAT?* [original emphasis].

The enthusiasm surrounding Neville's narrative significance becomes obvious when examining *how* fans respond to him. In this post, the fan expresses the (anti)climactic buildup of Neville through the series, before showing their excitement mid-sentence with the last three letters of "leading" suddenly changing to capital letters. The typography of this post mirrors the (somewhat) unexpected and sudden change in Neville's characterization. For Analyze It and Weep, "The truly empowering thing about Neville's transformation isn't the awesome things he does as the series comes to an end, but rather, the fact that he had it in him all along, and just didn't know it." Precisely as we have argued, reading the series through Neville (or Luna), as opposed to Harry, reveals a multitude of significant and "badass" characters.

Another fan to take up this point is DeviantART user nateneurotic. In nateneurotic's painting, 11-year-old Neville is shown facing right, holding a Mimbulus Mimbletonia in his left hand, with Trevor the Toad on his right shoulder. Neville looks frightened and sad as he stares into the distance. Behind him, his shadow is seventh year Neville cutting the head off Nagini with the Sword of Gryffindor, while the Sorting Hat floats to the side. This image encapsulates the evolution of Neville throughout the series and the Harry Potter generation's perception of him as a hero. This image demonstrates that Neville really does "[have] it in him all along."

While Neville appears to dominate online fandom, Luna too has her share of admiration. Much of the fan response to Luna expresses dissatisfaction with the omissions which characterize her adaptation from book to film.

Discussing the removal of the mural scene, Tumblr user mouserightsactivist explains:

luna isn't even made out to be one of harry's closest friends (not when he has Hermione and ron, anyway) but she puts him up there anyway. she puts hermione— who is constantly criticising her theories—and ron—who makes fun of her a lot, at least in the fifth book—up there too.

maybe it's because she finally has friends. maybe it's because she always treats those friends with love and respect, no matter what they say or do to her. maybe it's because she took the time to paint an entire mural dedicated to THEM—the people who finally befriended her. were nice to a girl who was previously bullied [sic; original emphases].

Fans appear to understand the significance of Luna's psychological character development. They see her compassion as necessary, not only to the narrative's resolution, but to Harry's (and the trio's) personal narrative(s). Luna is introduced as peculiar, but by the series' conclusion she is no longer simply an oddity, but an important person in the trio's (and fans') lives.

Henry Jenkins notes in *Textual Poachers* (1994) that fans construct meaning through "a social process" so that "individual interpretations are shaped and reinforced through ongoing discussions with other readers" (45). "Such discussions," he adds,

expand the experience of the text beyond its initial consumption. The produced meanings are thus more fully integrated into the readers' lives and are of a fundamentally different character from meanings generated through a casual and fleeting encounter with an otherwise unremarkable (and unremarked upon) text. For a fan, these previously 'poached' meanings provide a foundation for future encounters with the fiction, shaping how it will be perceived, defining how it will be used [Jenkins 1994, 45].

By sharing interpretations of Neville and Luna as significant characters, fans build upon and expand their interaction with them. Websites such as Tumblr and DeviantART allow fans to share readings of the texts with thousands of other users. When one fan shares their reading of Neville or Luna as important characters, future encounters of Neville and Luna by other fans are potentially altered.

In one piece of fanfiction aptly titled "An Untold Love Story: Luna Lovegood and Neville Longbottom," Wattpad user bands_and_demands embraces a romantic addition to the filmic representation of Neville and Luna that fans have overwhelmingly supported. This story has been read almost 20,000 times. The "untold love story" of Neville and Luna arises during the film *Deathly Hallows Part 2*, and is one of the many pieces of fan prose that reorients the events of the books. Ika Willis has shown that "through writing fan fiction … a fan can, firstly, make space for her own desires in a text which may not at first sight provide the resources to sustain them; and, secondly, recirculate the reoriented text among other fans without attempting to close the text on the 'truth' of her reading" (Willis 2006, 155). The same process occurs with the creation of Harry Potter fan art. Fans can be seen to be transforming the films to include their own desires to see Neville and Luna portrayed in a more substantial manner. By circulating these readings on sites such as Tumblr and DeviantART, fans are not "attempting to close the text on the 'truth' of [their own] readings" (155), but rather, highlight and defend the importance of characters who are often overlooked in both the narrative and in critical responses to the series.

The Harry Potter generation has grown up with Harry Potter. But we have also developed alongside Neville and Luna, and seen ourselves in them. When reading the narrative through Neville and Luna, it becomes apparent that Harry is only able to "save the day" because of all the support he is given throughout the series from supporting characters such as Neville and Luna. The transition to film, however, reduces Neville and Luna's narrative significance, pushing them to the margins. Nevertheless, fans have taken it upon themselves to bring to life Hermione's assertion: "Neville is not an idiot and Luna is not an oddity!" (*DH* 336). By transfiguring Neville and Luna back to a state in which they have greater significance to the overall narrative, fans have demonstrated the extent to which non-main characters are important to reader engagement. It is as a result of this process of resistant reading that fans have been able to/are able to challenge the dominant understanding of the Harry Potter story, and highlight the narrative significance of Neville and Luna. It is, we suggest, largely because of them that "all was well" (*DH* 831).

NOTE

   1. The concept of the ur-fan, initially raised in this chapter was expanded more fully in "The Ghost of J.K. Rowling: *Harry Potter* and the Ur-Fan" by McLeod and Holland, 2017.

REFERENCES

Analyze It and Weep. 2013. "Neville Longbottom: The Unchosen One." *Tumblr.* Last modified 31 Dec 2013. Accessed 25 July 2015. http://analyzeitandweep.tumblr.com/post/71800 345930/neville-longbottom-the-unchosen-one.
Anatol, Giselle Liza, ed. 2003. *Reading Harry Potter: Critical Essays.* Westport, CT: Praeger.
Bal, Mieke. 2009. *Narratology: Introduction to the Theory of Narrative.* Toronto: University of Toronto Press.
bands_and_demands. "An Untold Love Story: Luna Lovegood and Neville Longbottom." *Wattpad.* Accessed 2 August 2015. https://www.wattpad.com/story/8418664-an-untold-love-story-luna-lovegood-and-neville.
daily-harry-potter. "If Lily Potter had an abortion..." *Tumblr.* 28 Jan. 2013. Web. 02 Oct 2015. http://daily-harry-potter.tumblr.com/post/41689586911/if-lily-potter-had-an-abortion.
Frow, John. 2014. *Character and Person.* Oxford: Oxford University Press.
Galef, David. 1993. *The Supporting Cast: A Study of Flat and Minor Characters.* Philadelphia: Pennsylvania State University Press.
Harris, Maria. 2004. "Is Seeing Believing? Truth and Lies in *Harry Potter and the Order of the Phoenix.*" *Topic: The Washington & Jefferson College Review* 54: 83–92.

Harry Potter and the Philosopher's Stone. 2001. Directed by Chris Columbus. Burbank, CA: Warner Bros. Pictures. DVD.
Harry Potter and the Chamber of Secrets. 2002. Directed by Chris Columbus. Burbank, CA: Warner Bros. Pictures. DVD.
Harry Potter and the Goblet of Fire. 2005. Directed by Mike Newell. Burbank, CA: Warner Bros. Pictures. DVD.
Harry Potter and the Order of the Phoenix. 2007. Directed by David Yates. Burbank, Ca: Warner Bros. Pictures. DVD.
Harry Potter and the Half-Blood Prince. 2009. Directed by David Yates. Burbank, Ca: Warner Bros. Pictures. DVD.
Harry Potter and the Deathly Hallows—Part 1. 2010. Directed by David Yates. Burbank, Ca: Warner Bros. Pictures. DVD.
Harry Potter and the Deathly Hallows—Part 2. 2011. Directed by David Yates. Burbank, Ca: Warner Bros. Pictures. DVD.
Heilman, Elizabeth E., ed. 2009. *Critical Perspectives on Harry Potter.* New York: Routledge.
Hutcheon, Linda, and Siobhan O'Flynn. 2013. *A Theory of Adaptation.* New York: Routledge.
Jenkins, Henry. 1992. *Textual Poachers: Television Fans and Participatory Culture.* New York: Routledge.
_____. 2007. "Transmedia Storytelling 101." *Confessions of an Aca-Fan: The Official Weblog of Henry Jenkins.* Accessed 05 Oct 2015. http://henryjenkins.org/2007/03/transmedia_storytelling_101.html.
_____. 2008. *Convergence Culture: Where Old and New Media Collide.* Fredericksburg: New York University Press.
Lavoie, Chantel. 2003. "Safe as Houses: Sorting and School Houses at Hogwarts." In *Reading Harry Potter: Critical Essays,* edited by Giselle Liza Anatol, 35–49. Westport, CT: Praeger.
Lee, Jarry. 2015. "Who Is The Best 'Harry Potter' Character?" *BuzzFeed.* Accessed 30 July 2015. http://www.buzzfeed.com/jarrylee/who-is-the-best-harry-potter-character#.vmyZo9rELw.
Margolin, Uri. 2007. "Character." In *The Cambridge Companion to Narrative,* edited by David Herman, 66–79. New York: Cambridge University Press.
McCrum, Kirstie. 2015. "New Harry Potter Story Revealed by JK Rowling Is FREE to Read." *Mirror.* Accessed 28 Sep 2015.
McLeod, Dion, and Travis Holland. 2017. "The Ghost of J.K. Rowling: *Harry Potter* and the Ur-Fan." *MFCO Working Paper Series* 3: 1–20.
mouserightsactivist. 2015. "No Title." *Tumblr.* Accessed 7 August 2015. http://mouserightsactivist.tumblr.com/post/125635563976/things-i-am-mad-about-how-the-deathly-hallows.
nateneurotic. n.d. "Neville Longbottom." *DeviantART.* Accessed 15 July 2015. http://nateneurotic.deviantart.com/art/Neville-Longbottom-122360154.
Nel, Philip. 2003. "Lost in Translation? Harry Potter, from Page to Screen." In *Reading Harry Potter: Critical Essays,* edited by Giselle Liza Anatol, 275–90. Westport, CT: Praeger.
Niantic. 2017. "The Magic of Harry Potter is Coming to a Neighborhood Near You." *Nianticlabs.* Accessed on 8 Nov 2017. https://nianticlabs.com/blog/wizardsunite.
Pierce, Jeremy. 2010. "Destiny in the Wizarding World." In *The Ultimate Harry Potter and Philosophy: Hogwarts for Muggles,* edited by Gregory Bassham, 35–52. Hoboken, NJ: John Wiley & Sons, Inc.
Rowling, J.K. 1997. *Harry Potter and the Philosopher's Stone.* London: Bloomsbury.
_____. *Harry Potter and the Chamber of Secrets.* 1998. London: Bloomsbury.
_____. *Harry Potter and the Prisoner of Azkaban.* 1999. London: Bloomsbury.
_____. *Harry Potter and the Goblet of Fire.* 2000. London: Bloomsbury.
_____. *Harry Potter and the Order of the Phoenix.* 2003. London: Bloomsbury.
_____. *Harry Potter and the Half-Blood Prince.* 2005. London: Bloomsbury.
_____. *Harry Potter and the Deathly Hallows.* 2007. London: Bloomsbury.
_____. "Have just heard that James S Potter has been Sorted (to nobody's surprise) into Gryffindor. Teddy Lupin (Head Boy, Hufflepuff) disappointed." 1 Sept 2015, 11:18 a.m. Tweet.

_____. "I'm in Edinburgh, so could somebody at King's Cross wish James S Potter good luck for me? He's starting at Hogwarts today. #BackToHogwarts." 1 Sept 2015, 2:15 a.m. Tweet.

SlickGenius. "J.K. Rowling—'A Year in the Life' Part 5 (Elizabeth Vargus Documentary ABC NEWS-HD)." *YouTube*. 17 July 2009. Web. 12 August 2015. https://www.youtube.com/watch?v=bKWGKzfzV4o.

Whited, Lana A. ed. 2002. *The Ivory Tower and Harry Potter: Perspectives on a Literary Phenomenon*. Columbia: University of Missouri Press.

Willis, Ika. 2006. "Keeping Promises to Queer Children: Making Space (for Mary-Sue) at Hogwarts." In *Rethinking Fan Fiction and Fan Communities in the Internet Age*, edited by Karen Hellekson and Kristina Busse, 153–70. Jefferson, NC: McFarland.

Woloch, Alex. 2003. *The One vs the Many: Minor Characters and the Space of the Protagonist in the Novel*. Princeton: Princeton University Press.

Wolosky, Shira. 2010. *The Riddles of Harry Potter: Secret Passages and Interpretive Quests*. New York: Palgrave Macmillan.

Harry Potter and the Book Burners' Mistake

Suppression and Its Unintended Consequences

EMILY LAUER

At the turn of the millennium, the Harry Potter series surged so much in popularity throughout the United States that voices of dissatisfaction and dissent were almost bound to appear alongside the many which clamored eagerly for the next installment of the series. There were those who objected to adults reading children's books. There were those who said the novels were poorly written and derivative. There were those (often devoted fans of the series) who pointed out the ways that it could be more progressive in race, class and gender issues. And there was a group that got far more press than their actual numbers could account for: fundamentalist Christian leaders who feared the series was inducting the youth of America into godless witchcraft.

Although many scholars and pastors noted the ways that the Harry Potter story resembled the Jesus story, the popularity of books in which good characters perform magic offended a small, vocal subsection of fundamentalists. In her article "The Perils of Shape Shifting," Leanne Simmons explains this phenomenon:

> Despite … affinities with the essence of Christian hope, the fears of some conservative Christians have not been assuaged; many regard the books as "anti–Christ." In these circles, there are lingering suspicions that the popular series contains spiritual threats to basic tenets of Christian faith. Based on a perusal of websites, it appears that fundamentalist Christians have had the most militant anti–Potter reaction. Some fundamentalists have lobbied to ban the book from public institutions and, in the most extreme cases, have burned the books in protest [Simmons 2012, 53–54].

Compared to other book burnings throughout history, these were small events and few in number. However, that does not mean they were ineffective. In fact, they received a lot of attention from the national and international press because they combined two things that journalists consider inherently newsworthy: Harry Potter and book burning, which we associate with Nazis. Part of the goal of book burning is to create spectacle and thus, publicity. That goal was amply achieved.

Considering more long term effects, however, these book burnings and the press that surrounded them also achieved an effect contrary to the aims of the burners. The massive protests against the burnings demonstrated that the fanbase of Harry Potter could be fruitfully mobilized for progressive action. Symbolically "destroying" a text by burning individual copies of the physical book requires the burner to assume via metonymy that the physical books themselves have a huge amount of power. In general, the pageantry of book burning can be easily co-opted by champions of the books themselves because everyone involved in the exercise has already opted in to the performativity of the event. The fan backlash against burning the Harry Potter books dramatically overshadowed the bonfires they protested and thus the intended destruction actually ended up having a reifying effect: the power of the text over society was demonstrated and in fact intensified rather than reduced. Both fan activists and the wider observing world were able to see the potential for effect when Harry Potter fans mobilize. In this essay, I first discuss the motivations of book burners and how the cultural connotations of book burnings shape our reactions to them. Then I apply that discussion to explain why these burnings got so much press and how I believe they helped galvanize Harry Potter fans into a generation with a particular view of progressive activism: because the book burners mirrored the way evil is represented in the series itself, fans were able to embody the books' representation of good in response.

Harry Potter and the Pastors

According to Daniel Schwartz of the CBC, as of 2010, "There have been at least six book burnings involving Potter books in the U.S.," two of which emerge from the journalistic record as the most press-covered, both in 2001. In March of that year, Pastor George Bender led his congregation in rural Butler County, Pennsylvania in "a burning of the Harry Potter books, as well as Shirley MacLaine books, *Pinocchio* videos, and music by Bruce Springsteen and Pearl Jam" (Roggenkamp 2008). On its page about Harry Potter book burnings, the website religioustolerance.org also reports that this bonfire included copies of the movie *Hercules* and "pamphlets from Jehovah's Witnesses" (Robinson 2005). Then in December of that year, in Alamogordo, New Mexico, "a local church held a bonfire event to burn works written by J.K. Rowling and other 'offensive' works, including J.R.R. Tolkien novels, issues of *Cosmopolitan* and *Young Miss* magazines, and *The Complete Works of William Shakespeare*," led by Pastor Jack Brock (Roggenkamp). According to religioustolerance.org, "also destroyed were Ouija boards, Maxim magazines, Pokémon cards, ... personal problems written on pieces of paper [and] a statue of the Buddha" (Robinson 2005). Both of these bonfires clearly included so many different items that different news outlets reported different items as indicative of the range. However, both of the pastors and all the news outlets agree that burning Harry Potter was the main thing.

The burnings were a predictable response to their cultural context in a variety of ways. First of all, the burnings can be seen as more extreme versions of the pushback against the series evidenced by the many challenges to its inclusion in public school curriculum and in public library collections. According to a list of Harry Potter challengers maintained by Karen Roggenkamp, it appears that the challenges were often provoked by special events focused on the books due to their popularity. In classrooms and libraries, Harry Potter books were often the read-aloud book, or there would be a special push to finish the whole series to earn a certificate, or there would be some similar way in which a Harry Potter book seemed to be given special treatment by teachers and librarians. Thus, the protests were not always about the popular book's accessibility; challenges also focused on the endorsement of these books by figures of authority within the school or library.

The pastors who organized bonfires in order to burn Harry Potter books were extreme examples of these challenges to the series, but they were also explicitly motivated to destroy the books in retaliation against pastors who embraced the message in the series as wholesomely Christian. Simmons reports that around the same time that challenges to the series were on the rise,

> Evangelical writer Charles Colson (1999), who disappointed many evangelicals and fundamentalists when he refused to jump on the anti–Potter bandwagon, was correct to assert that the Harry Potter series has more to do with secularism than Satanism. [Furthermore,] Connie Neal (2002), noting the methodology by which some Christians choose selective passages to prove the books "demonic," cleverly decided to do the same with the books' Christian content. The result, her *The Gospel According to Harry Potter*, has been used by ministers as a study tool for Christian understanding. She is certainly not the only author to see a 'Christ-likeness' hiding under Harry's robes [55].

To justify his bonfire, Pastor Brock said of Harry Potter, "Behind that innocent face is the power of satanic darkness.... Harry Potter is the devil and he is destroying people." The *BBC News*, which quoted this line in its 2001 article about the book burning, also notes "Pastor Brock said he had never read any of the four Potter novels." Most challenges to books come from people who have not read them. Brock is not the minority in this respect. The simple explanation for the burnings offered or assumed in most news articles was the mere fact that these were books in which laudable characters performed witchcraft, something that was inherently intolerable to a certain subset of fundamentalist Christians who did not feel the need to read the books for the context of what they already knew they'd deplore.

A Fundamentalist Society Under Siege

However, there are a few complicating factors here. There were thousands of fantasy books in public schools and libraries before Harry Potter was published and almost all of the other media burned in Pastor Bender and Pastor Brock's bonfires predate Harry Potter. However, Harry Potter was popular enough, and the Harry Potter phenomenon was in the public consciousness enough, that religious fundamentalists felt it might pose a threat to their way of life in a way that required its destruction—and many other aspects of the culture might as well be purged, too. As Hans J. Hillerbrand points out in his address to the American Academy of Religion, intolerance increases when a society feels threatened. He cautions:

> societies become persecuting societies when they perceive a threat to the *status quo*, a threat that may be real or merely imagined. When perceiving a threat, society responds with restrictive measures, redefining ever more narrowly what is acceptable and what is unacceptable behavior. The wagons are circled and the barricades erected. Thus, causality exists between threat, perceived or real, external or internal, and intolerance [Hillerbrand 2006, 608].

This helps explain why fundamentalist reaction against Harry Potter was expanded to include other exempla of contemporary American culture: because as the borders of acceptability are perceived to be widening too much, they must instead be protectively tightened in order to strengthen them.

While a wider society might perceive book burning as violently reactionary, those doing the burning characterize it as a reaction justified by intolerable impurity. As Hillerbrand puts it, "those who burn books claim honorable goals and values, a fact that cannot be emphasized too much. The work of destruction is accompanied by declarations of virtue" (Hillerbrand 2006, 607). At Pastor Brock's burning, for instance, "Parishioner Jennifer Jaglowitz, 17, discarded a Backstreet Boys music tape, among other personal items. 'It [burning them] will help strengthen my life in Jesus Christ and my relationship with [H/h]im,' she told the Albuquerque Tribune" (Ishizuka 2002).

Historically, motivations for book burning have included activating the wholesome symbolic aspects of purging and cleansing by fire: "In the armamentarium of the fundamentalist—from Salamanca to Salem—fire has been a favorite means of eliciting the truth, cleansing souls, and eradicating the undesirable" (Cronin 2003). For the Nazis, incitements to burn books took on aspects of national and personal mental housecleaning akin to our current uncluttering trend, as there were "invitations to the public to clear out their own and other libraries and to bring books for burning to collection-points" (Ritchie 1988, 637). Descriptions of the Nazis' bookburning activities rely on words like "purge" and "cleansing" to convey their motivations. For instance, the United States Holocaust Memorial Museum website notes that "on April 6, 1933, the Nazi German Student Association's Main Office for Press and Propaganda proclaimed a nationwide 'Action against the Un-German Spirit,' to climax in a literary purge or 'cleansing' (*Säuberung*) by fire" ("Book Burning" 2016). In his article "Books are Weapons," Matthew Fishburn discusses how inevitable Nazi bookburning seems, in retrospect, when he remarks that,

> For the nascent Third Reich, which adopted the purifying fire as its fundamental symbol, it is scarcely surprising that it took less than four months before books were burnt across the country.... In lightly falling rain [Joseph Goebbels] spoke of his hope that from the ashes of the pacifist, defeatist, and un–German books that had been burnt, the phoenix of the new Reich would rise [Fishburn 2007, 223].

The idea of burning out impurities has a physical and sometimes medical precedent that is often embodied symbolically. When the phoenix rises from the ashes, for example, its aged, worn-out body is discarded and burned, leaving a purified object newly strengthened by its sacrifice. This hopeful aspect about the future after the purge, as Brock's parishioner hopes her relationship with Jesus will be strengthened and as Goebbels hopes Germany will be strengthened, leads to a sense of transcendental ecstasy about the act of purging.

That joy might account for some of the festival atmosphere around book burnings, since metaphorical purges and cleansings require pageantry in a way that physical and medical purging and cleansings do not. This has been true for staged book burnings at many points in history. David Cressy asserts that in early modern England, book burning "was primarily a symbolic punishment, not a suppression of text. It was a demonstration of authority, not an annihilation of forbidden words" (Cressy 2005, 374). We can thus see

> book burning as part of the public performance of power as well as a means of policing discourse and destroying words on paper. The public rituals of censorship formed part of the communications repertoire of the early modern state. The banning and burning of books involved dialogue and discourse, speaker and audience, spectacle and spectators in the making and transmission of meaning.... Book burning, I will argue, was both medium and message [Cressy 361].

Cressy notes that the spectacle, like the symbolism, is essential to the burners. This is because the spectacle is required to activate the metonymy of punishing or destroying ideas by destroying individual copies of the physical books that house them.

Burning Books in American Society

For those burning Harry Potter books, the shared, festival atmosphere assists the burners in achieving the metonymic cognitive leap that allows them to believe destroying the physical books means destroying the temptations their contents might represent in the lives of the congregation performing the burning. However, book burning is more than just a festive bonfire or medical purging. It is also an activation of the frightening and threatening aspects of fire that evoke violent, painful punishment and destruction. The book burning bonfire is a celebratory, warming fire for those doing the burning and it is also a display of an awesome amount of power: a barely contained, destructive force on the side of righteousness. The sociological use of book burnings as a show of force is a reactive one, a defense mechanism of a society that perceives a threat.

In turn, our society perceives staged book burnings as a threat to our freedoms. Our cultural associations with book burnings start with the Nazis, but also include other instances of state-sanctioned limits of knowledge throughout history and around the world. In an article about how the symbolism of book burning became codified and calcified in the U.S., Fishburn notes that,

> the years succeeding 1933 had witnessed a profusion of attempts to understand the attraction and the use of book burning as a political tool or a cultural symbol. In this period even those writers who attacked or dismissed the [Nazi book burning] event did not necessarily relinquish the possibility that it might be invigorating and new. As such, book burning was appropriated by everyone from staunch Communists and fellow travelers, to dystopian novelists and bored literary critics [Fishburn 2007, 225].

Fishburn goes on to explain how it wasn't until the second World War was actually being fought that book burning had its role firmly fixed by the Allies into a symbol of what the Nazis stood for: evil, intolerant fascism. He asserts that this meaning was finally solidified in 1941 in "George Orwell's famous broadcast in which he observed that book burning was the 'most characteristic activity of the Nazis'" (Fishburn 226). That statement helps us define both Nazis and book burning. It is as self-evident to state "Nazis are book burners" as it is to state "book burners are Nazis."

Thus, just as insults about being a stickler can append –nazi as an intensifier (feminazi, grammar nazi, soup nazi), for both history and fiction in the

United States, book burning is now almost shorthand for repressive fascism that threatens religious and intellectual freedom. Book burning is perceived to be not only evil, but also un–American. Interestingly, Fishburn notes that even while book burning was being codified as a near synonym of "Nazi," the U.S. government was documented burning subversive literature by the ton (234). However, that burning was not an event, not a spectacle, but rather disposal. Much more important to the United States cultural consciousness was the equation of publishing freedoms with other cherished freedoms, as when "a Pennsylvania high school interpreted the Book Week slogan of 1941, 'Forward with Books,' to be synonymous with 'Forward with Democracy,' [and] the editors of the *Library Journal* derived a motto: 'in America we do not burn books; we build libraries'" (Fishburn 234). The democratizing of access to literature is positioned in opposition to repressive censorship, and progressive constructive action (building) is positioned in opposition to destruction.

Of course, Nazis were not the only oppressive regime to burn books. "Since ancient times, people from virtually all religions and societies have burned books as a form of censorship, protest, or hate mongering. It is no accident that these violent acts have often been committed in parallel with gruesome executions of heretics, scholars, and enemies of the state" warns the University of Wisconsin–Milwaukee Libraries in its "Book Burning 213 BC–2011 AD" exhibit, which divides book burners into the categories of "Vandals," "Censors and Bigots" and "Anti-intellectuals." Under "Censors and Bigots," the librarians who curated this exhibit write, "Those burning books as an act of censorship on ideological grounds often display religious intolerance, such as that exhibited during the Spanish Inquisition or the reign of the Taliban" ("Book Burning, 213 BC–2011 AD"). Thus it is noteworthy that in an attempt to purge performatively, the burners of Harry Potter books chose to invoke an allegiance with those commonly painted as the villains of history.

Books Have Power

This should indicate that the symbolism inherent in book burning is multivalent. Even in just the motivations of the burners, there is a tension between the symbolism of cleansing, purifying fire on the one hand and overwhelming power of destruction on the other, even though both of these "meanings" of burning are considered just and justified by the burners. When we consider the wider society's equation of book burning with evil oppressive regimes as well, it is clear that the book burners and those who learn about the book burnings have very different views on what the activity "means."

However, there is one thing that both book burners and proponents of reading freedom agree on and that is that texts can be powerful. Book burning, whether it is considered as a metonymic destruction, punishment or repudiation of the contents of the text, requires a cognitive leap to consider a physical copy of a book to stand in for the text it houses—the concepts of its contents. Symbolically "destroying" Harry Potter by burning the books requires the burner to assume books are dangerous because they have a huge amount of power over the culture and over individual people's lives. Those who protest book burning do so because they, too, know books can act powerfully on a culture or individual. This acknowledgment of their power motivates their destruction for one group and their defense for another.

All of this multivalent symbolism, the tacit agreement to engage in metonymy, and the shared belief in the power of books to shape people's lives mean that the pageantry of a staged book burning can be co-opted by champions of the book. Cressy notes that while the spectacle is required by those burning books, it does not necessarily remain in the power of those staging the burning (361). In that way the pageantry of book burning is like the fire itself—it is started by the book burners, but not necessarily contained by them. The Harry Potter burnings staged by fundamentalist Christians in the United States at the turn of the millennium are an example of how the spectacle of the purging bonfires can surge out of control of those who started the fire.

The Harry Potter burnings had a variety of consequences that we can only assume were not intended by the bonfires' instigators. One consequence is that the intended repudiation of the book, theoretically removing it from the lives of the burners and from the wider society, actually had a reifying effect: the power of the text over society is made real instead of reduced. The burnings in fact helped solidify the important role of these books in our culture both by asserting their importance in the lives of the burners, and, as I'll discuss at length later in this essay, by suggesting to fans of the series that their fandom was a principled philosophical stance in opposition to petty fascism, rather than just enjoyment of a very popular thing.

The first part of reification of the books' power is actually the more complicated—the idea that by rejecting the books, the burners are asserting the books' importance within their own lives. As the concept of the anti-fan makes clear, it is still possible to have your life defined by your relationship to a text even if you are not a proponent of the text. As various burnings throughout history have shown, burning copies of the hated text does not reduce its hold on the burner. For instance, after burning works felt to have an un–German spirit in 1933, Nazis in Germany did not move on to lead peaceful, productive lives of quiet contemplation. They were still defined by their need to reject and destroy. In the case of the Harry Potter burnings, while on a much smaller scale, there was the added issue of the extensive press coverage of the bonfires: with our current technological advances, the names of those who have burned Harry Potter will be linked to his in perpetuity.

The media was not sympathetic to those burning Harry Potter, but it did help their publicity. A blurb about the burnings in the *Manawatu Standard* in 2001 was headlined "Book-burning foolishness" for instance, and a *Washington Times* article from 2003 quotes "The Rev. Don Peter Fleetwood, a member of the Pontifical Council for Culture who contributed to a recent Vatican document on New Age religions," as saying "'If I have understood well the intentions of Harry Potter's author, they help children to see the difference between good and evil'" (Galupo 2003). This quotation seems pointed in the context of the media's attitude about the book burnings. The same article, "Are witches wild about Harry?" explored whether actual Wiccans felt that the series might draw children to Wicca, as Christian fundamentalists were so afraid it might. The article quotes other practitioners of various neopagan belief systems and religions, including a woman who says Rowling's series "'clearly draws a line between people who behave well and people who don't behave well'" (Galupo). Similarly, the tone of the journalist seems clear when an article about the Pennsylvania bonfire notes that "Rev. George Bender says he never thought a little book burning would ignite so much publicity" and quotes him saying "'We were only out to make a little noise in the local community'"("Church book burning draws heat" 2001). The pastor's affected surprise that burning books would gain journalistic attention is undermined by his assertion that the goal was "only" to make "noise."

In what was probably a predictable turn of events, the media coverage of the burnings made a mountain out of a molehill as it led to what is called the "Streisand effect": in 2003, Barbra Streisand attempted to have a photograph of her home removed from a public record of 12,000 images to show coastal erosion. The very idea that it might be suppressed led to a huge upsurge of interest in the otherwise uninteresting photograph of a house on a coast. The Streisand Effect, then, describes the phenomenon of an increase in interest due to a threat of lack of access.

It is certainly true that when something is forbidden, it gains in popularity. As Blaise Cronin notes in "Burned Any Good Books Lately?," "The irony is that firebrands throughout history have probably done much more in the long run against censorship than for their own causes" (2003). Similarly, in his satirical article "In Defense of Book Burning," from 2002, Will Manley claims "book burnings bring big publicity. Nothing provokes public interest more than a fire, and nothing helps to sell books more than public interest." Banned books often have their sales and circulation boosted by being banned as people's curiosity is piqued, an effect which predates Banned Books Week by hundreds of years. In his examination of Tudor and Stuart England, Cressy notes that forbidding something, especially in such a theatrical way as a book-burning, increased demand for it:

> As an act of censorship, [book burning] was ineffective. The spectacle subverted its sponsors' intentions. Only part of the edition was destroyed, and surviving copies, though "gelded and mangled," could still be found on the market. Indeed, as Jacobean authorities recognized on other occasions, the publicity involved in burning a book endowed it with "importance" and caused it "to be sought." "The stir" of suppression made copies 'much more inquired after' and turned some of them into best sellers [Cressy 368].

An actual gain in the popularity of the Harry Potter series due to six bonfires in the United States was probably negligible since the number of readers was so astronomical already, but the overblown media coverage of the burnings did make people think Harry Potter needed to be defended from bigots.

Counter Protests—Good and Evil in Fiction and Action

Luckily for those who wished to defend Harry Potter, they had a built-in model for resisting evil suppression in the books themselves. In fact, in some ways the fundamentalists burning Harry Potter books gave fans of the series exactly what they wanted and journalists who needed to spin the Harry Potter phenomenon in new ways on a near-daily basis exactly what they needed: a villain whose trappings resembled Lord Voldemort and who was not going to win.

Both evil and good allegiances in the book series can be easily mapped onto those burning the Harry Potter books and those protesting the burnings. In the books, the villains are those who value purity over lived human lives. We are told that the last time such an evil was seen in the wizarding world, Dumbledore defeated the evil wizard Grindelwald in 1945. As Marian Yee discusses elsewhere in this volume, we are presented with a three-way equation: Voldemort is like Grindelwald is like Hitler. The Death Eaters, with their Nazi-esque aesthetic made even more prominent by the movie versions of the series, want to remove the "mudbloods" from their midst and exert total, fascist control over the lives of the wizarding community. The heroes, in contrast, stand up for freedom and diversity by asserting that fascist control has no place in their lives, nation, and community and taking a public stand to protect freedom. As Simmons notes, "Rowling, it seems, prefers a psychologically modernized form of virtue ethics that focuses on character formation" (57). In the Harry Potter series, free thinking that results in critically choosing brave and tolerant actions allows school children to become champions. Thus, through equating book burning with Nazis and Nazis with Voldemort, fans of Harry Potter could become champions *like* Harry Potter by protesting the burnings.

Counter-protests sprung up to defend the series, in response to the many challenges it received, including the burnings. Since book burners and book banners rarely have read the books they profess to hate, there was a disconnect between the knowledge base of the two sides of the argument that proponents of the series were able to employ to great effect for a news-consuming public who, of course, had also generally read the books, and who were not sympathetic to book burning to begin with. For instance, when Pastor Brock's congregation burned the books in Alamogordo, New Mexico, "several hundred people formed a counter-demonstration across the street to protest at the burning…. Some waved signs—including one reading 'Hitler—Bin Laden—Pastor Brock—what great company'" ("'Satanic' Harry Potter Books Burnt" 2001). Webcomic artist Jon Rosenberg created the slogan "Republicans for Voldemort" in 2003 and it has turned into a fully-fledged meme, popular ever since. The TopatoCo product page for five bumper stickers with this slogan says, "Keep four for you and give one to your Republican cousin who doesn't know what Harry Potter is." The assumption is clear that those on the "other side" of this argument do not understand the implications of their actions and allegiances.

Counter-protests for the book burnings were widely documented as part of the newsworthiness of the bonfires. In the article "Harry Potter Book Burning Draws Fire" in the *School Library Journal*, Kathy Ishizuka noted that at Pastor Brock's congregation's bonfire,

> Close by, the incident triggered the opposite reaction: the Alamogordo Public Library has decided to extend its current Harry Potter display, which was originally mounted to coincide with the November premiere of the feature film based on the first book of the series. By so doing, Library Director Jim Preston wants to reassure the public, particularly children "that Harry is alive and well at their library." … Since then, the public has made generous cash donations to the library, says Preston. "With this money we are purchasing additional copies of Harry Potter, Tolkien, and Shakespeare" [Ishizuka].

Thus, the publishers of the burned books and the library itself both benefit financially from these donations.

In 2003, Blaise Cronin wrote in the *Library Journal*, "One can only hope that the pathetic parochialism of Brock and Bender will at the very least galvanize the thinking public's commitment to the anticensorship fight." From our current longer perspective, we can see that it has, and encouragingly continues to do so. In addition to immediate counter-protests, fundamentalist arguments against the Harry Potter series also led to outspoken progressive support for the books in the form of organized, sustained book drives and increased involvement in "freedom to read" movements such as Muggles for Harry Potter, which had formed in 2000. According to their press release, Muggles for Harry Potter brought together "eight groups representing booksellers, librarians, publishers, teachers, writers and citizens [into] a national organization to fight efforts to restrict access to J.K. Rowling's bestselling Harry Potter books" (FEN Newswire 2000). Since then, responses to the burnings have modeled ways to galvanize the genuine enthusiasm of a generation that welcomes calls to action.

There are parallels here, too, between Bender and Brock's bonfires and Nazi book burnings. After the Nazi burnings, allies rallied to rescue and preserve other copies of the books that had been destroyed, which "culminated in the establishment of a Freedom Library for Burned Books in Paris, a practical and symbolic act which both encouraged banned writers in exile and infuriated the Nazis in Germany. In England similar initiatives were taken by H.G. Wells and others" (Ritchie 1988, 643). These efforts were successful in preserving the texts and in equating a repudiation of censorship with a repudiation of Nazism. They also had an additional effect of identity formation: "the Paris library was founded largely by left-wing German émigré writers who wanted to represent the "other" and better Germany, the Brooklyn library was an initiative of liberal upper- middle-class Jewish-Americans who felt called upon both as the People of the Book and citizens of the New World" (Von Merveldt 2007, 525). The constructive and preservative act of founding these libraries allowed their creators to re-establish themselves as not only anti–Nazi, but also constructing and preserving the good and strong elements of their own identities that the Nazis threatened.

Evolving over several years, fans of the series have, in various ways, asserted their belief that having a strong affiliation with the Harry Potter series is identity-forming. As fandom activity has grown in cultural prominence and acceptability over the past fifteen years, the connection between fan identity and political identity has also grown. As Henry Jenkins notes in his 2012 article, "'Cultural Acupuncture,'" the messages and morals in a text can resonate with the text's fans in a way they see reverberating in the real world. He writes that "fans of a particular franchise often choose to support specific causes because they perceive them as tied to the theme of the franchise" (Jenkins 2012). Harry Potter fans, therefore, are most likely to organize around issues they think parallel the issues in the Harry Potter books.

Hillerbrand, in his 2005 address to the AAR, notes that the Fundamentalist congregations that burned Harry Potter books were in the extreme minority, and not politically powerful. It would have been acceptable, he feels, for society as a whole to ignore these burnings: "if such rejection of certain ideas [by burning the books that espouse them] is expressed by a small group of individuals—a pastor, a congregation, a voluntary association—society at large can afford to ignore the happening. This happens in our day, when overeager pastors rally their congregations to burn Harry Potter books" (Hillerbrand 2006, 603). His focus is on bookburning activities of powerful regimes and he does not mention the Harry Potter burnings again. However, the disproportionate response to the Harry Potter burnings, the massive response to "defend" the books from the threat of burning, is itself noteworthy. At the Alamogordo book burning, there were over 800 counter-protesters arrayed in solidarity to "stand up to" the small number of people attempting to repudiate the most popular book in centuries by burning a few individual copies of it. Harry Potter won against Brock's alliance with Voldemort partly because Harry Potter was much, much bigger. This is what I mean about the book burners providing a storybook villain for those who supported Harry Potter and wanted to see themselves as champions like him. Bender and Brock were not going to win, just as Voldemort was not going to win. The stories were already written. And the fundamentalists were right: the Harry Potter series did threaten their *status quo*, and it did end up widening the boundaries of what is considered acceptable in our society in a variety of ways.

Fan Activism in the Harry Potter Generation

In impressive numbers, fans of the series not only leapt to Harry's defense at immediate counter protests but also stuck around to organize against censorship in long-lasting ways. This demonstrated not only the depth of people's investment in Harry Potter, but also their ability to be mobilized in support of causes they believe their heroes would support, and now the Harry Potter fandom is, in fact, noted for an "orientation towards civic virtue" (Ito et al 2013, 53). These kinds of responses paved the way for The Harry Potter Alliance (HPA), an organization that has used fans' knowledge of the wizarding world to champion progressive causes since 2005. As Katie Pryor reported in her college newspaper, Andrew Slack, a founder of the organization, was persuaded that "'many other people had always wanted to be part of a Dumbledore's Army in the real world,' Slack says. With that, the Harry Potter Alliance was founded in 2005 to demonstrate its founder's belief that 'fantasy is not just an escape from the real world; it helps create a better reality for the real world'" (Pryor 2012). Henry Jenkins writes, "Slack describes a conscious rhetorical strategy mapping fictional content worlds onto real-world concerns, what he calls 'cultural acupuncture'" (Jenkins 2012), providing access points that connect understanding a problem in the Harry Potter series to ameliorating a problem in the real world.

The HPA has since become a model organization for fan activism, as it "uses parallels from the fictional content world as an impetus for civic action. It mobilizes young people across the U.S. around issues of literacy, equality, and human rights, and in support of charitable causes" (Ito et al 49). Its founder believes its strength to be its effect on a generation: "fandom may represent a particularly powerful training ground for future activists and community organizers" (Jenkins). As Neta Kligler-Vilenchik notes in her 2013 study on fan activism, "Most, though not all, HPA members see themselves as fans of the series. Many describe having 'grown up with Harry Potter,' reading the books as they came out, and experiencing the gradually maturing story-line as they themselves were entering adulthood" (Kligler-Vilenchik 2013, 19), indicating that while the organization's reach is wider than one generation, the Harry Potter Alliance's core and focus is those who are mobilizing around the series because it was foundational for their sense of self. The *Connected Learning* research synthesis report on improving educational environments, which lauds the HPA, describes one representative HPA member this way:

> Anna leads a chapter of the Harry Potter Alliance in California. She started reading Harry Potter books when she was 11 and was immediately captivated by the story and characters. She continued to follow the books and movies through her teens and early adulthood. She first learned about HPA during her college years, at a Wizard Rock concert where HPA members were running their "Wrock the Vote" Campaign.
>
> After learning about HPA, Anna registered right away, and started participating as an individual in various campaigns. She describes how HPA linked her imagination of wanting to do "something awesome" that came out of the reading of fantasy and applied it "in such a good way that could appeal to so many people" [Ito et al 59].

The generational appeal of the HPA is clear. The organization is large and diffuse and uses social media natively to allow individual chapters to engage with different political causes local to them. It playfully maps elements of Rowling's wizarding world onto ours—sending "owls" and "howlers" through email and social media, for instance—in order to demonstrate the more serious ways that problems in Rowling's wizarding world map onto our own. It "engages with young people in a way that naturally fits in with their everyday lives, interests, and passions, and has been doing so for ten years.... Seventy-four percent say HPA is the first time they've participated in activism" (Phillips 2016). As Amber B. Vayo mentions in her essay, many young fans are critical readers as well as attentive ones, and their understanding of the books' messages can lead them to help make real change based on their internalizing of the series' messages. For the founder of the HPA, this is connected to their generation: "Slack argues that the Harry Potter books take young people seriously as political agents and thus can inspire youth to change the world" (Jenkins). A case study in *Connected Learning* quotes a participant in one of the HPA's campaigns saying "There is this huge fan group that has been moved emotionally by these Harry Potter books and by the idea that the weapon we have is love and that love ultimately is something that can change the world" (Ito et al 50). This belief has inspired fan led-campaigns to donate to disaster-struck regions around the world ever since.

To their alarm, Pastors Bender and Brock and their congregations would probably have agreed with the founders and members of the Harry Potter Alliance about a lot of things. They would all agree that the books are powerful, for instance. They would all agree that books have the capacity to change people's lives, and to change the world. Thus, both burning Harry Potter and becoming a progressive activist in an organization based on the series can be seen as two different ways of responding to the power of books.

REFERENCES

"Book Burning." 2016. *United States Holocaust Memorial Museum.* Accessed August 5. https://www.ushmm.org/wlc/en/article.php?ModuleId=10005852

"Book Burning, 213 BC-2011 AD" 2011. *University of Wisconsin–Milwaukee Libraries* exhibit. Accessed August 5, 2016. http://uwm.edu/libraries/exhibits/burnedbooks/

"Book-burning foolishness" 2001. *Manawatu Standard,* December 29, 2nd ed. sec. Features—Opinion.

"Church Book Burning Draws Heat as Harry Potter Tales Feed Flames." 2001. *Toronto Star,* March 28, section News.

Cressy, David. 2005. "Book Burning in Tudor and Stuart England." *Sixteenth Century Journal* 36 (2): 359–374.

Cronin, Blaise. 2003. "Burned Any Good Books Lately?" *Library Journal* 128 (3): 48.

FEN Newswire. 2000. "Muggles for Harry Potter to Fight Censorship." *The Ethical Spectacle.* Accessed July 16, 2016. http://www.spectacle.org/0400/muggle.html.

Fishburn, Matthew. 2007. "Books Are Weapons: Wartime Responses to the Nazi Bookfires of 1933." *Book History.* 223–251.

"Five Republicans for Voldemort Stickers." 2017. *TopatoCo* product page. Accessed March 31. https://www.topatoco.com/merchant.mvc?Screen=PROD&Store_Code=TO&Product_Code=GOAT-RFV-STICKERS&Category_Code=ALLSTICKERS.

Galupo, Scott. 2003. "Are Witches Wild About Harry?" *Washington Times,* June 21, section Arts.

Hillerbrand, Hans J. 2006. "On Book Burnings and Book Burners: Reflections on the Power (and Powerlessness) of Ideas" [2005 AAR Presidential Address]. *Journal of the American Academy of Religion* 74 (3): 593–614. doi:10.1093/jaarel/lfj117

Ishizuka, Kathy. 2002. "Harry Potter Book Burning Draws Fire." *School Library Journal* 48 (2): 27–28.

Ito, Mizuko, et al. 2013. *Connected Learning: An Agenda for Research and Design.* Irvine, CA: Digital Media and Learning Research Hub.

Jenkins, Henry. 2012. "'Cultural Acupuncture': Fan Activism and the Harry Potter Alliance." *Transformative Works & Cultures* 10. http://journal.transformativeworks.org/index.php/twc/article/view/305/259

Kligler-Vilenchik, Neta. 2013. "'Decreasing World Suck': Fan Communities, Mechanisms of Translation, and Participatory Politics." A Case Study Report Working Paper. Annenberg School for Communication and Journalism, University of Southern California.▉June 24.

Manley, Will. 2002. "In Defense of Book Burning." *American Libraries* 33 (3): 196.

Phillips, Janae. 2016. "The Harry Potter Alliance." *Journal of Digital and Media Literacy.* Accessed July 23. http://www.jodml.org/2016/06/27/the-harry-potter-alliance/

Pryor, Katie. 2012. "Harry Potter Alliance Creator Brings Motivation and Passion to Millersville." The Snapper. Accessed July 23, 2016. http://thesnapper.millersville.edu/

index.php/2012/10/24/harry-potter-alliance-creator-brings-motivation-and-passion-to-millersville/

Ritchie, J.M. 1988. "The Nazi Book-Burning." *Modern Language Review* 83 (3): 627–43.

Robinson, B.A. 2005. "Conservative Christian Responses to the Harry Potter Books: Introduction and Book Burnings." Ontario Consultants on Religious Tolerance. Last updated November 6, 2005. Accessed March 31, 2017. http://www.religioustolerance.org/pottera.htm.

Roggenkamp, Karen. 2008. "Harry Potter Series—Selected Challenges." Course material for ENG 406.001.

"'Satanic' Harry Potter Books Burnt." 2001. *BBC News World Edition,* December 31, section Entertainment.

Schwartz, Daniel. 2010. "The Books Have Been Burning." *CBC News.* Last updated September 8, 2015. Accessed August 5, 2016. http://www.cbc.ca/news/world/the-books-have-been-burning-1.887172.

Simmons, Leanne. 2012. "The Perils of Shape Shifting: Harry Potter and Christian Fundamentalism." *Pastoral Psychology* 62: 53–68. DOI 10.1007/s11089–012–0478–4.

Von Merveldt, Nikola. 2007. "Books Cannot Be Killed By Fire: The German Freedom Library and the American Library of Nazi-Banned Books as Agents of Cultural Memory." *Library Trends* 55 (3): 523–535.

The Disenchantment of Harry Potter

How Magic Died and the Wizarding World Became Modern

Marian Yee

"The fate of our times is characterized by rationalization and intellectualization, and above all, by the disenchantment of the world."

—Max Weber

In "Science as a Vocation," Max Weber (1946) asserts that rationalization and intellectualization has destroyed "the mysterious incalculable forces" that once ruled the world of "savages" (16). We live now in a time and place where "technical means and calculations" (6) perform the service once held by inexplicable, magical forces. In short, we live in a modern, disenchanted, Muggle world. In contrast, the world that J.K. Rowling creates in the Harry Potter series appears to escape such a fate: with its wands and spells, potions and invisibility cloaks, the wizarding world seems to be an enchanted existence where the irrational and mysterious reign supreme. However, the modern, ordinary Muggle world and the magical wizarding world may not be as different as they appear. Disenchantment not only marks the boundary between modes of knowing, but the division between knowledge that is approved and sanctioned as opposed to knowledge that is deemed invalid and illegitimate. If disenchantment means the triumph of the rational and measurable over the mysterious and inestimable, then it is more about leaving behind a way of conceiving and using knowledge than possessing a certain kind of learning. Demarcations between the legitimate and the unlawful, the good and the bad, the modern and the pre-modern are at the heart of Harry's battle with

Voldemort. Their fight to possess Hogwarts is a struggle to uphold how society is ordered, how identity is defined, and how knowledge is procured, organized, and practiced. Harry's conflict with Voldemort, in other words, is a struggle to assert the condition of modernity against its self-referential opposite: magic. By the end of the Harry Potter series, with Harry's victory over Voldemort and the future of Hogwarts assured, no significant differences exist anymore between the wizarding world and the Muggle one, really, except for differences in the modus operandi of each world's technology: wizards fly on brooms; Muggles fly in airplanes, and so on. By the end, magic dies, and the world of Harry Potter, too, becomes disenchanted.

Throughout the traditions of social thought, magic has operated not only as a foil for modern notions of religion and science but, more broadly, as scholars like Styers, Meyer and Pels, and Latour, assert, as a foil for modernity itself. From the European witch hunts, to the advent of the scientific revolution, to the triumph of Enlightenment rationality, to the colonialist suppression of local forms of shamanism, to the pathologizing of magical belief in the early 20th century—magic has served as modernity's antithesis, allowing modernity to construct itself as a dynamic, disenchanted, progressive force that has surpassed the superstitious and stagnant past. Nevertheless, magic's banishment is never complete. Meyer and Pels (2003) point out that "the radical distinction between magic and modernity is a form of modernist purification that is constantly being betrayed by the translations and mediations needed to relate the two" (32): i.e., magic slips out between the cracks of a seemingly impervious construct. Or another way to put it, as Meyer and Pels do, is to say that modernity is "haunted" by the magic it represses (30). In the attempt to differentiate and purify modernity from magic, Margaret Wiener argues that "colonialism *required* native magic, as its foil and ground" and that "the purifying moves of colonial discourse generated new and uncanny hybridities: forms of indigenous knowledge (trance, rumor) that the colonial order could not accommodate" (qtd. in Meyer and Pels 2003, 34). The specter of magic isn't merely an inconvenient reminder of the past; it is something scarier—an anarchic threat to the core unity and productive operation of modern society (Styers 2004, 198). Indeed, magic's entanglement with modernity is indicative of how provisional the condition of modernity is itself. By giving vent to unsocialized desire, magic threatens the seeming stability of modern social organization. Thus, though magic is repressed it is never really lost; it can erupt and threaten a modern way of life.

In the Harry Potter series, the opposition between magic and modernity is constructed within the conflict between the rogue wizard Voldemort and the rest of the wizarding world. The wizarding world is represented as a network of modern institutions that include ministries, hospitals, prisons, banks, and, of course, educational establishments like Hogwarts School of Witchcraft and Wizardry. This highly organized, rationalized modern society seeks to do what all modern societies do—to perpetuate itself by producing citizens who replicate and maintain the values held by that society. The same could be said of any society, for that matter, but for modern societies, ideological formation is embedded within its institutional structures rather than through the governance of dominant, individual leaders. There are strong leaders in the modern world, of course, but they are considered effective leaders insofar as they protect and promote the institutions they preside over. Hogwarts, then, is not only a school; it is, as Foucault (1977) would call it, an ideological producer. And the boy wizard, Harry Potter, is the embodiment of his society's modern values and beliefs. Voldemort, on the other hand, stands for the antithesis of everything that modernity represents. He seeks to use arcane, unschooled knowledge to concentrate power in his own hands and to dominate the world for his own purpose. His practices are hierarchical, secretive, unofficial, and anti-social. In short, Voldemort's battle with Harry and Hogwarts represents the struggle between magic and modernity.

Magic as the Other of Modernity

Weber's talk, "Science as a Vocation," delivered to science students at Munich University in 1918, proposes that it is possible our world has been post-magical since the time that the first caveman in Plato's *Republic* broke free from his chains and discovered the source of the mesmerizing shadows on the wall. He tries to tell the other captive cavemen that the sun is the cause of these enthralling images, but they do not believe him. Weber describes this moment as the revelation of true versus illusion-based knowledge, and the birth of the "conscious concept" (Weber 1946, 8), one of the great tools of all scientific knowledge. This conscious concept, precursor to the experiment, is an attitude and method of investigating the world and taking control of it instead of being the passive recipient of mysterious forces; it inaugurates the process of scientific progress and intellectualization that has brought us to our present modern condition (Weber 1946, 8). But although scholarly narratives of magic's evolution like Weber's have often posited magic as having been left behind as "the past of modernity" (Meyer and Pels 2003, 4) such linear narratives of magic's obsolescence overlook the extent to which magic and modernity have always existed in intertwined states rather than successive stages. In fact, whether the west has ever fully divested itself of magic and terminally arrived at modernity is a matter of contention for critics like Bruno Latour (1993), who argues that modernity's existence is dependent upon magic's continuing role as an oppositional, even antagonistic principle. Randall Styers (2004) points out in his study of magic's evolution that "far from being a primitive or medieval throwback or survival, belief in witchcraft and natural magic flowered in the very era in which Europe began its move toward modernity—the Renaissance, the Reformation, and the age of early modern philosophy, science, and capitalism" (28). Early modern concerns with witchcraft and magic have been implicated in the process of defining and categorizing emerging modern spheres of knowledge such as religion and science.

Leading anthropologists like James Frazer and Edward Tylor designate magic as the predecessor of religion based on the many shared beliefs and practices held by each order. Other theorists have considered magic as standing outside the category of religion altogether. Either way, "there has been widespread scholarly consensus that magic has often been considered 'the bastard sister of religion'" (Styers 2004, 6). As the illegitimate sibling of religion, "[m]agic has played a central role in scholarly efforts to define the nature of religion and to demarcate its proper bounds" (6). In other words, to know what religion is, we need to know what it is not. Yet historically, the boundary between magic and religion has never been easy to mark, and trying to establish these borders can be a bloody business, as the European witch hunts of the 16th and 17th centuries demonstrate. Randall Styers (2004) points out in *Making Magic* that "certain elements of the Reformation may have exacerbated popular concerns with witchcraft. Areas of Lutheran Germany and areas strongly influenced by Calvinist reforms ... were particularly hit by the persecutions. The concern over witchcraft spread through both Catholic and Protestant regions, reaching its height between 1560 and 1660 during an era of intense religious conflict" (38). Despite—indeed, because of—the intense competition with each other, Protestants and Catholics alike sought to distinguish themselves from occult forms of approaching the unknown, which were considered morally deviant and socially destructive.

Just as religion became the socially accepted form of the fear of invisible powers, science came to be the socially acceptable form of knowledge acquisition and practice. And the distinction between science and the occult, like the distinction between religion and superstition, is ultimately to be found in public sanction (Styers 2004, 48). Throughout the course of the seventeenth century, scientists and natural philosophers offered a range of competing views as to the specific natural forces that were to be "the proper subject of scientific inquiry and the precise nature of the emerging mechanical philosophy" (44). Nevertheless, science proved no less difficult to define than religion. As Bruno Latour pointedly states, "'Science'—in quotation marks—does not exist. It is the name that has been pasted onto certain sections of certain networks, associations that are so sparse and fragile that they would have escaped attention altogether if everything had not been attributed to them'" (qtd in Styers 2004, 6). Magic operates as an invaluable foil for bringing the boundaries of these indefinite networks into sharper relief. And, as Styers underscores, with magic positioned as a middle ground between religion and science, "it has functioned in the scholarly literature to mediate—even police—relations between the two" (6). Thus, how religion and science divided the labor of assessing the known and unknown world between them had great significance for emerging modern views of magic.

If "science," as Latour asserts, does not exist, neither does "magic." Magic, in this sense, functions provisionally as a marker of the illegitimate—defined more by its comparative, oppositional aspect than through its spells and enchantments. In *Dialectic of Enlightenment*, Horkheimer and Adorno (2002) note for instance how the Enlightenment's privileging of rationality was dependent on religion and reason outlawing the principle of magic as obfuscating and irrational (13). The outlawing of magic was also exported with colonialist expansion, motivating the colonialist suppression of local, shamanistic knowledge. Only enlightened, approved, *modern* forms of magic—science and religion—were sanctioned. As Meyer and Pels (2003) point out, "The attempt to define magic ... has to confront the problem that its constituent elements are the product of a specific history ... [moreover] ... any general definition of magic—or witchcraft, or fetishism, or shamanism— is itself the product of a history of Christian discipline and Occidental science (16–17). In other words, magic cannot be defined outside of its practices and power relationships. A study of what magic is, therefore, entails a study of practices that we generally classify as modern—and these modern practices both depend on and seek to suppress the magic that both defines and defies them.

Voldemort as Pre-modern Outsider

In *A General Theory of Magic*, the sociologist Marcel Mauss (2001) describes magical rites as performances that generally happen in out-of-the-way locations, away from dwelling places. He contrasts this to religious rites, which are performed openly, in full public view and are always "predictable, prescribed, and licit" (30). A magical rite, then, is "any rite which does not play a part in organized cults—it is private, secret, mysterious and approaches the limit of a prohibited rite" (30). Magical knowledge, like magical rites, is practiced outside the boundaries of society and nature—literally, in the woods. The Forbidden Forest, for example, which exists on the margins of the Hogwarts grounds, is the site of dangerous, illicit activity and the students are prohibited from entering it.

Consider, on the other hand, how magic is taught and used at Hogwarts. Hogwarts represents institutional learning, which comes with the assumption that magic can be taught and that anyone can learn to do it, given proper instructions and enough practice. The pedagogical structures that reinforce this assumption include lectures, designed labs, paper topics, testing, assessment, and placement. The lectures are sometimes delivered by ghosts, the labs include making magical potions, the papers are written on scrolls, the placements are designated as N.E.W.Ts or O.W.Ls, but the educational model of Hogwarts is more or less the same as a modern educational institution. And of course, an important part of this curriculum includes the use of textbooks. Textbooks are the conventional means of disseminating knowledge, and they function by standardizing the knowledge they disseminate: that is, everyone is supposed to learn the same material and to achieve identical results with it.

The *Advanced Potion-Making* textbook that sixth-year Hogwarts students use in their Potions class is an example of such a standardized text. This textbook, as it turns out, is flawed in several respects, but the students are required to follow its directions and to produce similar outcomes nevertheless. In *Harry Potter and the Half-Blood Prince*, Hermione, a stickler for rules, is particularly vexed when she cannot brew a proper Draught of Living Death potion based on the book's instructions. Harry, meanwhile, discovers an alternative set of instructions scribbled in the margins of his borrowed textbook and by following those unofficial, handwritten directions, he achieves the goal of the lesson (*H-BP* 188–93).

This incident illustrates two different kinds of knowledge acquisition: one that is official and standardized, and one that is unauthorized and marginalized. The kind of learning done in schools is a sanctioned, legitimate form of knowledge acquisition shared by the members of the community that the educational establishment serves. It is the school's function, moreover, to train people to become effective members of that society by instilling in them its rules and values. This is in opposition to the knowledge that Harry discovers in the margins of his textbook. The notes he finds there are written by hand rather than printed; this handwritten knowledge is secret, existing literally along the edges rather than at the center of the text. Moreover, when Harry harms Malfoy with a spell he finds from this book (*H-BP* 522–523), it becomes clear that the peripheral, unofficial knowledge written in it was never meant to be shared. This hoarded knowledge is anti-social, in contrast to institutionalized knowledge, which is widely distributed in order to constitute a community.

In the Harry Potter books, secretive, anti-social, unlawful ways of practicing magic are most closely identified with Voldemort, who spends a great deal of time in secret, hidden places, including the Forbidden Forest. As Mauss (2001) explains, "[t]he magician is a being set apart and he prefers even more to retire to the depths of the forest" (30). It turns out, too, that

Harry's borrowed textbook belonged to Snape, who is also the author of the marginal scribblings that Harry finds. Snape, like Voldemort, practices dark (i.e., unauthorized) magic, and despite his position as a teacher at Hogwarts, he is a suspected figure at the school who keeps to himself. The lack of a community is the fundamental difference between magic and religion, Durkheim contends: "The magician never establishes the social bonds that would create a moral community with those who seek out magic; the magician has only a clientele" (qtd. in Styers 2004, 93). Insofar as the magician has social relationships with others, it is of a hierarchical, authoritarian kind. Indeed, many critics have noted the similarities between Voldemort and Hitler. Hitler himself was obsessed with the supernatural; in *Morning of the Magicians*, Louis Pauwels and Jacques Bergier (2007) examine the magical nature of fascism and the preoccupations of Hitler and various Nazi intellectuals with occultism. The notion that magic is fundamentally reactionary "fits seamlessly both into scholarly traditions emphasizing the authoritarian nature of magic and into traditions stigmatizing occultism as reprehensibly anti-modern" (Styers 2004, 202).

In contrast to the magical knowledge that is taught at Hogwarts, which is transferable, replicable, and ultimately transformative of the learners themselves, Voldemort's mode of acquiring knowledge is largely self-taught and unschooled, and begins and ends with himself. His refusal to share his secret knowledge with others gives him power over those who do not know or what he knows or do not have what he has. Moreover, he uses this advantage to terrorize others and subject them to his will. But as a technique of power, Voldemort's methods are distinctly pre-modern insofar as he has no system in place for efficiently reproducing his dominance. Thus, while his secretive hoarding of knowledge gives him some measure of power, it also defines the limits of his ability to reproduce and multiply his power efficiently. In regard to techniques of modern power, the French philosopher and sociologist Jacques Ellul speculates in *The Technological Society* that "[i]f we imagine that magic and science were once 'one,' then we can create a narrative of their split; one path went the way of technique, into technology; material technique leads to a multiplication of discoveries, each based on the other and, thus, writes in itself a myth of progress" (qtd. in Appelbaum 2003, 43). But magic, Ellul contends, takes the other path, and promotes only "endless beginnings" (43). These endless beginnings, can be seen, for example, in Voldemort's horcruxes—those singular magical objects which house parts of his soul and which are meant to ensure his immortality. The nature of such objects is that they are singular: each one is unique, and Voldemort's power significantly declines as Harry and his friends hunt down and destroy each one. In other words, Voldemort has no reproducible, systematic way of multiplying his dominance; his power rests in singular objects that once destroyed are gone forever. As Max Weber shows, "a disenchanted world is more effectively sub-ject to exploitation by capitalism and rationalized modern science.... As the sacred [and the occult] evaporate into a dematerialized fog, all objects, loca-tions, and identities are rendered equally subject to the regimentation of the market" (Styers 2004, 224).

Magic and non-magic can be differentiated on the basis of practices that affect modes of thought, behavior, and production. Insofar as Voldemort embodies anti-rationalized learning, anti-social approaches, and anti-market processes, his brand of anti-modern magic provides a foil for the rationaliz-ing, commodifying, and homogenizing social structures of the modern wiz-arding world.

Hogwarts and the Creation of the Modern Subject

In the modern wizarding world, techniques of power do not operate through physical domination and threat of pain and death as they do for Voldemort, but through regulation, surveillance, and mandates. Power is not concentrated in the hands of an individual but deployed through a network of institutions that control and regulate every aspect of social life. This world is a fully bureaucratic enterprise with an elaborate system of law and fully equipped with operations and directives, divisions and assignments. Its organizations include a Committee for the Disposal of Dangerous Creatures, an Accidental Magic Reversal Squad, Departments of Magical Law Enforce-ment, offices of Muggle Artifacts and Magical Transportation, and even a Department of Mayhem as well as a Department of Mystery. All movement is monitored: transportation devices and networks like Portkeys and Floo networks must be authorized and coordinated. Those who do not fit in easily with the magical mainstream, like Animagi, are registered. These modern management systems are much more effective and efficient in exercising power because, like Bentham's Panopticon, they do not rely on exterior force, as Voldemort's methods do, but operate by internalizing obedience. As Fou-cault (1977) explains in "The Eye of Power," the Panopticon that Jeremy Ben-tham conceived at the end of the eighteenth century is a security device designed to optimize surveillance and control behavior by placing a watch-tower at the center of a circular prison. A single guard within the watchtower can survey the entire prison at all times while remaining unseen himself. In fact, the prisoners could never really know whether the guard was in the watchtower or not, and thus would always have to behave as if they were under scrutiny for wrongdoing. The Panopticon illustrates the operation of modern ideology, in which the tyrannizing gaze is internalized via external structures that shape internal subjection and, indeed, define the modern subject (146–165). Nor would storming the prison and taking over the watchtower change anything, for simply replacing the guard would not alter the relations of power. Voldemort crucially misunderstands this when he takes control of the Ministry of Magic via his minions and Imperius-controlled bureaucrats. He uses the Ministry as an extension of his dominating tactics: approving Inquisitorial Squads, making arrests, instilling a state of fear that is externally rather than internally coercive. As a result, rebellions spring up everywhere: in *Harry Potter and the Deathly Hallows* underground movements are organized, and alternative media sources like *Potterwatch* pop up in resistance (*DH 437–445*).

As Foucault (1977) points out, a violent form of power risks provoking revolts with "resistance and disobedience … develop[ing] in the interstices" (155). This, he says, "was how monarchical power operated" (155). And in fact, Voldemort's aim is to rule as a monarchical dictator, using violent forms of power to achieve his goals in essentially pre-modern ways. But multiplying violence only multiplies the revolts: exterior control is not only ineffective, it's inefficient. Thus, when Foucault discusses the elusive and diffuse power of the Panopticon, he could also be describing Voldemort's problem with trying to use the offices of the Ministry to exert personal dominion: "One doesn't have here a power which is wholly in the hands of one person who can exercise it alone and totally over the others. It is a machine in which everyone is caught, those who exercise power just as much as those over whom it is exercised.… Power is no longer substantially identified with an individual who possesses or exercises it by right of birth; it becomes a machinery that no one owns" (156). In other words, when the system itself is totalitarian, it foregoes the need for a dictator.

The person who understands this best in the Harry Potter series isn't Voldemort, but Ministry official Dolores Umbridge, who first makes her appearance in *Harry Potter and the Order of the Phoenix* (Rowling 2003). While Voldemort uses the Ministry to terrorize the rest of the wizarding world, Umbridge uses her authority as a Ministry official to stamp out nonconformists. Both Voldemort and Umbridge seek to exert control, but Voldemort seeks control for himself while Umbridge acts on behalf of the institutional machine. Indeed, she identifies with the machine. In this regard, Dolores Umbridge actually has more in common with Hogwarts Headmaster Albus Dumbledore in that both are custodians of a very important institutional machine: education. As a modern educational institution, Hogwarts is organized to produce modern subjects, just as a Muggle school is. This subject, as Styers (2004) notes, "conforms to distinctive norms of individual agency and autonomy (seeing itself as fundamentally independent from other individuals and the natural world), while tempering that autonomy with a suitably submissive attitude toward the social order.... Subjects who fail to conform to these norms are denigrated as trapped in decidedly non-modern and subversive forms of magical thought" (13). Styers, building on Foucault, maintains that "while 'freedom' from magic is certainly invoked as a constitutive element of modern modes of subjectivity, this freedom is purchased only at the price of potent new forms of social control and regimentation" that often contradict the very values they espouse (13). In this way, schools use pedagogical structures and architectural arrangements to suppress individuality and autonomy. Students are mentally disciplined to adhere to standardized textbook learning, and are further physically disciplined by the confines of classroom spaces arranged in linear rows of desks designed to focus attention on the authority of the instructor.

As the face of the educational machine, Dumbledore is certainly the more human and more likeable representative of it, but what he does, and what Umbridge does when she presides over Hogwarts, is different only in degree: both discipline, control, and regulate the students. So while it may appear that Umbridge has hijacked Hogwarts, she's only doing, in a less benevolent form and with a much harsher touch, what Dumbledore has always done. Umbridge conveniently gives an unpleasant face to the more unpleasant functions of institutions, which include issuing decrees, compelling compliance with rules, outlawing unapproved behavior, stamping out nonconformity, and expelling, imprisoning, or eliminating transgressors. That Umbridge is authorized to punish dissenters using violent means exposes the fact that all institutions are supported by violence in the end, as Azkaban prison attests.

To the extent that modern subjects can resist the consolidation of their subjectivity they need both an alternative mental and physical space. Consequently, when Harry and his friends decide to rebel against Umbridge, they not only reject her narrow and conservative pedagogy, but they seek a space that evades the gaze of power and the physical structure of domination. In "The Eye of Power," Foucault (1977) implies that such spaces do not exist: modern subjects are securely inscribed in the material foundations of their world. To evade Umbridge, Harry and his friends would need to find a space that does not physically exist. And that is exactly the kind of space that they find in the Room of Requirement, a space that materializes only when it is needed, to those who need it; it ceases to exist when these conditions no longer hold true. This is where Dumbledore's Army goes to practice an alternative and subversive pedagogy—one where there are no authority figures or set curriculum, and the students teach each other what they need to know (*OotP* 390). The Room of Requirement is, in other words, a space that defies all temporal, material, and rational conventions: it is an impossible space. Harry and his crew of rebels are being their most magical when they go there—which is to say, when they are acting against the normative conventions of their society.

In the end, however, Dumbledore's Army supports Hogwarts: the rebellion against Umbridge is not a rebellion against the educational establishment itself, but the artless decrees that she heavy-handedly throws about. Support of Hogwarts, indeed, fighting to save Hogwarts from Voldemort, is effectively a battle to save the modern world that Hogwarts stands for.

The Death of Magic and the Re-enchantment of the Modern World

Saving the school, then, is equivalent to saving the modern world. In the battle between Hogwarts and Voldemort, Voldemort seeks to assert his individuality and to break free from institutional norms. He's not just fighting one under-aged wizard, he's up against the entire modern establishment, which Harry embodies. There's a part of Harry himself that sympathizes with this rebellious aspect of Voldemort; Harry's propensity for rule-breaking is an expression of the ambivalence that many hold towards institutions and their conformist culture. But once that culture is threatened, there is no ambivalence: Harry and his friends do not hesitate to fight for the world they know. A happy ending to the Harry Potter series is marked, in the epilogue, by the beginning of another school year.

When Voldemort dies, magic, as modernity's opposite, also dies. In the end, Harry Potter is like other western children's fantasy stories in which the found magical world (Narnia, Neverland) is lost to the child when he or she crosses the line that separates childhood from adulthood—a line marked by acceptance of a rational, secular, conformist world—because only children, the insane, and outsiders are allowed to continue believing in magic. It may not appear that Harry is exiled from the wizarding world since we see him as an adult at the end of the series. But the truth is, there is no need to separate Harry from the magical world since there is no longer a magical world at the end. There are only two modern worlds with similar institutions, conventions, and norms. And though the technologies of each world are different, they achieve the same results: they fly on brooms, we fly in airplanes; they have potions, we have pharmacies; they have delivery owls, we have the postal service; they have the Marauders' Map, we have the *Find my Friends* app, etc. In the end, the wizarding world is as disenchanted as our modern one.

For the Harry Potter generation, the death of magic at the end of the series is not necessarily experienced as a loss, however. Readers of the series, and those in particular who journeyed with the boy wizard and came of age alongside Harry, return at the end to a Muggle world in which Muggle technologies and a modern way of life can now be recognized as magical in its own right. We can see the wizarding world reflected in our own through the ordinary things we do, such as back-to-school shopping (at Target or Staples, instead of at Diagon Alley); the rites of passage we undergo, such as learning how to transport ourselves (in cars, instead of through apparating); or even in the transition to adulthood and choosing a career (a lawyer or doctor, perhaps, instead of an Auror or an office job at the Ministry of Magic). Through reading the Harry Potter books, we may subsequently discover the re-enchantment of our own modern way of life.

REFERENCES

Appelbaum, Peter. 2003. "Harry Potter's World: Magic, Technoculture, and Becoming Human." In *Harry Potter's World: Multidisciplinary Critical Perspectives,* edited by Elizabeth E. Heilman, 25–51. New York: RoutledgeFalmer.
Find My Friend, Apple, www.apple.com/ios/app.store/.
Foucault, Michel. 1977. "The Eye of Power." In *Power/Knowledge: Selected Interviews and Other Writings 1972–1977,* edited by Colin Gordon,146–165. New York: Pantheon Books.
Horkheimer, Max and Theodor W. Adorno. 2002. *Dialectic of Enlightenment: Philosophical Fragment,* edited by Gunzelin Schmid Noerr. Translated by Edmund Jephcott. Stanford, CA: Stanford University Press.
Latour, Bruno. 1993. *We Have Never Been Modern,* translated by Catherine Porter. Cambridge, MA: Harvard University Press.
Mauss, Marcel. 2001. *A General Theory of Magic.* New York: Routledge.
Meyer, Birgit and Peter Pels, eds. 2003. *Magic and Modernity: Interfaces of Revelations and Concealment.* Stanford, CA: Stanford University Press.
Pauwels, Louis and Jacques Bergier. 2007. *The Morning of the Magicians.* London: Souvenir Press.
Rowling, J.K. 2003. *Harry Potter and the Order of the Phoenix.* New York: Scholastic Press.
_____. 2005. *Harry Potter and the Half-Blood Prince.* New York: Scholastic Press.
_____. 2007. *Harry Potter and the Deathly Hallows.* New York: Scholastic Press.
Styers, Randall. 2004. *Making Magic: Religion, Magic, & Science in the Modern World.* New York: Oxford University Press.
Weber, Max. 1946. "Science as a Vocation." In *Max Weber: Essays in Sociology,* edited and translated by H.H. Gerth and C. Wright Mills, 129–156. New York: Oxford University Press.

Cloaked in History

Magical Heritage Sites in the Harry Potter Series

EMILY LOHORN

"Any sufficiently advanced technology is indistinguishable
from magic."
—Arthur C. Clarke, *Profiles of the Future*

In twentieth-century Western children's literature, magic is something
that lives in the past. Due to magic's dissociation from the modern age, witchcraft and other displays of supernatural power often occur in pre-industrial
settings removed from the present, such as dank medieval castles or faraway
ancient lands. In the early twentieth century, sociologist Max Weber published
his theories of the rationalization and resultant demystification of the Western
world. Weber argued that the process he named the disenchantment of the
world birthed a set of "paradigm shifts [that] have inaugurated a more rational
understanding of events … [and] ultimately resulted in a decline of the use
and belief in magic, God, and myth" (Shull 2005, 61). One of the most significant paradigm shifts came in the form of the scientific revolution of the
fifteenth century, which marked the beginning of the end for the cultural
legitimacy of magic.

The Harry Potter series provides a nexus of magic, time, and technology
in children's fantasy that speaks to the gulf between magic and modernity.
The books show that magic exists uneasily in a contemporary setting because
a magical society is marked by a significant investment in its own historical
discourse. Although the Harry Potter series takes place in present-day
England (i.e., the events of the first book commence in 1991), J.K. Rowling
has constructed a magical world with strong connections to its beginnings.

81

Thus, although Rowling's wizarding world operates in a contemporary society, it still cloaks itself in the trappings of an ancient tradition. Their society draws power from an unbroken link to its own origins, evidenced not least of all by the role of applied history in the novels and Rowling's use of what I call magical heritage sites. There is a remarkable anachronism in the magic of the Potterverse, which in turn provides an analogy for how readers of Harry Potter might interact with their own cultural heritage.

The concept of a heritage site has been popularized due to the United Nations Educational, Scientific, and Cultural Organization's (UNESCO) initiative to catalog and protect locations significant to human heritage. The result of this initiative was the World Heritage List, a directory with entries for all significant sites, and the World Heritage Fund, which provides monetary assistance for protecting the nominated sites. A world heritage site, then, is a place that locates some telling trace of humanity's past. When a site has been marked as a carrier of cultural and historical value, it is set aside for preservation. A site holds significance in the arena of cultural heritage when, according to the 1972 UNESCO Convention, it exhibits "outstanding universal value from the historical, aesthetic, ethnological or anthropological point of view" ("Convention Concerning"). UNESCO's heritage site initiative demonstrates a societal imperative to protect symbolic locations. The push to preserve these locations reveals an association between their cultural value and their unspoiled link to the past.

I suggest that J.K. Rowling's work exhibits the same social imperative to concentrate cultural meaning in preserved places, and I have thus labeled these places magical heritage sites. A magical heritage site is a location steeped in history that has great cultural value in the wizarding world. These sites are explicitly protected from outside influence and remain largely unchanged over time due to their emblematic status. In the series, magical heritage sites help to define the common experience of being a wizard in Britain. Furthermore, the various functions of these magical heritage sites suggest that the layering of eras evoked by Rowling is not a haphazard postmodern pastiche, but rather an organic accumulation of history growing towards and through our current time.

Hogwarts School of Witchcraft and Wizardry stands as one of the most significant magical heritage sites in the text. The school is an ancient institution of magic, and its illustrious history is inscribed in the very walls. The ghosts of witches and wizards long since deceased roam the castle and act as the school's most explicit, direct link to the past. Their presence establishes Hogwarts as a place where history plays an omnipresent part in everyday life. The ghosts maintain a bridge between past and present times at the school and prove to be a valuable resource for amateur historians such as Harry, Ron and Hermione. As it turns out, Hogwarts is littered with primary sources. When Harry combs the grounds for the Horcruxes that contain Voldemort's soul, he faces an obstacle when told "Nobody has seen [the object he seeks] in living memory" (*DH* 601). Although no man alive can tell him what he needs to know, Harry has the privilege of turning to the castle's ghosts for information to aid his search. He consults Nearly Headless Nick and the ghost of Rowena Ravenclaw, whose assistance leads him to successfully recover the Horcrux. With this interchange, it becomes clear that ghosts act as cultural retainers who preserve historical knowledge for the coming generations.

Notably, the books remain curiously silent as to the exact date of the school's founding. Although it has been in continuous operation since its establishment, there remains only a murky incertitude regarding the timeframe. Even the History of Magic professor, a ghost himself, concedes that "the precise date is uncertain" (*CoS* 150). Joyce Carol Oates (1998) speaks to the trope of the ambiguous past in fantasy, remarking that the traditional phrasing "*Once upon a time*—uses bland, blurred, stereotypical language that thwarts the more vigorous intellectual desire to know *when, where, how, why*" (264). She sees the setting of an unspecified past as a narrative device that dissuades interrogation. Oates argues that the use of constructions like "long ago and far away" signals complacency and the resignation to ignorance. Jack Zipes (1988) instead claims that authors use the device as a gesture toward hope where "[t]he once upon a time is not a past designation but futuristic; the timelessness of the tale and lack of geographical specificity endow it with the utopian connotations—utopia in its original meaning designated no place" (10). While Rowling's a-historicizing of the school's founding achieves the timelessness that Zipes refers to, it wants for nothing in terms of geographical specificity. Hogwarts lies less than a day's travel by train north of London where its students and teachers speak the King's English.

Of course, both the aforementioned critics concern themselves with fairy tales, which Rowling's stories are not. They more closely fit the definition of the fairy tale's cousin, what Zipes (1988) calls the "*Zaubermärchen* or the magic tale" (7). The magic tale relies on the wonderment of the reader to move her through unfamiliar channels (an attribute confirmed by its other name, the wonder folk tale). Rowling accomplishes the "sense of wonder" necessary to both the magical tale and portal fantasy by "embroider[ing] continually" with fantastical details that render the present unfamiliar. Mendlesohn (2008) contends, however, that the Harry Potter series is an example of such embroidery "taken to excess ... in which almost all of the imaginative material is in the worldbuilding," resulting in a serious case of "*diegetic overkill*" (9). Rowling's worldbuilding does expend a lot of imaginative energy in drawing heavily from the past, then making it fantastic. But the accumulation of such details functions as more than aesthetic fluff.

Wizards on the Internet

It doesn't take much consorting with a search engine to find dozens of Harry Potter fan forums. These forums host public discussion threads where readers register their opinions and hypotheses on the series and are a virtually endless font of close textual readings. They can be a source of cogent arguments about the books, made by fans of all ages who subject the text to rigorous critical inquiry at times. While considering the critical context that informs the aesthetic choices of authors like Rowling, it seems wise to also examine the fan discussions of Rowling's own explanations for a rift between magic and contemporary society.

In response to a thread titled, "Electricity in hogwarts?" (2004) CoSForums user fakesky pondered the conspicuous lack of Muggle technology in use at the school of witchcraft and wizardry:

> I wondered about the library though. Wouldn't researching your homework be soo much easier if there was a computer that had all the books encoded by topic? Harry wouldn't have stayed up looking for something to enable him to breathe underwater.... I believe I read somewhere that there's so much magical energy surrounding wizarding places, it just corrupts technology and it doesn't work [sec. 30].

Even the most casual reader of the Harry Potter series will notice that the wizarding world, with the exception of a few technophiles like Arthur Weasley, actively shuns the use of Muggle technology—and it turns out that the reader's claim for a technology-banishing magical fog is substantiated in *Harry Potter and the Goblet of Fire*. In a discussion of whether Hogwarts could be bugged with hidden microphones, Hermione, as usual, provides the definitive answer. Modern recording devices could never operate properly at the school because, as she explains, "All those substitutes for magic Muggles use—electricity, computers, and radar, and all those things—they all go haywire around Hogwarts, there's too much magic in the air" (*GoF* 548). This passage enables a reader to visualize the tension between post-industrial technology and the magical world. At a place like Hogwarts where there is a great concentration of many witches and wizards, the massive output of energy takes the form of something like a magical current. Electrical gadgets go on the fritz when they encounter this current. In the conflict between the two, magic is a blanketing force, stronger than the derivative, counterfeit power that Muggles call electricity.

The magical fog theory provides an explanation consistent with the internal logic of the Potterverse for why wizards do not take advantage of search engines when writing term papers or researching famous alchemists. Interestingly, however, magic's prohibitive force does not exclude all technology that originates in the non-magical world. Gadgets that operate by clockwork or any machinery that predates the spread of electricity can function without difficulty. For this reason, the students can use a steam-powered train, the Hogwarts Express, as a mode of transportation to and from the castle.

The Hogwarts Express is a token of industrial technology, but it does not quite represent the age of electronics and thus does not offend the school's sensibilities so greatly as a computer would. Rather, it is an artifact of intermediacy. Fittingly, it can bridge the distance between 1990's London and the drafty, medieval castle in the Scottish Highlands. The train represents an intermediate technology that can make limited contact with the magical realm. While this would suggest flexibility and fluidity, students must first cross a decidedly solid barrier before gaining entrance to the train. Harry learns in his first year that in order to reach the Platform 9¾ to board the Hogwarts Express, one must "walk straight at the barrier between platforms nine and ten … best [done] at a bit of a run" (*SS* 93). Here, the brick wall of the barrier stands guard to the magical world. The sentry function of Platform 9¾ is reminiscent of Farah Mendlesohn's portal theory. In her encyclopedic survey of the genre, *Rhetoric of Fantasy,* Mendlesohn (2008) uses the label of portal fantasy as an umbrella term for those stories where a character travels to a fantastic world by the use of a portal, which marks the "transition between this world and another; from our time to another time." A clear delineation between two separate spheres is key. As her comment about the passage from one time to another also denotes, there is an association between the portal and time travel as well. She considers the "archetypal portal fantasy [to be one in which] … the fantastic is *on the other side* and does not leak" (Mendlesohn 2008, 1). The condition of insularity then defines the portal fantasy, with the imagery of the seal between worlds being watertight. Rowling's portal of bricks and concrete embodies this insularity and solid state.

While the train may be granted a special magical allowance to make a stop on the grounds, it does not have permission to convey the students all the way to their destination. As the Hogwarts Express cannot abut directly with the school, the final leg of the journey must be completed by boat. Small passenger boats ferry the first-year students to the main entrance in *Harry Potter and the Sorcerer's Stone.* As the students approach the great craggy rock that Hogwarts is built upon, they all must duck "their heads [while] the little boats carried them through a curtain of ivy that hid a wide opening in the cliff face" (*SS* 112). This curtain marks the final demarcation between the life they leave behind and the ancient magical tradition they are about to be initiated into. It is imperative that they cross this barrier without the aid of contemporary technology, so the train is jettisoned.

The liminal, intermediary zone that the Hogwarts Express occupies means that it is not subject to the same alienation from magical spaces as other modern technology. In the second book of the series, a more contemporary car, however, does not fare nearly so well at Hogwarts. When Harry and Ron see themselves barred from entrance at Platform 9¾ in *Harry Potter and the Chamber of Secrets*, they opt to take Mr. Weasley's flying Ford Anglia instead. At the crucial moment of touchdown on Hogwarts' grounds, the car is denied contact. The Anglia is physically accosted and restrained from landing by the Whomping Willow. The massive tree batters and beats the car with "a branch as thick as a python" while the tree's "gnarled boughs were pummeling every inch of the car that it could reach" (*CoS* 75). The Whomping Willow's assault on the Anglia overtly dramatizes the conflict between magic and technology, the tension between tradition and progress. The tree sends the modern intruder fleeing, acting as a defender of tradition.

Noel Chevalier (2005) interprets this scene differently in "The Liberty Tree and the Whomping Willow: Political Justice, Magical Science, and Harry Potter." He frames the willow's barrage as a function of its role as a "weapon and a violent dispenser of punishment" for the school, part of the disciplinary body that rules over students. In Chevalier's view, the Whomping Willow symbolizes justice and authority, and metes out punishment to Ron and Harry for their misstep in stealing the car. While I consider the incident representative of the magical space rejecting the presence of industrial technology, I can agree with the assessment of the tree's secondary function as "a guardian, an authority figure planted over a secret passage" (Chevalier 2005, 406). The Whomping Willow protects the integrity of the wizarding community by acting as a sentry, maintaining Hogwarts' insularity. The tree is part of the school's apparatus for fending off unwanted outside elements, including technology.

Elsewhere, Chevalier (2005) speaks to the separation between modern technology and the magical settings in the Harry Potter series by theorizing that "Rowling removes the technological complications of the contemporary world not out of nostalgia for cultural stability, but to reveal that, without the veneer of technology, the world wrestles with the same social and political questions in the 1990s as it did in the 1790s" (402). Chevalier responds to critics who have written off all of the books' anachronistic touches as nothing more than a pastiche, a wistful nod to the Edwardian era. Instead, he claims that Rowling excises technology from the wizarding world in order to facilitate a discussion of Enlightenment-era social mores. Though Chevalier suggests that Rowling models her world after the era of the Enlightenment, I find that the Harry Potter series at once invokes the more recent past (in the form of the Edwardian nods) and also reaches back much further than the 1790s. I suggest that this far-reaching historical resonance speaks specifically to the Harry Potter generation and their relationships with both magic and modernity.

First of all, wizarding clothing conveys a distinct impulse toward medieval garb. Harry learns in his welcome letter from Hogwarts that the school uniform entails "Three pairs of plain work robes (black) [and] One plain pointed hat (black) for day wear" (*SS* 66). Harry must make a dramatic change in wardrobe while immersed in magical society during the school year, which helps to make the division between his Muggle life on Privet Drive and his magical life even clearer. It is a significant aesthetic choice on the part of J.K. Rowling to clothe her protagonists in the cloaks and hats emblematic of the European tradition of pagan witchcraft. Her design of the school uniform reflects what Seth Lerer (2008) refers to in *Children's Literature: A Reader's History from Aesop to Harry Potter* as "the medievalizing of children's literature itself." Medieval Europe was dismissed by Enlightenment thinkers "as a childish time, a kind of cultural formation moment in the history of the West that they, more modern figures, had outgrown" (Lerer 2008, 13). The Enlightenment–like stance on the medieval period presumed that people who came before the Age of Reason lived in infantile societies where the specter of magic teemed in the cultural imagination, clouding an understanding of nature. Therefore, the Western literary traditions that grew out of the Enlightenment and developed into the forms we see today conserve this association between childishness and the medieval period. Tokens and artifacts from this time are woven into children's stories as motifs—knights, dragons, witches on broomsticks—far more frequently than they appear in literature written exclusively for adults.

Lerer (2008) refers to this tendency of children's book authors to embroider their stories with the relics of medieval culture as an attempt "to coat their adventures with the patina of the exotic" (14). His statement implies a sense of artifice. If the patina is, as he says, only a coating, it cannot be an integral part of the action; storytellers can slip in and out of this time period disingenuously, skimming a few details here and there. Rowling certainly appears to be playing at being medieval with at least one foot firmly grounded in the present. As Harry and Ron prepare on the train to arrive at Hogwarts for their first year, they don their robes. They do, however, continue to wear their more casual and contemporary travel outfits under the long cloaks. Ron has changed into the uniform that Hogwarts students have worn for centuries, yet as his robes "were a bit short for him, you could see his sneakers underneath" (*SS* 110). The present era might consent to being wrapped up in an historical costume, but it will not allow itself to be totally subsumed. The still-visible sneakers are a last rebellious wink from the modern age before it is packed away for the school year. The boys now enter a world of turrets and torches where they will write their compositions with quills on parchment scrolls, but retain their modern sensibilities. The sense of play aids contemporary child readers in imagining themselves as Hogwarts students.

The (Applied) History of Magic

The tug of war between the ancient and the modern is not confined to fashion choices. Hogwarts, under the administration of Albus Dumbledore, weighs the mantle of tradition against the need to recognize innovation. The series expresses a tension between traditional, theoretical modes of teaching and novel methods of applied study. This tension reveals itself most prominently in the students' attitude toward the study of history. When it comes to explicit instruction, grounded within classroom walls, the History of Magic constitutes the children's least favorite class, earning the label "most boring": a ghost who "droned on and on while they scribbled down names and dates" administers this yawn-inducing course, a fact that serves to reinforce the outdated mode of instruction (*SS* 133). The unappealing nature of the class is directly linked to its conservative method of pedagogy, which involves a great deal of lecturing followed by examination where students are expected to reproduce this content.

All three of the young protagonists, Ron, Hermione, and Harry, reject this heavily theoretical format in favor of the applied study of historical discourse. They express keen interest in matters of history despite their dissatisfaction with school-issued curriculum. They instead take it upon themselves many times to execute independent historical research projects in the library. In the first novel, their search for information on the alchemist Nicholas Flamel and the sorcerer's stone has them sneaking into the book stacks after hours. *Harry Potter and the Chamber of Secrets* sees the group charged with uncovering knowledge of the school's mythological history in order to vanquish an ancient monster. Their historical research is, in part, what allows them to change the course of history. For example, Harry successfully slays the basilisk inside the Chamber of Secrets with the help of information that Hermione discovers. The children have great enthusiasm for the study of an applied history, a history that is still unfolding.

This desire to interrogate history is not uncommon at Hogwarts since the school itself is a magical heritage site. The student body at large takes interest in matters of applied history. During Harry's second year, the rumor that the heir of Salazar Slytherin has unleashed a mythic, bloodthirsty beast means that "[a]ll the copies of *Hogwarts, a History* have been taken out.... And there's a two-week waiting list" (*CoS* 147). The students show a reflexive interest in the history of the school when they see the ways that historical discourse, myth, and legend reach forward into and shape the experiences of the current generation of students. The demand for the book is symptomatic of a school-wide culture that values the independent investigation of history.

Crucial to this investigatory spirit is the condition of unsupervised access to history. The level of supervision marks the difference between dull, rote classroom instruction and the engagement with applied history. For example, Harry can use his invisibility cloak to peruse the Restricted Section without adult interference. The cloak is but one of a series of objects that facilitate Harry's unimpeded movements throughout the castle. While he may break the school's rules of conduct in his search for information, the ends always seem to justify the means when Harry uses the knowledge he earns to act heroically. When Harry wakes up after battling Quirrell in the dungeons at the end of his first year, he confesses to Professor Dumbledore that he learned independently of the Sorcerer's Stone and the enchantments protecting it. Dumbledore does not try to hide his pleasure, and he praises the boy, "sounding quite delighted. 'You *did* do the thing properly, didn't you?'" (*SS* 297). Implicit in his praise is an admiration for Harry's depth of research and his agency in pursuing historical knowledge. Harry's problem-solving with the use of research, as well as Dumbledore's reaction, highlight the value of engaging with history. Knowledge of the past is an important form of cultural literacy in the wizarding world.

Scholars recognize that the Harry Potter series emphasizes a young person's right to access history. Roni Natov (2001) praises the books for exemplifying the ways that "[e]ven the child, without the experience of the adult, without perspective afforded by hindsight, can glean something valuable from the lessons of the past—not those set in stone to be received unquestioningly but [rather those] to make meaning of" (325). Particularly here she refers to Harry's use of the Pensieve in Dumbledore's office to view the imprints of past events stored within. When a young person has unsupervised access to history, she is allowed to make meaning and order the world for herself. The Pensieve is a primary source that grants the user the ability to observe history firsthand, uncorrupted by a narrativizing discourse. The device helps Harry to move away from an absolute view of history and towards a more critical stance. Applied history appears in the Harry Potter series as problem solving, the manipulation of data to come to independent conclusions.

David Jones (2009), in his essay "'Interpret Your Findings Correctly': Harry's Magical Self-Discovery," expands upon the role of the Pensieve as a primary source. He describes it as a tool that debunks absolutes and encourages critical thought about the past. He notes that in *Harry Potter and the Half-Blood Prince*, Dumbledore uses the device as a means of "training Harry in the fine art of inferential reasoning" (198). Harry must piece together a patchwork of information from disparate sources, beginning with the memories stored in the Pensieve, in order to succeed when he ultimately faces Voldemort. In this way, "Harry's education is more than a rote understanding of the past…. Synthesizing information from the fractured narrative of Riddle/Voldemort provides nothing useful without interpretation and inference—exegesis of stories to form plausible conclusions" (201). While the Pensieve, like any primary source, provides valuable information in the form of discrete facts, the story it tells is woefully incomplete. Harry has to then fill in the gaps by his own interpretive act. Because the device requires such interpretive leaps of its user, it facilitates the critical interrogation of history.

That the Harry Potter series shows resistance to an absolute historical discourse marks it as a departure from the archetypal fantasy. Farah Mendlesohn (2008) remarks that the portal fantasy genre "is filled with assumptions that the 'past' is inarguable, that it just *is,* and that 'knowledge' is to be rediscovered rather than generated" (16). A sense that history is infallible and finished, a monolith that holds the answers to all the questions of the ages, pervades this type of fantasy. In the Potterverse, though, the meaning of history still seems to be very much up for grabs. The knowledge of the past is revered, but history has not yet reached the end of its rope. As a result, the discourse is still being written and rewritten as a living document.

Repello Muggletum: The Preservation of Magical Heritage

If history lives in the wizarding world, it must be thanks in part to the cultural geography and prevalence of magical heritage sites. Shops that comprise the marketplace of Diagon Alley, as well as Harry's birthplace of Godric's Hollow, and Hogwarts School of Witchcraft and Wizardry all meet my criteria for magical heritage sites.

For example, the wand shop, Ollivanders, heralds itself as an historical site of significance for the magical community. From its first appearance in *Harry Potter and the Sorcerer's Stone,* the store's sign acts as an announcement of its deeply rooted presence with "[p]eeling gold letters over the door [that] read Ollivanders: Makers of Fine Wands since 382 B.C." (*SS* 82). Ostensibly, this one business has provided witches and wizards with the same service for over two thousand years. Hagrid informs Harry that "it's the only place fer wands, Ollivanders," (81). Hagrid could mean that the store is literally the sole location in which a person can buy a wand, or he could be simply expressing a value judgment. Either way, a visit to Ollivanders is an integral part of the British wizarding experience, a rite of passage that is introduced as universal. In keeping with this role, the shop advertises itself as a singular site, and a community institution.

Ollivanders has a potent atmosphere, not in small part due to the promise of an unbroken lineage stretching back into ancient times. The shop's status as a long-standing cultural institution denotes its potential for great magic. Dust and clutter characterize the description of Ollivanders. There is a sense of endless accumulation—of cobwebs, years, power. Harry picks up on the peculiar energy of the space, finding that "[f]or some reason, the back of his neck prickled. The very dust and silence in here seemed to tingle with some secret magic" (*SS* 82). The dust itself, imbued with magic, suggests that the age of the place gives it great power.

Ollivanders represents only one of the many stalwart shops that line Diagon Alley. The marketplace functions as the center of British wizard commerce, and as such, it introduces Harry to the magical community in the first book. Beginning with its name, a loose anagram of the word "diagonally," Diagon Alley suggests transection and the upending of previous assumptions. Seth Lerer (2008) relates the site to the Victorian expression "Queer Street," which commonly "describe[d] someplace awkward or where you would find yourself in trouble, debt, or illness" (196). This definition comes closer to Harry's experience with Knockturn Alley in the second book, but Diagon Alley is a queer street nonetheless, a place that transgresses norms and never fails to surprise. Diagon Alley's cobbled lanes and profusion of magical paraphernalia, "with barrels of bat spleens and eels' eyes, tottering piles of spell books, quills, and rolls of parchment, potion bottles, [and] globes of the moon" that spill into the street, serve as Harry's real initiation to wizarding culture (*SS* 72). The exhaustive lists that provide the first descriptions of Diagon Alley suggest a feast for the eyes and help to create the immersive experience of Harry's first exposure to a new culture. The location meets both of the basic criteria for a magical heritage site: significant historical and/or cultural value, and the protection from corruption by outside influence. Diagon Alley hides in plain sight, its entrance a humble pub in London protected by enchantment from prying Muggle eyes.

No place embodies both the heritage site's historic-cultural significance and the imperative to preserve quite like Godric's Hollow. In the final book, Hermione researches Godric's Hollow with the aid of Bathilda Bagshot's *A History of Magic*. She learns that the village where Harry was born and his parents died has great historical import for the series. The town boasts an illustrious past as that "Most celebrated of these half-magical dwelling places … [the] village where the great wizard Godric Gryffindor was born" (*DH* 319). Since its circa 1689 establishment, the village has gathered acclaim as the birthplace of heroic men as well as the great wizarding pastime, Quidditch. Its graveyard collects generations of blue-blooded wizarding families' bones—the Dumbledores, the Peverells, the Potters. These facts alone could merit the designation of magical heritage site. However, Bagshot's book fails to include a reference to the most significant historical event to occur in the Hollow, the infant Harry's deflection of Voldemort's Killing Curse that ended his first reign of terror.

Astute Hermione recognizes the constraints of static sources like

Bagshot's account when compared with her own experience of living history. She notes the conspicuous absence of any mention of Harry and his parents in the list of the town's famous inhabitants "because Professor Bagshot doesn't cover anything later than the end of the nineteenth century" (*DH* 319). It seems one must continually revisit and revise history in order to maintain its usefulness as a discourse. Harry and Hermione's visit to Godric's Hollow demonstrates not only the series' leaning toward applied historical revisionism, but also suggests that the actions of young wizards and witches are capable of making and becoming history.

The preservative impulse that marks a magical heritage site reveals itself first in the form of a statue that commemorates the sacrifice of Harry's parents, James and Lily Potter. Harry and Hermione spot "what looked like a war memorial in the middle" of the lane, but upon closer inspection, "[i]nstead of an obelisk covered in names, there was a statue of three people, [the Potters]" (*DH* 323–4). At first glance, the memorial has been bewitched for the Muggle inhabitants of the Hollow to resemble the sleek monuments that attest to the heroes and victims of a Muggle war. But wizards can see past this enchantment to the real statue of the martyred Potters. The memorial for the young couple exhibits a curious compulsion of the magical community to simultaneously display and conceal. The statue acts as a public demonstration of reverence and affection, yet the disguising charm occludes its true nature. Godric's Hollow exists in a negotiated state, balancing the need to preserve and recognize wizarding history with the necessity to live in peaceful secrecy among Muggles. The unique constraints of the wizarding community require multivalence from even a memorial statue, which must then take on multiple historical significances.

The weightiest moment in Godric's Hollow comes when Harry stumbles upon the remains of his parents' home, seemingly untouched for the sixteen years since their deaths. For Harry, the place has obvious emotional significance, but it has symbolic importance for the rest of the community as well. When he first sees the wrecked shell of a cottage where his parents sacrificed their lives, Harry wonders that no one ever cleared the rubble or repaired the damage. But as he moves in for a closer look, a sign springs from the ground bearing the following message:

> On this spot, on the night of 31 October 1981,
> Lily and James Potter lost their lives.
> Their son, Harry, remains the only wizard
> ever to have survived the Killing Curse.
> This house, invisible to Muggles, has been left
> in its ruined state as a monument to the Potters
> and as a reminder of the violence
> that tore apart their family [*DH* 332–3].

The Potter home's preserved ruin attests to the magical community's continued engagement with its own historical discourse. The protective charms transform the cottage into something of a curated display, a site that inscribes both literal and symbolic meaning as a testament to the carnage of war. The expository sign posted out front further contributes to the sense of the home as a museum exhibit; it provides information and contextualizes the display much in the same way a docent would.

Significantly, though, the cottage lacks the austere sterility of a typical museum. Visitors to the Potter home interact with the display by amending it with their own messages. While a few "had merely signed their names in Everlasting Ink [,]" others leave comments that revise the sign's official message to include the Dark Lord's return and the resistance effort currently led by Harry. Though the signers register their support of the movement and leave words of encouragement, Hermione bristles at the unauthorized revisions. She complains that the original sign should have been left intact, but Harry disagrees: "It's brilliant. I'm glad they did" (*DH* 333). He takes pleasure in the site's re-inscription as a symbolic place of resistance to Voldemort's renewed campaign of bloodshed. In this way, the house becomes a multivalent memorial like the obelisk/statue in the town square, honoring the casualties of the First Wizarding War while simultaneously rallying the troops of the Second.

Rowling's reader community seems to take Harry's position on the resistance-themed graffiti. A thread from CoSForums titled "The graves, house, and memorial at Godric's Hollow" (2007) records many readers' responses to the scenes depicting the memorial at the Potter house. Responses to these passages vary from great satisfaction to almost unbearable poignancy. Referring to the visitors' inscriptions on the sign, user Elysia makes a connection between the Potter home memorial and the site of a generation's most symbolic national trauma: "[They] reminded me of all the memorial notes after 9/11, which made this chapter even sadder than it already was" (sec. 13). American readers of the Harry Potter series who came of age at the time of the series' initial publication will likely have vivid memories of the September 11th terrorist attacks. While the reader does not elaborate, it is possible that by memorial notes she is referring to the letters left by visitors at the World Trade Center site in the days and weeks after the towers fell. Her comments demonstrate an associative link between the two locations; both act as symbolic retainers of trauma and represent a significant, though somber, moment in a culture's history. This reading of a parallel between Godric's Hollow and the site of terrorism reveals the import these fictional locations can hold for a generation of readers who consider the cartography of the series as they process their own world.

The overlay of the past and present is substantive. It not only comments upon the ways to mediate tradition with progress, but also investigates the relationship of a society with its own historical discourse. And the same intensity of detail that suffocates some readers, enchants others with the realness it suggests. As peculiar proof of this realness, several of the magical heritage sites that I reference—Ollivanders Wand Shop, as well as the Hogwarts Castle—now have real world analogs in the form of theme park attractions at Universal Studios Orlando and Hollywood, explored by Dennis J. Siler in his essay of this collection. By grounding her stories in places with a palpable sense of history, Rowling takes on the role of cartographer as well as historiographer, mapping out an irresistibly complete world that will undoubtedly charm generations of readers to come.

References

Chevalier, Noel. 2005. "The Liberty Tree and the Whomping Willow: Political Justice, Magical Science, and Harry Potter." *The Lion and the Unicorn* 29 (3): 397–415.
"Convention Concerning the Protection of the World Cultural and Natural Heritage." *UNESCO World Heritage Centre.* November 23, 1972. http://whc.unesco.org/en/conventiontext/.
"Electricity in hogwarts?" *CoS Forums.* Last modified July 7, 2004. http://www.cosforums.com/cosarchive/archive/index.php/t-29304.html.
"The Graves, House, and Memorial at Godric's Hollow." *CoS Forums.* Last modified July 24, 2007. http://www.cosforums.com/archive/index.php/t-108548.html.
Jones, David. 2009. "'Interpret Your Findings Correctly': Harry's Magical Self-Discovery." In *Hog's Head Conversations: Essays on Harry Potter,* edited by Travis Prinzi, 189–205. Allentown: Zossima Press.
Lerer, Seth. 2008. *Children's Literature: A Reader's History from Aesop to Harry Potter.* Chicago: The University of Chicago Press.
Mendlesohn, Farah. 2008. *Rhetorics of Fantasy.* Middletown: Wesleyan University Press.
Natov, Roni. 2001. "Harry Potter and the Extraordinariness of the Ordinary." *The Lion and the Unicorn* 25 (2): 310–27.
Oates, Joyce Carol. 1998. "In Olden Times, When Wishing Was Having: Classic and Contemporary Fairy Tales." In *Mirror, Mirror on the Wall: Women Writers Explore Their Favorite Fairy Tales,* edited by Kate Bernheimer, 260–83. New York: Anchor Books.
Rowling, J.K. 1997. *Harry Potter and the Sorcerer's Stone.* New York: Scholastic.
_____. 1999. *Harry Potter and the Chamber of Secrets.* New York: Scholastic.
_____. 2000. *Harry Potter and the Goblet of Fire.* New York: Scholastic.
_____. 2007. *Harry Potter and the Deathly Hallows.* New York: Scholastic.
Shull, Kristina Karin. 2005. "Is the Magic Gone? Weber's 'Disenchantment of the World' and its Implications for Art in Today's World." *Anamesa* 3 (2): 61–73.
Zipes, Jack. 1988. "The Changing Function of the Fairy Tale." *The Lion and the Unicorn* 12 (2): 7–31.

Wizarding World Tourism

Numinous Experiences of the Harry Potter Generation

DENNIS J. SILER

Over a decade after publication of the last book of J.K. Rowling's Harry Potter series, enthusiasm among the fandom shows no sign of waning. The books are re-read loyally and the films are re-watched and compared to the books by passionate Potterites worldwide. Websites dedicated to the Potter-verse span the continuum from the official *Pottermore*, overseen by J.K. Rowling herself, to sites for academic discussion of the books, to repositories for Potter memes, and even fan fiction that would boggle the minds of less-fervent followers. As of 2010 new physical manifestations of the Potterverse have appeared. Since their inception the Wizarding World of Harry Potter (WWHP) theme parks and London's Warner Brothers' "The Making of Harry Potter" Studio Tour (WBST) have enjoyed massive popularity. In 2014 a new park opened in Japan to wild enthusiasm and massive crowds. WWHP Orlando drew 8.3 million visitors in 2014 alone, and a new park which opened to great fanfare in Hollywood in 2016 promises to give California's iconic Disneyland a run for its money. Similarly, Warner Brothers' Making of Harry Potter Studio Tour has far outstripped even the legendary Stonehenge to become one of the most successful tourist attractions in the UK ("Theme Park").

Just what is it that makes these attractions so attractive? Why do excited members of the Harry Potter generation shell out £33.00 (about $45.00 U.S. at this writing) to visit, catching a series of trains and buses to get to the Studio Tour, or perhaps paying even more for a ticket on the specialized tour bus from central London? Why do millions of Potter fans travel to Florida, fight Orlando traffic, and pay $165.00 U.S. plus lodging to visit a 20 acre plot of land that represents a portion of the fictional wizarding world? And why

95

do they keep coming back again and again? I would argue that the draw of Harry Potter tourism, and indeed, the attraction of *Pottermore*, the films, wizarding world merchandise, and all things Harry Potter, is inextricably tied to the desire of those who grew up with these books for a "numinous experience." But that word, "numinous," may be problematic.

Two weeks after the release of *Harry Potter and the Order of the Phoenix*, the *New York Times* published a vitriolic attack on J.K. Rowling's popular series with A.S. Byatt's article "Harry Potter and the Childish Adult." In the article, which *Salon* described as a "goblet of bile," Byatt states:

> Ms. Rowling's magic world has no place for the numinous. It is written for people whose imaginative lives are confined to TV cartoons and the exaggerated (more exciting, not threatening) mirror-worlds of soaps, reality TV and celebrity gossip [2003].

This quote, perhaps more than any other in the article, fired up the energetic rebuttal that followed. Bloggers and journalists of many stripes leapt into the fray, often keying on the term "numinous" in their rejoinders and rants. But a quick scan through a dozen or so of the responses to Byatt quickly shows the word "numinous" being used in several different (and not necessarily compatible) ways. It was an apples and oranges free-for-all, with emotion so high nobody seemed to realize the problem of semantics at the core of the argument. In the immortal words of Inigo Montoya, "You keep using that word. I do not think it means what you think it means."

There are good reasons for confusion on the meaning of "numinous." A little research shows it has been in use since the mid–1600s, but in the 20th century it was adopted, adapted, and applied extensively in different ways by different fields. For example, the word was brought into the field of theology by Rudolph Otto in 1923. Otto employs "numinous" in referring to the "non-rational mystery behind religion and the religious experience"; he called this mystery, which he posits as the basic element in all religions, "the Numinous." For Otto, the Numinous is "wholly other"—unlike anything else we experience in ordinary life (Otto 1928, 23).

On the other hand, and in another field, Carl Jung's definition of "numinous" carries different connotations:

> Descriptive of persons, things or situations having a deep emotional resonance, psychologically associated with experiences of the self. Numinous [...] comes from Latin numinosum, referring to a dynamic agency or effect independent of the conscious will. [...] The *numinosum* is either a quality belonging to a visible object or the influence of an invisible presence that causes a peculiar alteration of consciousness [Jung 1966, CW 11, par. 6].

As if these two variations were not confusing enough, several other definitions from yet other fields turn up. For example, British dictionaries variously define numinous as "arousing spiritual or religious emotions" or "mysterious or awe inspiring," or even "arousing one's elevated feelings of duty, honor, loyalty, etc." Perhaps more interesting is what may be gleaned from a glance at a thesaurus, where no less than 298 synonyms for numinous are listed, grouped under the following categories: metaphysical, miraculous, mystic/mystical, secret, esoteric, sacred, holy, blessed, and supernatural. Under a few of the larger categories appear these words: magical, mysterious, awesome, visionary, witchlike, and wizardly, along with many others frequently invoked by Harry Potter readers to refer to their experiences. Obviously, the word has myriad definitions and connotations.

It follows, then, that much of the confusion about whether or not anything is or isn't "numinous" is entirely dependent on exactly what one means by the term as well as several other factors including, significantly, the observers themselves. But that ambiguity won't serve our purposes. After all, no useful dialogue can take place if we simply parrot Humpty Dumpty's equivocation in *Through the Looking Glass:* "When I use a word […] it means just what I choose it to mean—neither more nor less."

For our purposes here, the definition of "numinous" in question comes not from the fields of theology or psychology, but from the relatively new theories of historical interpretation and public history. While heritage sites are focused on historical or cultural events and objects, I will argue that examining the parallels between public history and literary tourism, more specifically tourism related to Harry Potter sites, can be most illuminating.

In 2002 Catherine Cameron and John Gatewood coined the term "numinous experience" to describe the "accidental discovery" of what many visitors to particular historical museums and attractions indicated they sought from their time at these sites. After extensively surveying visitors, Cameron and Gatewood identified three larger categories of motives people may have for choosing particular heritage sites: (1) numen-seeking, (2) information-seeking, and (3) fun-seeking. While the nature of the latter two categories is evident, the numinous experience as defined in this study was uniquely categorized:

Conceptually, numen can be said to involve three aspects:
(1) Deep Engagement—a transcendental experience in which one often loses the sense of time passing, something that Csikszentmihalyi and Csikszentmihalyi (1988) call flow;
(2) Empathy—a strongly affective experience in which the individual tries to conjure the thoughts, feelings and experiences, including hardships and suffering, of those who lived at an earlier time; and
(3) Awe or Reverence—an experience of being in the presence of something holy or of spiritual communion with something or someone [Cameron and Gatewood 2003, 242].

Cameron and Gatewood's investigative study, published in *Ethnology* in the winter of 2003, involved asking

> … a combination of closed-ended and open-ended questions that assessed people's interest in historical sites. […] One open-ended question asked people to describe what might enhance their experience at historical sites, and another asked what they seek to get from such visits.

It was the information gleaned from these two survey questions that helped the researchers determine that people sought more than just information and entertainment from their outings. One of the more important findings of this study is that visits to these sites have a "strong affective component" for some visitors, who wish to have a more personal and emotional connection with a place/experience. These people, Cameron and Gatewood found, wish to, "transcend the present and engage with the past in a highly personal way." It is this particular group who make "a personal connection with a site that may be manifest as a deep engagement, empathy, or spiritual communion."

One way to better understand this particular effect was demonstrated in a Historical Interpretation class that took place a few years ago at the University of Arkansas–Fort Smith. A guest lecturer began the class by passing around two old, worn wheat pennies. Students were asked to examine the pennies and evaluate them. Their responses indicated that the coins were old, yes, but too worn to have any real numismatic value, even if they had been of a rare date or mint mark. Once the coins had made their way all around the class, the lecturer then told the students that these particular pennies had been part of a stash of coins that notorious gangster Charles Arthur "Pretty Boy" Floyd robbed from a Fort Smith bank and hid on the presenter's family property. After Floyd's death two of his descendants found the stash in the old well. The second time the coins were passed around the students had a very different response to them. This emotional and intellectual connection, a sense of awe or of being in the presence of something ineffable, is at the core of the numinous experience.

Methodology

Following the lead of Cameron and Gatewood, I created a survey that asked both closed-ended and open-ended questions, but instead of focusing on heritage sites this study focused on Harry Potter tourism sites, specifically the Wizarding World of Harry Potter theme parks and the Making of Harry Potter Studio Tour. Over 100 subjects responded to this survey, which identified the respondents according to age categories, level of interest in Harry Potter sites, and whether or not they had visited such sites before.

The three questions that produced the majority of the data for this study are as follows:

(Question 1)   "If you have not already visited a Harry Potter site, what would make your time there more enjoyable?"

(Question 2)   "If you have not already visited but would like to visit a Harry Potter tourism site, what do you want to get from your visit?"

(Question 3)   "For those who have visited a Harry Potter site, what were your impressions? Please go into detail about what you thought and felt there."

Once the survey responses were all collected, replies were evaluated by a method similar to that used by the heritage tourism researchers. Comments were classified into the various categories of Authentic, Information, Connection, Physical Setting, and Other. In actual practice, many of the categories blurred together. In those cases, responses were logged into each of the categories that applied. The comments referring to the Authentic and Information groupings were fairly easily identified by the use of certain key words and expressions. Likewise, the Physical Setting category was tallied any time responses mentioned anything from accessibility of the site, to crowd control, to food and merchandise. The Connection category was tallied whenever a response indicated the subject wished to experience (or had experienced), in the words of Cameron and Gatewood, "a personal connection with a site that may be manifest as a deep engagement, empathy, or spiritual communion." In actual practice the remarks in the Connection (read "numinous experience") category were easily identified as such. Below are a few of the comments (from "Enjoyment" (Q1) section) that represent the sense of intimate connection that classifies as a numinous experience:

From "Enjoyment" (Q1) Section

"Being able to see the movies and books come alive and in person would be what I would like. I want to just see the sets and relive the story for myself."

"I want to interact with the set and feel like I'm in the books."

"[…] I'd also like some sort of immersive quality like walking through Diagon Alley, stepping into the bungalow."

"I want to feel magical."

"[…] I would also like an immersive experience. I would love to get my letter and start my journey."

From "Want" (Q2) Section

"Everything. The books helped shape who I am as a person. I read SS when I was 11, and I have grown up with Harry, Ron, and Hermione. I've learned more about family, love, and bravery from these 7 books than I ever have in a church service. I want an experience that doesn't trivialize the books. I want something sentimental, fun, and dare I say ... magical."

"The feeling of being connected to a story or scene from one of the books."

"I want to see everything and feel like I'm living in the wizard world."

"I want to be immersed in the wizarding world."

"Anything that can give me that feeling that I am actually a student at Hogwarts."

"I want to escape reality and feel a part of the magical world."

"The biggest thing I would like to get out of my visit would be the renewing of the love for the series by feeling the magic all over again!"

"I would like to feel like part of the magic and story."

"I would be in awe."

"A sense of wonder."

"I want to be able to pretend like I am a student of Hogwarts, regardless of age."

The desire for deep connection and personal identification is evident in these comments, as is an almost religious devotion to the Potterverse. It is important to remember that these comments are taken from the responses of those who have not actually visited a HP site. The comments from those who have experienced a visit to the Potter attractions appear later in this article. First, however, an examination of the specific questions and their responses is in order. For ease of reference, this article will refer to the three questions as Q1, Q2, and Q3.

The First Question (Q1)

The first open-ended question was, "If you have not already visited a Harry Potter site, what would make your time there more enjoyable?" The written responses to this question were evaluated and classified into categories paralleling those of the heritage site study.

Figure 1.1: Total Categories by Percentage: "What would make your visit to a HP site more enjoyable?"

Categories	Percentage
Authenticity/Authentic	12%
Authenticity/Artifacts	4%
Authenticity/Not commercialized	4%
Information/Guides or Tours	14%

Categories	Percentage
Information/Signs or Displays	4%
Connection/Cognitive	17%
Connection/Emotional	34%
Physical setting/Friendly People	4%
Physical setting/Aesthetics	2%
Physical setting/Access	17%
Physical setting/Services	12%
Other	8%

It should again be noted that not all respondents to the survey answered this question, and that some responses ticked the boxes for more than one category. This chart [Fig. 1.1] shows the frequency of the responses by set with each section color coded to reflect the larger categories of *Authenticity, Information, Connection, Physical Setting,* and *Other*. The percentages are calculated according to the number of those who responded and are thus not representative of the entire sample.

The survey data indicates 51 percent of respondents anticipate cognitive or emotional *Connection* as most important to their enjoyment, while 35 percent identify aspects of the *Physical Setting* as elements that would enhance their pleasure. The next highest category, *Authenticity,* (20 percent) comes in just ahead of *Information* (18 percent). It bears noting that several comments specified *Authenticity* as crucial in forming an experience of *Connection* to the site.

The Second Question (Q2)

The next question, again mirroring the original heritage tourism survey question, asked participants, "If you have not already visited but would like to visit a Harry Potter tourism site, what do you want to get from your visit?" The resulting table [Fig. 1.2] shows the percentage breakdown from all responses to this question.

Figure 1.2: "If you have not already visited but would like to visit a Harry Potter tourism site, what do you want to get out of your visit?"

Categories	Percentage
Authentic: True to book/films	13%
Information: Tours/guides/Signage	23%
Connection: Cognitive/Emotional/Escape	63%
Physical Setting: Accessibility/services/merchandise	27%
Other	8%

While the percentages in parallel categories in this data set to some extent echo basic trends of the first, there are notable differences. For example, while 20 percent of those responding in the first set identified the *Authenticity* as important for enjoyment, only 13 percent indicated it was part of what they wanted from the experience of visiting a Harry Potter site. The *Information* category was closer, with only 5 percent more choosing this category in the second group, but in the next category fully 12 percent more emphasis was placed on *Connection*. Finally, respondents in this set placed 7 percent less emphasis on the *Physical Setting* than the first group.

The Third Question (Q3)

The final open-ended question was directed specifically toward those who have visited either a Wizarding World of Harry Potter theme park or the Warner Brothers Studio tour in London: "For those who have visited a Harry Potter site, what were your impressions? Please go into detail about what you thought and felt there." These 34 responses, while fewer in number than those in other categories, were frequently lengthy and full of telling comments. The two highest categories were again *Authenticity* (29 percent) and *Connection*, (59 percent), with the lowest percentages in *Information* (12 percent) and *Physical Setting* (6 percent) of the three. Placed side by side in a graph, [Figure 1.3] the consistency of these factors becomes evident.

Looking at the overall data it is obvious that expectations held for these sites by those who have not visited them and reports of actual experiences do not match up exactly, nor do predictions of what *will be* most important in a visit and stories of what *was* most impressive once a visit actually took place. While discrepancies such as these are not necessarily unexpected, the degree to which categories vary is interesting. For example, the highest percentage mentioning the *Authenticity* category occurs with those who have actually visited a site, (9 percent higher than Q1, 16 percent higher than Q2). Conversely, those who have visited a site register the lowest interest in the *Physical Setting* category, (28 percent lower than Q1, 21 percent lower than Q2). The one relative constant is the comments that describe a cognitive or emotional *Connection*, with the 59 percent tallied in Q3 falling just 4 percent below the percentage for Q2 and 8 percent above the score for Q1.

The above results are open to interpretation, but one thing seems certain: seeking the sort of intimate connection that our definition would classify as "numinous experience" is both highly valued by those who wish to visit a Harry Potter site, and frequently reported by those who have visited one. If we choose to follow the lead of those respondents who insisted authenticity is a necessary part of that sense of deep connection, the percentages designating numinous experiences rise to 71 percent for Q1, 76 percent for Q2, and 88 percent for Q3.

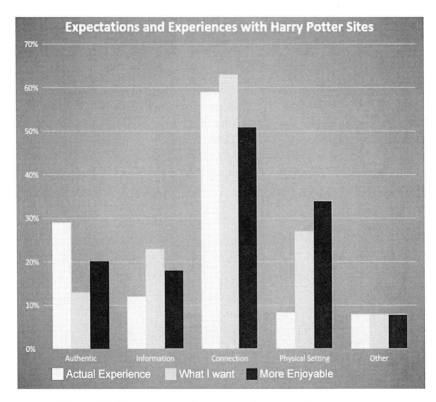

Figure 1.3: Comparison of responses from the three questions.

There are also differences between an imagined *Connection* predicted by those who wish to someday visit a wizarding world attraction, and actual experiences described by those who have done so. A sampling of comments gleaned from Q3 makes the differences evident:

"I felt *amazed*. It was an *incredible experience*, sort of like having a childhood fantasy come to life. It's really *hard to describe* it, except to say that I would love to do it again at some point."

"I felt like I had finally made it to my second home of Hogwarts, Hogsmeade, and the like. I grew up reading those books and watching those movies, waiting eagerly for the next one to come out, and I had already been to all of these places in my mind. They all had a *special place in my heart*, so walking into the pages of my favorite books was *very emotional for me*. The Harry Potter books taught me life lessons and life morals that I still *believe strongly* in today. It's *more than just a story*. The tourist sites take this feeling of the books being more than just bound pages to a whole new level."

"*I felt great* while I was there. It was like *I was part of the Harry Potter world*, and *I hated to leave it*."

"It was *magical and awesome*."

"It was a *wonderful experience* getting to be in a world that started out on paper. Growing up with Harry Potter and loving the series, *it was like a pilgrimage to a special place.* I loved the *translation of text to reality* from a book I loved so much." [Emphasis mine.]

The numinous quality of these experiences is made evident in the language of the comments. Note how often the descriptions employ the vocabulary of deep, personal connection, sometimes even using terminology that might just as easily be applied to religious experience. If, as the data above suggests, the Harry Potter generation seeks numinous experiences, the creators of these attractions must be doing something right in their efforts to provide them.

The Age Factor

While the results of the Cameron and Gatewood study showed no variation in respondents according to age, an interesting effect appears in the breakdown by age of respondents in Question 2, "If you have not already visited but would like to visit a Harry Potter tourism site, what do you want to get from your visit?" For this reply responses showed sometimes startling differences in the wishes of potential site visitors in various age groups. While this is only one survey with a limited sample size, the trends it reveals within the various age groups are interesting and perhaps illuminating.

Figure 1.4: "If you have not already visited but would like to visit a Harry Potter tourism site, what do you want to get out of your visit?" Data grouped by age.

	Under 18	18–24	25–30	31–35	36–40	41–45	46–50	51 and above
Escape/go to another time or place	0	16%	25%	0	16%	0	0	0
Experience Authenticity	0	11%	25%	0	16%	25%	0	0
Gain Connection	0	44%	50%	66%	83%	25%	100%	100%
Memories/Souvenirs	66%	22%	25%	0	0	0	0	0
Information	0	27%	25%	66%	0	25%	0	0
Fun	33%	22%	50%	0	33%	0	0	0
Relaxation	0	0	0	0	0	25%	0	0
Aesthetic Enjoyment	0	5%	0	0	0	0	0	0
Other	0	5%	25%	0	0	100%	0	0

Several interesting patterns come to light in this table. The first three categories, *Escape, Experience Authenticity,* and *Gain Connection* represent aspects of the numinous experience. It is noteworthy that the respondents under 18 universally mentioned "souvenirs" as what they most want from their visit, but *none* mentioned any of the numinous aspects. This demographic was also the one primarily enticed by the rollercoasters and other rides.

The second age category, 18–24, was the largest demographic in responses and also wrote the most of any group per capita. While none of the under 18 group specified a desire to gain connection or escape or go to another place as part of their responses, fully 44 percent of this group chose *Gain Connection* as what they most wanted from their visits, and 16 percent identified *Escape* as one of their goals. *Authenticity*, which, as we have seen, is another indicator of numen-seeking, was mentioned by 11 percent of those responding. Another new category appearing with this age group is the desire for *Information*, which totes up 27 percent. This age group rounds out with *Fun*, at 22 percent, and finally, *Aesthetic Enjoyment* with 5 percent.

Category three, age group 25–30 was even more interested in numinous experience, with 50 percent seeking *Connection*, and 25 percent each naming *Escape* or *Authenticity* as what they want from the visit. Another 25 percent named *Information* and Memories/souvenirs (*Physical Setting*) as important. Curiously, this group also placed the most importance on the *Fun* category, with 50 percent of respondents mentioning it specifically.

While category four, age group 31–35 also frequently supplied answers supporting numen-seeking, all responses were focused on *Gain Connection* alone, with no responses mentioning *Escape* or *Authenticity*. The only other category declared, *Information*, received exactly the same number of mentions.

Category five, age group 36–40, is even more slanted toward numen-seeking than previous groups. Fully 83 percent of this demographic specifically mentioned a desire to *Gain Connection*, while 16 percent each mentioned *Escape* and *Authenticity* as important. The only other category mentioned was *Fun*, with 33 percent identifying it as important.

With category six (age group 41–45) an interesting new development appeared. While a significant percentage appeared to be numen-seeking, (25 percent wanted to *Gain Connection* and 25 percent sought *Authenticity*), another 25 percent chose *Relaxation* as important. Significantly, this was the only group to do so. Also, 25 percent chose *Information* as significant to the experience. Perhaps most remarkably, every single participant from this age group mentioned "family" in their responses. Some indicated their own interest in attending a Harry Potter site was only a function of their family members' wish to do so. Others indicated that their desire to attend a Harry Potter site was directly tied to seeing family members participate in the experience together.

The final two categories, age groups 46–50 and 51 and above, were almost identical in their responses, and, surprisingly, both designated 100 percent in the personal *Connection* category. Unfortunately, the sample size in these two areas was lower than necessary to avoid possible skewed data, so they are omitted from the data in the graph below. Another survey to include more subjects from these age groups is warranted.

As we have seen, the first three categories, *Escape*, *Experience Authenticity*, and *Gain Connection*, combine to form the numen-seeking experience. Focusing just on numen-seeking responses by age category reveals some interesting patterns (Fig. 2.1).

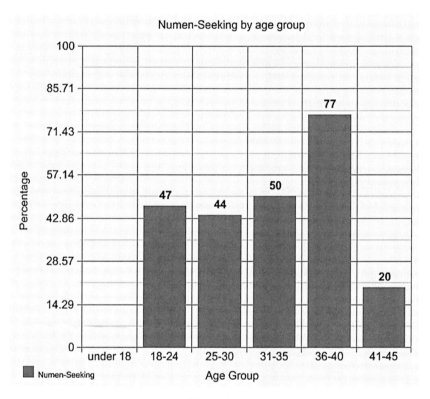

Figure 2.1

As shown above, the under 18 age group made no mention of a desire for deeper connection with the site, preferring in almost every case to describe what souvenirs they wished to receive and/or which roller coasters they wanted to ride. In the 18–24 age group, however, there was an ample percentage who sought deep engagement or a sense of identification with the attraction or the world it represents. Comparable percentages of 25–30 and 31–35-year-olds also identified the desire for some sort of numinous experience as a primary motivation for going to a Harry Potter attraction. The highest percentage of numen-seekers, however, appeared in the 36–40 age group. Among this demographic, a remarkable 77 percent described a desire for communion with the wizarding world. The magnitude of this percentage is even more startling when compared to percentages from the next age group, the 41–45-year-old subjects. This group posted only 20 percent interest in numen-seeking, the second-lowest percentage in the entire study. It also seems significant that this group almost unanimously specified that their interest in attending an attraction was unwaveringly tied to having a family experience; often their children's interest in the attraction was the only reason the subjects wanted to visit a Harry Potter site at all.

Conclusions and Observations

What are we to make of this graph? Why did the subjects under 18 make no mention of a desire for numinous experiences, and why did the 35–40 age group value such experiences so highly? It may be best to begin with the 35–40-year-olds.

One might reasonably assume that first time Harry Potter readers would most closely identify with the characters of their own age. In other words, one might expect an 11-year-old reader would relate more easily to the adventures of 11-year-old Harry, Hermione, and Ron. By extension, it might be tempting to assume that an 11-year-old reader encountering *Sorcerer's Stone*, (in which Harry and company were themselves 11), soon after its release would feel an even stronger sense of identification. The same effect might be true for 12-year-old readers of *Chamber of Secrets*, 13-year-old readers of *Prisoner of Azkaban*, and so forth. While the first Harry Potter book was released in the United States in 1998, the following books did not necessarily come out one-per-year afterward. For example, 1999 saw the release of the second *and* third books, but no books came out between 2000 (*Goblet of Fire*) and 2003 (*Order of the Phoenix*). Consequently, an examination of the book release dates shows a character/reader age correlation with those who were, at the time of the survey, (2015) between 25 and 29 years old. Obviously, this range does not match the data for numen-seeking gleaned from the survey responses. In fact, the respondents who were 25–29 fall directly into the third lowest demographic on the graph.

If not the books themselves, then perhaps their film versions have most strongly influenced viewers of the same age as the heroic trio. Again, this hypothesis fails to match up with the results of the survey, since the age range for numen-sympathetic viewers would be 22–25, and while that group does identify the importance of obtaining a personal connection as the primary reason for attending a site at between 44 percent and 47 percent, the numbers still fall far below the 77 percent of the 36–40-year-old age group who do the same.

If not a correlation of age, what other factors might contribute to the tendency to seek numinous experiences at Harry Potter attractions? Perhaps this effect is not a direct parallel between the reader's and character's ages, but rather certain circumstances of the reader which caused him or her to encounter the series at a particular age. For example, many of today's avid Harry Potter fans were unaware of the books when they were 11, or perhaps they were not allowed to read them for whatever reason. In my Harry Potter course at the University of Arkansas–Fort Smith I have encountered many students who did not read the books until they graduated from high school. Some tell me they were forbidden to read them while they still lived at home. Others had read none of the books until they started the class, in which we read all seven books, (as well as extensive theory and background material), in just 17 weeks. I have encountered similar stories in the continuing education class I taught in the summer of 2015: readers who did not encounter the series until they were older, sometimes much older, than the main characters of the books.

If my theory that readers are affected most when they share experience with the characters has merit, then the target group's age range of 18–23 at the publication of the first book makes some sense. This age range encompasses those who have graduated high school, (college students in particular), who may have had a first opportunity to take on a book series that parents did not sanction at home. A series of books representing a boarding school atmosphere might be particularly affective for someone away at school for the first time. The experience of living in a dormitory, braving isolation from family, struggling with difficult new academic subjects, and learning from sometimes eccentric professors would seem quite familiar to these readers.

Along similar lines of thought, one might point out that survey respondents under 18 were not yet born when the first Harry Potter books appeared in the United States. Unlike older readers, who were likely to have discovered the books through friends or on their own, the youngest group in this survey most likely heard about Harry from their parents or teachers. By the time this younger demographic encountered the wizarding world it was old hat. Far from stirring controversy in daily newspapers and inflaming fundamentalist groups as discussed by Emily Lauer elsewhere in this volume, the books were generally seen as positive, a reading to be encouraged even in some private religious schools, and the movies now just fodder for endless television reruns. Compare the enchantment in reading something controversial, perhaps even a bit dangerous, on the advice of a friend to the disinclination a student might feel toward reading a book recommended, possibly even thrust upon him or her, by a parent or teacher. It is not hard to see why some from this group might have a different attitude toward the Harry Potter books, and by extension the attractions which have grown from them.

It may also bear mentioning that this age group (under 18) most likely first encountered the wizarding world through the films rather than the books. This order of contact, first seeing an impressive and realistic representation of Harry's world complete with countless unique props and special effects might influence the desire for tangible goods over the numinous experience. Conversely, for those visualizing Hogwarts, Diagon Alley, the Burrow, Hogsmeade, and the like via their movie experience, acquiring tangible goods that look identical (read "authentic") to those in the films might actually be part of an immersive and numinous experience in itself, just one of a different type than those sought by members of other age groups.

Whatever the motivation one need only visit WWHP or the WBST to witness the experiences of visitors who seek and find the numinous there. I was able to take a group of 19 students to the W.B. Studio Tour as part of a 15 day literary tourism course in May 2015. The students spanned the continuum of Harry Potter interest and experience levels, including devout Potterites who had read all the books and seen all the films multiple times, to less enthusiastic readers who had seen the films but had not read all (or any) of the books. There was even one student who had read none of the books and seen none of the films.

Observing the reactions of these students to the vast and impressive studio tour was enlightening and often powerful. Some students who had been vocal and sociable at other sites we had visited meandered off by themselves to view the displays. Given the opportunity to take their time and wander at will, many of the students who would ordinarily have clung to the group went off on their own, lingering over sets or props that obviously had meaning to them in the Great Hall, the Burrow, or Dumbledore's office. Some stood for a long time looking at the mannequins of Dobby, Hedwig, or the only-too-realistic figure of the dead Dumbledore. One nearly universally reported numinous experience was the reaction to the enormous and minutely-detailed model of Hogwarts at the end of the tour. The room cycles through continuous day and night lighting sequences while sweeping theme music from the films plays above. Almost everyone seemed transfixed by the sight, wiping tears, walking around the castle to take in every detail, and speaking only in whispers.

Afterward the students recorded their impressions in class journals. A sample of their comments may help convey the profound nature of their experience:

> "Seeing the Hogwarts model towards the end of the tour was heart wrenching—I'm still too uneasy to talk about it. To see that novels written by a single person brought so many people together and created not only a subculture but an entire world that can be experienced is beyond any comprehension of mine."

"Warner Brothers Studio Tour was nirvana."

"As I took a picture of myself facing into the Mirror of Erised, I couldn't help but think how appropriate the reflection was: me standing in that place. Definitely a dream reflected back at me into a reality."

"It caught me completely off guard to step into the large room with Hedwig's Theme swelling to crescendo and seeing a huge "miniature" of Hogwarts School of Witchcraft and Wizardry. It nearly brought me to tears, I was so amazed and thankful to see it."

"Seeing the Hogwarts Express and having a seat inside Ron's blue Ford Anglia was almost heartbreaking it was so beautiful to experience."

"HOLY COW. Talk about connecting with a piece of literature. When the doors of the Great Hall opened, tears were shed. I was in the Great Hall. I walked by Harry, Dumbledore, and Snape. I was there."

"I stayed until it was almost dark outside. I could not imagine ending the tour better than they did: You round one final corner and there it is. A huge replica of Hogwarts [...] stood right in front of our faces. Immediately, people in the group, including myself, broke out in tears."

Having witnessed the reactions of my students and numerous other visitors to WBST, not to mention my previous experiences at WWHP, I think it beyond argument that many who go to these sites are indeed having numinous experiences as the term is defined by heritage tourism scholars like Cameron and Gatewood. The creators of these slices of the wizarding world certainly know what they are doing, and what they are doing resonates with visitors who pursue close personal connection with a site. While it is certain that these magical places satisfy many numen-seekers, what may still be in question is why the unique effect of numen-seeking, a term devised to describe experiences of guests at historic sites and museums, would apply so aptly to what amounts to an amusement park and a preserved movie studio. Why, in other words, does a trait found amongst historical site guests show up so palpably in Harry Potter site visitors?

Discussion and Further Implications

This is a difficult and convoluted question, but one possible answer might stem from a direct linguistic connection between the two fields represented in the various sites, the genres of history and literature themselves. The commonalities between these genres are so deeply ingrained that our very grammar evinces it. To demonstrate this shared effect one need only examine the way verb tenses are used in writing about these two fields. In any other writing, events that are taking place now are in present tense and events that have already taken place are referred to in the past tense:

"Today, I go to work." (Present tense)

"Yesterday I went to work." (Past tense)

Two notable exceptions to this rule take place in the historic present tense and the literary present tense. In these conventions, both historical and literary events are referred to in the *present tense*, without regard to when they occur. For both fields, history and literature, those speaking or writing about an historical event or a literary work bring all happenings into the here and now. The effect of doing so is an immediacy with one's audience, a proximity of time and place that exists in few other circumstances. The text transcends time, providing a means of identification and connection for the audience. The literary (and historical) present tense is a grammatical reflection of a numinous experience, which in this case, translates well from the page, to the screen, to the site.

This linguistic and historical shift in the time/space continuum may find echoes in the theories of some postmodern critics and from their adherents who have written about Disney and Harry Potter theme parks. While I would argue that Disney parks and Harry Potter parks hold significant differences, they both display some of the functional qualities of simulacra. A simulacrum is, at its most basic definition, a copy or reproduction of something real. However, according to Postmodernist social theorist Jean Baudrillard, a simulacrum is not just a copy of something real, but becomes truth in its own right. He calls this effect Hyperreality. Drawing on the concept of simulacrum, Kyle Bubb describes the H.P. theme parks as "a simulated re-creation of Rowling's novels, and [...] a virtual reality that blurs the distinction between the real and the unreal for fans of the Harry Potter series"(Bubb 2015, 49). But, as Bubb later points out, the definition of simulacrum as a "re-creation of something real" cannot fit these theme parks, since they are designed to reflect works of fiction rather than reality. I would argue that closer scrutiny will show yet another layer of complexity in seeing the Harry Potter theme parks as simulacra. Not only are they not re-creations of something "real," neither are they direct re-creations of Rowling's novels, but are in almost every case based on the Harry Potter *film series*. Since the films are themselves simulacra of the novels, so the theme parks are actually simulacra of other simulacra! This is perhaps most reminiscent of a concept suggested by Postmodern critic Frederic Jameson, who offered photorealism as an example of artistic simulacrum, where a painting is created by copying a photograph that is itself a copy of the real. Yet even here the analogy is not perfect, since Jameson's photo was of something real, whereas the films that inspired the theme park were in turn inspired by the fictional world of a series of novels.

Meyrav Koren-Kuik discusses the same effect in the Disney parks, where she argues that Disneyland creates a particular "sentimental utopia" that "is by definition a simulacrum of what Baudrillard terms 'the third order,' one residing in the realm of the hyperreal without a tangible origin within consensus reality"(Koren-Kuik 2013, 150). Koren-Kuik goes on to argue that the "spatial immersion Disneyland offers is marked by the connection between desire and the fictional world. This connection supports both spatial and temporal dimensions and projects a unique chronotope—a unique space/time construct of immersion experience"(150). Mikhail Bakhtin's definition of chronotope is "the intrinsic connectedness of temporal and spatial relationships that are artistically expressed in literature"(Bakhtin 2002, 15). From here it seems fairly straightforward to see that the relationship between the linguistic effect of time/tense in the literary and historic sites discussed above is a direct parallel to the chronotope intrinsic to Baudrillard's "third order" simulacrum. This is also a direct tie-in to the principle of Deep Engagement—the "transcendental experience in which one often loses the sense of time passing" essential to the numinous as defined by Cameron and Gatewood.

So the question of whether or not Harry Potter books contain the numinous has come full circle. It is obvious to anyone who has experienced it that there is something of the numinous here, and whatever it is must be contiguous throughout all parts of the tangible and intangible wizarding world. But it is just as obvious that the numinous experience, whether within the books, the films, or the sites, is not accessible to everyone. This should come as no surprise. Indeed it is in the nature of all experiences from all fields that use the word "numinous" in all its definitions and iterations. What is a numinous experience for one will not evoke numen for all. The key might just lie in the word "fan" so often used to describe Potter devotees. Tanya R. Cochran contends that the term "fan" derives from the Latin *fanaticus*, meaning insane, mad, or possessed by the gods" (qtd. in Barton 5). While the original definitions may reach beyond what most Potterites would own up to, the spirit of the word is still present. There is an ecstatic element, an out-of-the-ordinary (if not out-of-body) experience of immersive, almost religious elation in these descriptions written by fans who have visited a Harry Potter site. The numinous effect is certainly subjective, whether the word is used to describe a religious ecstasy, a feeling of inspiration, or awe, or a sense of duty, no one book, event, work of art, or historic site can move all observers equally, if at all. But, for those who have memories of their own numinous experiences within the cosmos conjured by Rowling's books and the subsequent films, a physical manifestation of the wizarding world provides a new level of numinous experience, best described by Elizabeth Gramlich, one of the students who visited the Studio Tour with my literary tourism class:

> Seeing the Hogwarts Express and having a seat inside Ron's blue Ford Anglia was almost heartbreaking, it was so beautiful to experience. […] But this made me stop and wonder why? Why am I loving this so much? Why am I getting emotional when

I look at these silly robes that Daniel Radcliffe, not the actual Harry Potter, wore in the first movie? Why does this matter? And I have come to the conclusion that as real and as close to our hearts as some stories are, they can never be so real or so near and dear to us as they are when we experience them firsthand. Reading about something and actually experiencing it are two totally different things, maybe both equally important, though. That's why the Harry Potter set has thousands of visitors. Not because someone is really fascinated by the cut of Daniel Radcliffe's robes (probably), but because they love the story and meaning of Harry Potter, and the set allows them to connect to it and experience it in a whole new way.

Elizabeth's analysis is astute, and rife with the language of the numen-seeker. To A.S. Byatt and all those who question the numinous quality of the Harry Potter series and all its ideological and physical offspring, I say this: regardless of which definition is used, it must be noted that numen is in the experience of the beholder, and millions of seekers have found it, and will continue to find it, in the wizarding world.

REFERENCES

Bakhtin, M.M. 2002. "Forms of Time and of the Chronotope in the Novel: Notes Toward a Historical Poetics." In *Narrative Dynamics: Essays on Time, Plot, Closure, and Frame,* edited by Brian Richardson, 15–24. Columbus: Ohio State University Press.

Barton, Kristin M., and Jonathan M. Lampley, eds. 2013. *Fan CULTure: Essays on Participatory Fandom in the 21st Century.* Jefferson, NC: McFarland.

Bubb, Kyle. 2015. "The Simulated World of Harry Potter." *A Wizard of Their Age: Critical Essays from the Harry Potter Generation.* Albany: SUNY Press.

Byatt, A.S. 2003. "Harry Potter and the Childish Adult." *New York Times,* July 11.

Cameron, Catherine M., and John B. Gatewood. 2003. "Seeking Numinous Experiences in the Unremembered Past." *Ethnology* 55.

Carroll, Lewis, and John Tenniel. 2000. *The Annotated Alice: Alice's Adventures in Wonderland & Through the Looking-glass.* New York: Norton.

Csikszentmihalyi, I. and Csikszentmihalyi M. 1988. *Optimal Experience: Psychological Studies of Flow in Consciousness.* New York: Cambridge University Press.

Jung, C.G. 1966. *Psychology and Religion.* New Haven: Yale University Press.

Koren-Kuik, Meyrav. 2013. "Desiring the Tangible: Disneyland, Fandom and Spatial Immersion." In *Fan CULTure: Essays on Participatory Fandom in the 21st Century,* edited by Kristin M. Barton and Jonathan M. Lampley, 146–58. Jefferson, NC: McFarland.

Otto, Rudolph. 1928. *The Idea of the Holy; an Inquiry into the Non-rational Factor in the Idea of the Divine and Its Relation to the Rational.* Translated by John W. Harvey. Oxford: Oxford University Press.

The Princess Bride. 1987. Directed by Rob Reiner. Los Angeles, CA: Twentieth Century Fox Film Corp. DVD.

"Theme Park Attendance Skyrockets at Universal, Sinks at SeaWorld." 2015. *Theme Park Attendance 2014: Universal Skyrockets, SeaWorld Sinks.* Accessed 3 Aug. 2015. http://www.mynews13.com/content/news/cfnews13/on-the-town/article.html/content/news/articles/cfn/2015/6/3/theme_park_attendance_2014.html.

Filling in Memory Gaps with Love

Harry Potter on Tumblr

HEATHER URBANSKI

All stories have gaps. That's the nature of narrative and this nature is counter-intuitively enhanced in long-running series such as Harry Potter. Fans want to know what's happening off-screen, off-page, between installments, before the series started, and, of course, after the stories "end." This impulse fuels fan fiction and fan art but also the less well-known phenomenon of headcanon. As its name implies, headcanon is primarily a private and personal mini-story created by a fan for their favorite series, usually focusing on beloved characters. A key element of this fan production is that it doesn't change the established narrative of the "official" canon, unlike alternate universe (AU) fan fiction. It fills in the gaps, but doesn't contradict the established storyline.

The traditions of fan art and fan fiction are decades, if not centuries, old, depending on how you characterize and categorize the activity. We are now seeing, however, new wrinkles within this tradition made possible by the social nature of digital media. In many ways, digital media has changed the nature, or at least the distribution, of memory objects produced by fandom. Fan memory is on display in nearly every aspect of fandom and it is undeniable that many of our practices, including fan fiction and fan art, depend on the need to remember the canon of the original narrative. The headcanon examples I will examine in this essay demonstrate the blurring of the line between producer and receiver that's been established within fandom research for decades but with a new twist: Tumblr and other sites allow for increasing collaboration in that users submit ideas for Harry Potter headcanon for translation into production on various Tumblr blogs.

When it comes to creating headcanon, Harry Potter fandom remains active over a decade after the seventh novel's release. I believe modern interpretations and explorations of the ancient rhetorical canon of memory (such as Paul Booth's description of the current digital rhetorical situation as one of "a postmodern restructuring of truth and history as eternally constructed and constructing" [2009, 337]) can be combined with narrative theory and the contemporary fandom concept of canon to examine the gaps in the Harry Potter saga. My analysis relies on the interactions between canon, knowledge, and memory with the complicating notion that both canon and memory have gaps and it is in those gaps that the fan practice of headcanon lives. In other words, Harry Potter headcanon exists where narrative theory meets fan production, especially for the generation who grew up with Harry Potter, since so many of them were introduced to narrative by J.K. Rowling.

Canon as Knowledge

There are few words within fandom that carry as much weight, even reverence, as *canon*, which Karen Hellekson and Kristina Busse define for fandom studies as "the events presented in the media source[s] that provide the universe, setting, and characters" of the narrative (2006, 10). For the purposes of this analysis, I am limiting the information on the Harry Potter narrative to what is included in books 1 through 7 and omitting the *Cursed Child* play and script, which, as a time-travel tangent to the original narrative, did not shape the Harry Potter generation in its formative years. Booth, meanwhile, describes canon as the "diegetic history" of a popular culture text (2009, 340) and advocates seeing "story canon as something akin to a fictional fact" (341). This intractable set of features, events, characters, and even beliefs that defines our beloved franchises, however, relies on a complex human phenomenon: memory.

The fandom definition of *canon* builds on a much older one in function if not form: the classical rhetorical "canon" of *memory*, which is one of the five traditional elements of rhetoric along with invention, arrangement, style, and delivery. In the ancient rhetorical tradition, memory and *kairos* (the sense of time and place) are closely linked and, I contend, a focus on this double meaning for *canon* provides an incredibly useful lens through which to understand and appreciate the fan experience.

In many ways, the double meaning of canon I'm invoking here is nothing new. Classical rhetoric was predicated on rhetors training their memory of commonplaces and shared cultural stories. But in a digital age of convergence culture, these centuries-old concepts are rapidly being adapted to reflect the postmodern understanding that all knowledge and memory is partial, mediated, and constructed. Thus, Harry Potter headcanon, and many other types of fan production, complicate the classical conception of rhetorical memory. A foundational premise for this essay, therefore, is that if memory is a classic rhetorical canon and canon is a defining element of fandom, then the work of rhetoricians, classical as well as contemporary, can help us better understand twenty-first century Harry Potter fandom.

We begin this analysis of the role of canon in fan production with Mieke Bal's three-part narratological system, though with Bal's reminder that these layers do not "exist independently of each other" (2009, 7) and cannot be wholly separated, firmly in mind:

> *Text*: "in which an agent … ('tells' the reader) a story in a particular medium."
> *Story*: "the content of that text [that] produces a particular manifestation, inflection, and 'colouring' of a fabula."
> *Fabula*: "a series of logically and chronologically related events that are caused or experienced by actors" [5].

Using this theoretical construction, it is my contention that fan production of headcanon identifies the gaps within the "story" level of the Harry Potter narrative and then creates or expands the events experienced by the characters of the fabula to fill in those gaps. This is a never-ending process because, as H. Porter Abbott argues, a complete sense of the narrative is impossible because narrative "at one and the same time fills and creates gaps" (2007, 44).

Abbott argues that those necessary reader insertions are what give "the experience of narrative much of its power" (2008, 91). Thus, as Abbott explains, "in seeking to fill the gaps of what happens in the storyworld we must cope not only with what is left out of the narration but also what is given" (2007, 45). Similarly, Marie-Laure Ryan identifies, referencing the work of Todorov and Bremond, "events that do not happen are as important to the understanding of narrative as events reported in the factual mode" (1999, 118).

Those gaps, which can be either temporary or permanent, according to Emma Kafalenos, can be examined using the Formalist and early structuralist "view of fabula as a material: a set of events from which a *sjuzhet* is made … [that is] conceived as finite … [and thus] available as a totality for analysis" (2010, 37). By defining fabula instead as "a construct that readers make from a *sjuzhet*," Kafalenos argues, we can assign "the constructing of the fabula to perceivers" and thus allow for the "possibility not only of comparing individual perceivers' fabulae but of directly addressing the instability of the fabula as it grows and changes during individual perceivers' process of perception" (37). This construction of fabula by the readers is, in many ways, at the heart of fan production in general, and headcanon in particular.

Booth refers to the work of David Herman and Richard Walsh to remind us of the "inherent paradox at the heart of the fabula/sjuzhet divide," which he delineates as "the fabula only exists because it has appeared, however, briefly, within the nature of the sjuzhet. At the same time, however, there must be an inherent difference, for the fabula exists as separated from the sjuzhet experientially" (2009, 336). It is this notion of experiencing a text that is particularly useful for study of headcanon because as Booth also describes, "to fill in the gaps in the sjuzhet by expounding the fabula becomes one key aspect of fandom" (336).

Knowledge as Memory

As Tomasz Mazur summarizes, "In ancient Greece, memory constitutes the very core of knowledge. To discuss memory is, then, to discuss knowledge itself" (2011, 237). So, if canon is knowledge, then canon is also inextricable from memory. But, memory can no longer be (and never really was) value-neutral. As Booth argues, "memory itself is shaped by the multitude of cultural codes that go into the collective memory" (2009, 337). Similarly, Tara Brabazon defines memory as "a composite construction" that "finds a fertile incubator in popular culture" but also warns, "Memory is not safe: it is messy, corrosive and/or empowering" (2005, 70).

For example, Jan Assmann identifies the disorganized nature of "socially-mediated memory" as "a high degree of formlessness, willfulness, and disorganization…. Every individual memory constitutes itself in communication with others. These 'others,' however, are not just any set of people, rather they are groups who conceive their unity and peculiarity through a common image of their past" (1995, 127). Approaching this concept from the classical tradition, Mazur uses the stories of Apollodorous and Socrates from *Symposium* to illustrate that memory is "fragmented, shaped and even distorted according to audience profile" (2011, 241). A key distinction in Mazur's construction is between "memory work" and memorization (239) where, "as a result of these contingencies, the stories are changed constantly in the process of memorizing and re-memorizing. The Socratic word for this reshaping … is 'practising'" (241). Thus, we can definitely view canon as an element of memory practice that is central to the fandom experience.

Similarly, Mazur identifies that "according to Plato, knowledge is only memory in a specific modus or constellation" (2011, 239). In this way, if canonical knowledge can be seen as a pattern of memory, then headcanon interrupts that pattern, individualizing it while also adding to the community understanding of the canon.

Canon, in many ways, can be distilled down to narrative knowledge that influences the reading or viewing experience. Memory in classical rhetoric was also about knowledge in being able to recall applicable information (names and facts) as well as commonplace structures at the "right time" (Crowley and Hawhee 2004). Conventional wisdom often sees memory as unnecessary in a print literacy culture, a view made even stronger, for some, in the age of digital media, since nearly all accumulated knowledge is readily available. And yet when we look at memory through the fandom lens, there seems to be no question that this canon is still rhetorically relevant. Fan memory is constantly invoked in fandom practices, where the reading and writing, consumption and production, of the activity cannot be separated from the need to remember the canon of the original narrative.

Several scholars, including Susannah Radstone (2011), have observed that memory as a rhetorical canon is in the midst of a resurgence. Classical rhetoric was predicated on rhetors training their memory of commonplaces and shared cultural stories. The classical canons of rhetoric—invention, arrangement, style, memory, and delivery—have traditionally been used to help writers and speakers manage the time and place of their situation, their *kairos*, to achieve their particular goals. *Kairos* is a distinct notion of time separate from *chronos*, which is the more familiar concept: when referencing *kairos*, we mean the opportunity, the time, the place of the communication … in other words, the context of the situation.

When considering the fan experience, however, our focus shifts from the memory of the rhetor to that of the audience. While classical rhetoric sees memory as almost entirely the province of the rhetor, memories of canonical knowledge on the part of the fan/viewer is a significant factor in the headcanon experience. But we now understand both knowledge and memory to be dynamic, even unstable (as Booth (2009) identifies) and situated within complex social and collaborative endeavors. Brabazon further observes, "Remembering requires a conscious selection of events and people" (2005, 72) and the fan authors of headcanon make such choices and selections all the time.

Fan fiction, especially headcanon, relies on memory and invention to fill in the narrative gaps identified by narrative theory; thus, headcanon is a manifestation of Jason Mittell's (2006) narrative complexity not only in that complex narratives turn audiences into "amateur narratologists" but also into amateur rhetoricians as well. While Mittell is concerned principally with television serials in opposition to "standalone" films, his observations regarding narrative complexity also apply here. Mittell contends that narratively complex series "convert many viewers to amateur narratologists, noting usage and violations of convention, chronicling chronologies, and highlighting both inconsistencies and continuities across episodes and even series" (38) in ways that require "procedural literacy" (39). If we extend Mittell's analysis, it would seem that many fans of Harry Potter engage in the narratologically complex task of filling in the gaps: rather than simply reading between the lines, they inscribe these spaces with their own writing. The Harry Potter generation has grown up with this type of fan activity being commonplace, leading, as discussed elsewhere in this volume, to a collaborative view of meaning-making.

Fan Production in the Digital Age

Another way to approach this collaborative assembly as memory practice is through Charles Soukup's description of memory as "History, as a shaper of identity and community, [as] dispersed and endlessly reconfigured based upon the pleasures of play" (2010, 89). Similarly, Mazur also examines Plato's *Philebus* for its "dialogue concerning the notion of pleasure" where "Plato's … main thesis is that pleasure is not the main motive for human action. Rather, memory motivates us, because what and how we remember matters most. All motives related to the search and desire for pleasure are located in memory" (2011, 244). Fandom involvement exists at this intersection of identity (such as the #Potterheads on social media platforms), community, play, and pleasure and so a key element of fandom research is to approach this subset of the Harry Potter audience within rhetorical situations that carry specific, distinct cultural knowledge and memory.

Booth refers to the landmark work of Henry Jenkins and Pierre Bourdieu to observe, "The signs that [the] audience decodes are influenced by the type of cultural system in which the audience sits: one cannot 'decode' outside of one's own cultural system" (2009, 333), thus we cannot separate fandom from canon as they are entwined in a deeply contextual subcultural system. In other words, the nature of canon as knowledge can be seen as based in part on the shared cultural memory from a subculture that is fandom.

Assmann also argues, "Cultural memory … always depends on a specialized practice, a kind of 'cultivation'" (1995, 131), going on to define cultural memory as "that body of reusable texts, images, and rituals specific to each society in each epoch, whose 'cultivation' serves to stabilize and convey that society's self-image" (132). Thus, we can see the canon of a fandom as a heritage that is cultivated by a wide variety of specialized audiences: fans, producers, scholars, etc. Contemporary postmodern perspectives have already made these distinctions blurry and fraught, to say the least. In particular, questions are being raised regarding the nature of collective socially-mediated memory within our connections to group and social identities. This notion of "memory work" within a rhetorical situation (Monaco 2010) points toward an increasingly complex, constructed, and mediated understanding of the cultural memory involved in the *kairos* of a text (Enos 2012). Brabazon further identifies that the "careful recycling of popular culture—particularly music—has frayed the textual fibres of remembering and forgetting" (2005, 69).

So what happens when we consider the connections among memory, time, and place from the fan perspective? Many scholars, including C. Lee Harrington and Denise D. Bielby (2005) and Radstone (2011), have raised this question and found strong connections among feelings of home, identity, and a space of belonging rooted in fandom and our experiences with the texts that are the objects of our fanship, to use Harrington and Bielby's term.

As Assmann identifies, a significant characteristic of "cultural memory" organization is both the "institutional buttressing of communication … through the formulization of the communicative situation in ceremony" and "the specialization of the bearers of cultural memory" (1995, 131). Digital tools and platforms such as Tumblr provide structures to create and transmit knowledge and memory that are incredibly complex within decentralized fandom to assist us with the memory work. As Booth observes in his analysis of fan wikis, we are continuing to experience a "changing dynamic between production and consumption in the digital age" (2009, 333). A significant portion of this dynamic is what Booth calls "active audience" response: "Rather than a centralized, singular 'meaning' that emerges from a text, active audience studies posit that audiences have the power to read texts in their own way, constructing personalized meaning from elements within the text" (333). These personalized meanings form the foundation of headcanon.

As the owner of Tumblr page "headcanonsforpotterheads" describes, "They are head canons, meaning they are only canon in the person's head. Head canons are used 'to describe something that hasn't yet happened, or has not be described or explained, yet it has happened/is happening in the [head-canon] writer['] s head." Thus, we see the posts to this page, and the many similar to it, as filling in narrative gaps within the Harry Potter canon. This is a collaborative activity, with a feature on the page for fans to submit head-canons that the owner of the page then transforms into posts. Thus, the digital media tools lead us to ask, Whose memory? Whose invention? On April 29, 2012, for instance, the blog showed a post declaring, "Charity Burbage and Severus Snape were actually rather close. He had warned her not to publish in the Prophet but she refused to cower" (tumblr.com)—an idea never alluded to within the series proper, but one that is not contradicted by the canon.

Headcanons on Tumblr

When we pull all these pieces together, then, we can see headcanon on Tumblr posts as a mash-up of fan production, collaboration, and digital media among members of a self-identified subculture. Tumblr is such a decentralized and dynamic platform that any attempt to conclusively categorize the posts shared there would be a blurry picture at best, as any particular hashtag on the site is a continually moving target. What follows, therefore, cannot in any way be considered a comprehensive categorization of the posts on any individual Tumblr, let alone the entire platform. Instead, my analysis will rely on a selection of posts taken from three Tumblr users' pages, chosen because they directly invite collaborators to send in ideas that are turned into posts, to demonstrate the manifestation of headcanon using Brabazon's characterization of popular culture as preserving "something of a life lived, pleasures shared, joyous laughter or empathetic tears. It is not accurate or verifiable, but it is affective" (2005, 67).

The three Tumblr users I have chosen can be found at the urls:

- hp-headcanon.tumblr.com (abbreviated HPHC in this essay)
- headcanonsforpotterheads.tumblr.com (PH)
- pottersheadcanons.tumblr.com (PHC)

Most of the posts on these Tumblrs use a consecutive number system, which is indicated in text, but some from Headcanons for Potterheads do not have numbers. In those cases, the date the post was loaded is used for reference. These Tumblr users are using the fan activity of headcanon to "preserve" for their beloved Harry Potter characters the life events, pleasures and joy shared, and tears shed. They are collaboratively filling in the gaps of the Marauders' all-too-short lives and of both major and minor characters as they respond to the aftermath of the Battle of Hogwarts and try to have the "lives lived" Barbazon (2005) identifies. Fans mourn the deaths of beloved characters through their headcanons, imagining the process of picking up the pieces and dealing with the trauma of what they've experienced, and celebrate moments of joy on behalf of characters they love, as the Harry Potter narrative continues to expand for them, in their own "heads" and on Tumblr. As fans so often say, these headcanons are "all about the feels."

Life Events

One of the more prominent, and optimistic, expressions of headcanon fills in the tantalizing narrative gap in *Deathly Hallows*: those eighteen years between the end of the Battle of Hogwarts and the Epilogue. In particular, fans imagine the details surrounding the births, weddings, and other milestones encountered by the students we followed from year one to the final battle. For example, several posts deal with Hermione's pregnancy with Rose, suggesting that she told Harry before Ron because she wasn't sure how he would react (PHC #52) and then broke her husband's finger during labor and delivery (HPHC #965). We also learn that Teddy is named Lily Luna's godfather out of respect for Remus choosing Harry for Teddy (PHC #48) and Hagrid receives pictures from Charlie of Norberta's dragon children (HPHC #905). Related milestones captured by headcanon include Harry teaching Teddy how to produce his patronus, as Remus did for him (HPHC #821) and passing along the Marauder's Map to his godson as a legacy from both himself and Remus (PHC #9). And one fan imagines Ginny's first professional Quidditch match being attended by her loyal friend Luna, in her familiar lion's hat (HPHC #985).

But those times are not perfect, at least as these fans imagine them. For example, Ron proposes to Hermione sooner (in Australia after retrieving her parents, per PH #120) than they are ready to be married, according to one headcanon (HPHC #868), because she needs that reassurance as she heals from the trauma experienced during the war. George's wedding to Angelina, meanwhile, acknowledges Fred's absence by a missing Best Man among the groomsmen (PHC #189) and Fleur's sister, Gabrielle, meets her husband, Dennis Creevey, at a memorial service for the Battle of Hogwarts (HPHC #744). Other minor characters, such as Oliver Wood, Katie Bell, Alicia Spinnet, Lavender Brown, Parvati Patil, and Cho Chang, all get spouses, in various combinations: Oliver marries Alicia (PHC #28) but then again, so does Katie (HPHC #918).

This latter pairing brings us to what is sometimes termed the "queering" of canon by fans. For several years, multiple continuing online discussions have directly taken on the lack of diversity, along many axes, in the Harry Potter series, including the fan fiction described in Balaka Basu's *Magic from the Margins: Harry Potter and the Postcolonial Experience* in this collection. Many interpret the queering of characters in headcanon as a response to this but that is a subject deserving of its own dedicated analysis from those more qualified than I am in such scholarship. For this essay's purpose, therefore, I will note that character same sex pairings popular as headcanon include Dean and Seamus (PHC #187, #211, #224; PH #063) and Lavender and Parvati (HPHC #788). Other characters imagined to have at least experimented with queer relationships include, of course, Harry (with Draco, HPHC #707; and George, HPHC #703), Ginny and Luna (HPHC #710), and even Lucius Malfoy and Arthur Weasley while at Hogwarts (PH 22 Apr. 2012). Both Oliver (HPHC #921) and Charlie Weasley (PHC #212) are imagined to be asexual by some fans while another post identifies Bellatrix Lestrange as experiencing gender dysphoria (HPHC #872). And these are just a very small sample of characters who are presented as non-heteronormative in headcanon posts on the three examined Tumblrs.

Looking further back to those life events that occurred before *Philoso-*

pher's Stone begins, fans imagine the Sorting Hat granting Peter Pettigrew's request to be sorted into Gryffindor House, despite finding it a bad fit (HPHC #841), while also rejecting Severus Snape's similar plea that same year, after Lily was placed in Gryffindor (PH #85). We also get a glimpse of Lily and James's wedding, which one post indicates was much less traditional and grand than Lily had dreamed of (PH #075) where another user imagines Sirius introducing himself to the Evans family as James's brother (PHC #174).

And while the "official" narrative ends with the Epilogue in *Deathly Hallows*, headcanon can fill in gaps after this as well as before. Fans create milestones both happy and sad for the characters. For example, multiple posts predict Hermione becoming the first Muggle-born Minister of Magic (HPHC #758 and PH 27 Apr. 2012) and Hagrid remaining at Hogwarts until Lily Luna graduates, to keep Harry's kids as safe as students can be at Hogwarts (PHC #47). Finally, many fans project ahead to the final moments and/or afterlife for the characters. Harry, for example, is imagined to be the first among his friends to die (HPHC #880) while another fan saw a deathbed conversation between Harry and Draco in St. Mungo's (PH 22 Apr. 2012). When he crosses over into heaven, where his family and friends stay close to each other, his mother knows he is on his way before the others because "a mother always knows when her baby is coming home" (HPHC #796). A later post on that same Tumblr imagines George reverting back to his twenty-year-old self and finally reuniting with Fred in the afterlife (HPHC #862) while another fan imagines Minerva McGonagall passing away quietly surrounded by old friends who have gathered to mark her retirement from Hogwarts the same day (PH #087).

Pleasures and Joys Shared

Another enticing gap in the Harry Potter narrative for fan headcanon to fill is the adventures of the Marauders' generation: James Potter, Sirius Black, Remus Lupin, and Peter Pettigrew, and Lily Evans as well as others at Hogwarts at the same time. Fans frequently imagine this band of mischief makers singing loudly, often drunkenly (PHC #75; PHC #108; PHC #157; and PHC #44), with Sirius particularly interested in Muggle punk rock (PH #077). More details are also provided for the relationship between Sirius and James's parents who welcomed him during summer and other holidays (PHC #168; PHC #125; and PHC #124) as well as the beginnings of the romances for Narcissa and Lucius Malfoy (PHC #70) and Arthur and Molly Weasley (PH #062). The relationship between James and Hagrid is filled in by a headcanon that James was the one who bought Fang for the gamekeeper at Hogwarts (PH 6 Dec. 2011). In addition to envisioning James being well-received by Lily's parents, especially in contrast to Vernon Dursley (PHC #95), Lily's kindness is extended to Luna's mother whom she also befriends while at Hogwarts (PH 23 Apr. 2012). Perhaps these types of headcanons can be compared to Rowling's own tweets about her ideas of what happens off the page. An argument can be made, for instance, that Dumbledore's sexuality is Rowling's headcanon, but not actual canon.

The intersection between the wizarding world and the modern Muggle world during the events of the seven books is also an area ripe for headcanon, particularly on the hp-headcanon Tumblr, which was still actively posting in fall 2016. Fans imagine what it would be like for Muggle-borns to attend Hogwarts without working access to their digital devices and predict complicated attempts to resolve the problem (HPHC #979; HPHC #956). Outside of the grounds of Hogwarts, one headcanon imagines the meeting between Arthur Weasely and Dr. Granger, once their children get engaged, and finds unexpected kindred spirits with Hermione's father as interested in the magical world as Arthur is about Muggles (PHC #183). One fan, meanwhile, imagines what would happen if Hermione took Ron to a showing of *Lord of the Rings: Return of the King* but forgot to mention the scenes with a cave full of spiders (HPHC #941). These few examples in particular demonstrate the underlying role of memory in understanding fan productions like headcanon: they rely substantially on a robust knowledge of the franchise canon, rewarding those fans with prodigious memories of the minute details of the Harry Potter universe.

Empathetic Tears

But there is no getting away from the reality that perhaps the most emotionally wrenching elements of Rowling's canon involve the loss of loved ones and friends to both wars against Voldemort. Several fans focus on the remaining Marauder, Remus, as he wanders Hogwarts grounds when he is an instructor there, to feel closer to his lost friends (PH #050) and occasionally imagines he can feel James and Sirius in their Animagus forms during full moons (PHC #84). Many fans also engage with the long-term effects of those wars on the characters who survive the Battle of Hogwarts. For example, one post imagines that Neville's Boggart (and thus his greatest fear) transforms from Snape, as we saw in *Prisoner of Azkaban*, to his family and friends being tortured by the Cruciatus Curse (PH #015) while another anticipates Hermione's difficulty sleeping without Ron and so creates a headcanon that she is allowed to live in Hogsmeade rather than the castle when she returns for her final year so that he can be with her at night (HPHC #765). And while much fan fiction, and indeed a lot of headcanon, predicts a romantic relationship between Rose and Scorpius Malfoy, one fan instead interprets her character to be so attuned and close to her family as to realize that Ron could never bring himself to forgive the Malfoys for all the pain they caused and so she resists anything more than friendship with Draco's son (PHC #65).

It is likely not a surprise, then, that many headcanons imagine the mourning and memorialization process the survivors experience both during and after the events of the main narrative. While individual posts imagine the quiet, personal mourning of Snape for Lily (PH #090; PH #056), Draco for Crabbe (PH #119), and Charlie for Tonks (PHC #74), the grief over Fred Weasley's death is a much more frequent subject of headcanon for fans. Some fans imagine George encountering the Mirror of Erised (PH #104; PH #032) or being unable to produce a patronus because all of his happy memories include his twin (PH #059), while others focus on Molly's response over the years to the realization of her greatest fear (as we saw in *Order of the Phoenix*): a family member's death. In some of these headcanons, she continues to knit sweaters with an "F" on them (HPHC #836; PH #103) and in others she slips and calls out to Fred when she really means George (PH #013), even continuing to set a place at the family table for her missing son for the rest of her life (PH #123).

As Emily Lohorn discusses elsewhere in this volume, memorial sites are important to the wizarding world. Thus, it should come as no surprise that the physical commemorations of the dead are also a focus for fan headcanon, including frequent predictions that the Marauder graves (minus Peter Pettigrew and plus Fred Weasley) are engraved, "Mischief Managed" (HPHC #900; HPHC #938). Another fan envisioned a coordinated effort sometime between the events of *Goblet of Fire* and *Deathly Hallows* to present the TriWizard Tournament cup to Cedric Diggory's father. The Hogwarts grounds are also imagined as a location of memorial in other posts, such as the annual gathering on May 2 in the Room of Requirement for survivors of the Battle (PH 20 Apr. 2012) and the empty place setting left on each house table during feasts in the Great Hall representing those who have been lost (HPHC #705).

As I said above, it's all about the feels. Thus, while it is unlikely that each of these headcanons will resonate with each member of the Harry Potter generation—or, indeed, even with each Harry Potter fan—the inextricable connections among knowledge, canon, and memory are all in play to fill in the gaps in the narrative that fans just cannot let go.

REFERENCES

Abbott, H. Porter. 2007. "Story, Plot, and Narration." In *The Cambridge Companion to Narrative,* edited by David Herman, 39–51. Cambridge: Cambridge University Press.
_____. 2008. *Cambridge Introduction to Narrative.* 2nd ed. Cambridge: Cambridge University Press.

Assmann, Jan. 1995. "Collective Memory and Cultural Identity." Translated by John Czaplicka. *New German Critique* 65: 125–33.

Bal, Mieke. 2009. *Narratology: Introduction to the Theory of Narrative*. 3rd Ed. Toronto: University of Toronto Press.

Booth, Paul. 2009. "Time and Relative Dimensions on Line: *Doctor Who*, Wikis and the Production of Narrative/History." *Interactions: Studies in Communication and Culture* 1(3): 331–49.

Brabazon, Tara. 2005. *From Revolution to Revelation: Generation X, Popular Memory and Cultural Studies*. Hants, England: Ashgate.

Crowley, Sharon, and Debra Hawhee. 2004. *Ancient Rhetorics for Contemporary Students*. 3rd Ed. New York: Pearson/Longman.

Enos, Richard Leo. 2012. *Greek Rhetoric Before Aristotle*. 2nd Ed. Anderson, SC: Parlor Press.

Harrington, C. Lee and Denise D. Bielby. 2005. "Flow, Home, and Media Pleasures." *Journal of Popular Culture* 38 (5): 834–854.

Hellekson, Karen, and Kristina Busse. 2006. *Fan Fiction and Fan Communities in the Age of the Internet*. Jefferson, NC: McFarland.

Kafalenos, Emma. 2010. "Across the Curriculum: Image-Text Studies." In *Teaching Narrative Theory*, edited by David Herman, Brian McHale, and James Phelan, 98–106. New York: MLA.

Mazur, Tomasz. 2011. "A Value of Memory—Memory of Value: A Mnemonic Interpretation of Socrates' Ethical Intellectualism." In *Memory and Migration: Multidisciplinary Approaches to Memory Studies*, edited by Julia Creet and Andreas Kitzmann, 235–48. Toronto: University of Toronto Press.

Mittell, Jason. 2006. "Narrative Complexity in Contemporary American Television." *The Velvet Light Trap* 58: 29–40.

Monaco, Jeanette. 2010. "Memory Work, Autoethnography and the Construction of a Fan-Ethnography." *Participations: Journal of Audience and Reception Studies* 7 (1): 102–42.

Radstone, Susannah. 2011. "What Place Is This? Transcultural Memory and the Locations of Memory Studies." *Parallax* 17 (4): 109–23.

Ryan, Marie-Laure. 1999. "Cyberage Narratology: Computers, Metaphor, and Narrative." In *Narratologies: New Perspectives on Narrative Analysis*, edited by David Herman, 113–41. Columbus, OH: Ohio State University Press.

Soukup, Charles. 2010. "*I Love the 80s*: The Pleasures of a Postmodern History." *Southern Communication Journal* 75 (1): 76–93.

Tumblr Posts Referenced (all accessed 27 Sep 2016).

hp-headcanon		*headcanonsforpotterheads*		*pottersheadcanons*	
Number	Date posted	Number	Date posted	Number	Date posted
985	23 Sep 2016	224	21 Feb 2015	123	17 Mar 2012
979	21 Sep 2016	212	9 Feb 2015	119	16 Mar 2012
965	13 Sep 2016	211	8 Feb 2015	106	9 Mar 2012
956	3 Sep 2016	189	24 June 2014	104	6 Mar 2012
951	2 Sep 2016	187	22 June 2014	103	6 Mar 2012
941	31 Aug 2016	183	1 June 2014	090	1 Oct 2011
938	30 Aug 2016	174	23 May 2014	087	30 Sep 2011
921	26 Aug 2016	168	21 Apr 2014	077	29 Sep 2011
918	26 Aug 2016	157	20 Mar 2014	075	27 Sep 2011
900	18 Aug 2016	142	5 Mar 2014	063	27 Sep 2011
880	6 Aug 2016	125	21 Jan 2014	062	27 Sep 2011
872	2 Aug 2016	124	20 Jan 2014	059	27 Sep 2011
868	31 July 2016	120	11 Dec 2013	050	29 Aug 2011
862	14 July 2016	108	11 Nov 2013	032	25 Aug 2011
841	20 June 2016	95	25 Oct 2013	015	24 Aug 2011
836	19 June 2016	88	14 Oct 2013	N/A	27 Apr 2012
821	14 June 2016	84	12 Oct 2013	N/A	23 Apr 2012

hp-headcanon		headcanonsforpotterheads		pottersheadcanons	
Number	*Date posted*	*Number*	*Date posted*	*Number*	*Date posted*
796	22 Apr 2016	75	9 Oct 2013	N/A	22 Apr 2012
788	20 Apr 2016	74	9 Oct 2013	N/A	20 Apr 2012
765	14 Apr 2016	70	9 Oct 2013	N/A	6 Dec 2011
758	12 Apr 2016	65	29 Sep 2013		
744	9 Apr 2016	52	24 Sep 2013		
710	5 Mar 2016	48	23 Sep 2013		
707	3 Mar 2016	47	23 Sep 2013		
705	2 Mar 2016	44	22 Sep 2013		
703	1 Mar 2016	28	18 Sep 2013		
9	15 Sep 2013				

Magic from the Margins

Harry Potter and the
Postcolonial Experience

BALAKA BASU

J.K. Rowling makes no effort to hide her personal politics from the world: she is liberal, supports the welfare state which she herself benefited from as a single mother, and she speaks on behalf of minority populations. As the author of the Harry Potter series, her voice—on Twitter, on the official Pottermore website, in interviews—carries enormous weight among fans of the series. Those fans who are members of the Harry Potter generation have grown up with her words resounding in their ears. Indeed, as discussed elsewhere in this volume, critics like Andrew Gierzynski and Loris Vezzali suggest that the series has come to form a moral compass for such readers, ostensibly pointing them away from bigotry and towards friendship and tolerance. While Rowling's personal politics do furnish the broad strokes of these lessons, the novels remain inscribed with traces of the imperialist rhetoric and politics of those nineteenth century novels that form the bulwark upon which her creation rests. When Rowling shifts the setting of her narrative to the United States for the Fantastic Beasts film series, this colonial subtext becomes almost impossible to miss. In this essay I will address the ways the fantasy of Britishness and colonialism in the series can be detrimental to a progressive reading of the original series and the ongoing growth of the Potterverse.

Harry Potter and the Idea of Britishness

Similar to other popular British cultural exports like *Sherlock, Downton Abbey,* and *Doctor Who*, the Potterverse privileges a Britishness that is gentrified, charming, imperialist, classist, and mostly white. For example, the wizarding world, where most of the action of the novels takes place, is a society based on slave labor, where the work is done by house-elves, who must physically self-injure to punish themselves if they disobey their wizarding masters' orders (*CoS* 14); it touts segregation as an acceptable and viable form of government; it believes in its superiority and rule over "uncivilized" magical creatures (house-elves, goblins, centaurs, and so on) who, like wizards and other humans, are also entirely sentient beings. It is a society encoded with species-prejudice, exemplified in attitudes towards Remus Lupin, a werewolf, and Hagrid, a half-giant, as well as codified officially within the walls of the wizarding world's governing body, the Ministry of Magic, where:

> Halfway down the hall was a fountain. A group of golden statues, larger than life-size, stood in the middle of a circular pool. Tallest of them all was a noble-looking wizard with his wand pointing straight up in the air. Grouped around him were a beautiful witch, a centaur, a goblin, and a house-elf. The last three were all looking adoringly up at the witch and wizard [*OotP* 116].

At the end of the novel in which this ironically named Fountain of Magical Brethren is introduced, Dumbledore warns the wizards that "The fountain we destroyed tonight told a lie. We wizards have mistreated and abused our fellows for too long, and we are now reaping our reward" (*OotP* 767). If Dumbledore's statement is true, and the novel certainly leads us to believe that it is, then the series' moral compass surely ought to demand an upheaval of epic proportions. Somehow, though, the narrative never fully delivers on this promise: the other magical species are never integrated into the world; their importance continues to be measured in terms of their loyalty to human wizards' interests. At the end of *Deathly Hallows*, one of two significant house-elf characters is dead and Harry wants the other to serve him a sandwich. Yet, somehow, the novels still maintain an idyllic viewpoint, which seems to argue that the world is benignly spectacular, troubled only by a single evil that can be fought and overcome, after which it will return to a pre-lapsarian state—alarmingly close to sentiments espoused by Britain First and other right-wing nationalist groups, who bank on exactly this kind of nostalgia in order to block immigration and foreign aid.

Harry Potter and the Nineteenth Century Novel

As Marian Yee discusses elsewhere in this volume, Rowling's wizarding world is a mélange of past time-periods. Medieval images abound: her wizards wear robes and swear by Merlin; they write on parchment scrolls with quills and ink. Renaissance-era alchemy figures heavily in the first novel, *Harry*

Potter and the Philosopher's Stone, as does a ghost of that period, Nearly-Headless Nick. The overarching conflict between pureblood and Muggleborn wizards throughout all seven volumes seems to echo the witch trials of the seventeenth century, as well as the Nazi regime of the 1930s and early 40s. Speaking literarily, however, Harry's narrative is peopled with Dickensian characters like his dreadful Dursley relatives, and dotted with Dickensian themes like Harry's own orphaned, abused childhood under the stairs. In fact, alongside the middle ages, it is the nineteenth century that most dominates the world of Rowling's novels. Her literary precedents from this era are clear, as some elements of the series evoke the horror of the gothic novel, while others echo the whimsy of Lewis Carroll's *Alice's Adventures in Wonderland* and *Through the Looking Glass,* as discussed in our prologue to this volume. What is perhaps the series' most obvious literary antecedent likewise hails from the Victorian period: Thomas Hughes' introduction of "muscular Christianity" in *Tom Brown's School Days.*

The first British public school novel, *Tom Brown's School Days* is a love-letter to Hughes's own school, Rugby, and its headmaster, Dr. Arnold. Like Harry, Tom has the name of a British everyman and is designed to be easy for other boys of his age to identify with. The Browns, we are told—much like the Potters, no doubt—form the solidly prosperous and gentrified backbone of England:

> For centuries, in their quiet, dogged, homespun way, they have been subduing the earth in most English counties, and leaving their mark in American forests and Australian uplands. Wherever the fleets and armies of England have won renown, there stalwart sons of the Browns have done yeomen's work [Hughes 1857, 1].

Even in the very first paragraphs of the novel, Hughes makes his colonial enterprise clear. For him, the educational work of the British public school is not to teach Greek and Latin from textbooks, but to form citizens who will extend and colonize the far flung reaches of empire. While the Duke of Wellington probably did not say that the Battle of Waterloo was won on the playing fields of Eton, this apocryphal quotation sums up Hughes's perspective neatly: the public school is where boys can learn the values and discipline that will allow them to literally conquer the world.

Tom Brown, therefore, does not really bother about academic excellence; instead he is far more engaged with pursuing team sports like cricket, and of course, rugby. Victorian educators were among "the staunchest advocates" of this form of learning because they thought it propagated "the muscular Christian values of fellowship, honor, and service" (Putney 2001, 15). In his sequel, *Tom Brown at Oxford,* Hughes explicitly uses the term:

> The least of the muscular Christians has hold of the old chivalrous and Christian belief, that a man's body is given him to be trained and brought into subjection, and

then used for the protection of the weak, the advancement of all righteous causes, and the subduing of the earth which God has given to the children of men [Hughes 1868, 170].

This sentiment is echoed when, as Tom finishes school as a young man of nineteen, Hughes closes with a cricket match. Tom, at the pinnacle of his school career, is captain of the Rugby eleven. As the match continues to its end, he has a conversation with his friend, Arthur, and one of the younger school masters, who tries to convince Tom that if he had applied himself to Greek as he did to cricket, he would have learned to enjoy and appreciate Aristophanes just as well as the game. The boys, however, set him straight:

> "…But [cricket's] more than a game. It's an institution," said Tom.
> "Yes," said Arthur, "the birthright of British boys old and young, as habeas corpus and trial by jury are of British men."
> "The discipline and reliance on one another which it teaches is so valuable, I think," went on the master, "it ought to be such an unselfish game. It merges the individual in the eleven; he doesn't play that he may win, but that his side may."
> "That's very true," said Tom, "and that's why football and cricket … are such much better games than fives or hare-and-hounds, or any others where the object is to come in first or to win for one's self, and not that one's side may win" [Hughes 1857, 394].

The emphasis that Arthur places on cricket as an institution and birthright of *British* boys signifies the reification of both British sport and British culture, which Rowling will echo in the Harry Potter series. A little further on, the schoolmaster describes Rugby as a microcosm, a "little corner of the British empire" (Hughes 1857, 395) where the school sports prepare students for war and administration. As Julia D. Morris observes in her essay of this volume, Quidditch in the Potterverse functions in a very similar fashion for Harry, who inherits his preternatural sporting talent from his father, an Old Boy (the term for alumnus of public schools like Rugby and Hogwarts). As is true for Tom Brown and his comrades, Harry's skill in sport saves him on numerous occasions, and his experience of education focuses much more on military preparedness, teamwork, and leadership, than it does on the actual curriculum. It's unremarkable that Harry and his friends don't actually graduate from Hogwarts in the pages of the original series; like Tom and Arthur, they are concentrating on the battle to protect and conserve British wizarding society, rather than on book learning.

If we want to see the results of a complete Hogwarts education, we need look no further than the careers of the three eldest Weasley boys. As Giselle Anatol states, they appear to "echo the British colonial enterprise" (Anatol 2003, 164). Percy works for the Ministry of Magic; Charlie works with dragons in Romania; Bill is a curse breaker for the goblin bank, Gringotts, working in Egypt. Percy's solid, boring job as a civil servant within wizarding bureaucracy is the least glamorous of the three, but he is still functioning as one of the cogs of empire, albeit in an administrative capacity. Charlie is exploring the "uncivilized" world of eastern Europe, where creatures like dragons are accepted as they would not be in the confines of Britain (excepting the Common Welsh Green?). Bill, however, seems to represent the worst parts of colonialism: when quizzed by his mother about his earring and wild clothing, he simply replies that no one at his work cares, so long as he brings treasure home. Bill's job, then, is to mimic the Victorian "Egyptologists" who took the treasures of Egypt and brought them "home" to England.

Great Britain on Screen

As part of the work of empire is to bring treasure home, another part is to export culture. Long before the series was completed, Harry Potter was already one of Britain's most influential exports. In the 2003 romantic comedy, *Love Actually*, the British prime minister, played by the ever diffident Hugh Grant, stands up for his country against the smooth-talking, sexual harassment lawsuit who is the president of the United States by saying:

> Britain. We may be a small country, but we're a great one, too. The country of Shakespeare, Churchill, the Beatles, Sean Connery, Harry Potter. David Beckham's right foot. David Beckham's left foot, come to that [Curtis 2003].

Although the film's list represents achievements by a small subset of modern Britain—every person named is white and male—it is nevertheless a moment designed to uphold Britishness and its glory to the world. Even as audiences laugh at the joke, the moment makes the audience of the film want to stand up and cheer for the white men chosen to represent Britishness in Hugh Grant's rallying cry, especially since film audiences of the time were responding to heavy handed U.S. foreign policy that was making waves across the globe.

When the Harry Potter films were being produced, casting directors were faced with a "Brits only" rule that prevented them from casting Robin Williams as Hagrid, a role the actor was eager to play (*The Guardian*, 2 Jan 2017). Rowling was anxious to make certain that her stories were not "Americanized," and if one looks at the cinematic landscape of the late nineties—including terrible American adaptations of quintessentially British properties like the television show *Doctor Who*—her fear for the setting and atmosphere of her series seems well-founded. At the time, this rule also provided much needed opportunities for British thespians to get mainstream movie roles that had until then usually been cast out of Hollywood.

Harry Potter's immensely popular film franchise set a precedent. As of

2015, films, television shows, and video games that pass a "cultural test" for Britishness can receive tax relief in the United Kingdom. Productions score points on the test if they are set or produced in the UK, employ British "cultural practitioners" (actors, directors, writers, etc.), and if they otherwise demonstrate "British creativity, British heritage and/or diversity" (bfi.org). While such an initiative obviously helps the British economy, the Harry Potter version of Britishness that is being exported globally through cinematic and visual iconography—including the tweed worn by Remus Lupin; the teapots used by Professor Trelawney and Mrs. Weasley; the bowler hat worn by the minister of magic, Cornelius Fudge; the arching spires of Oxford that stand in for the towers at Hogwarts—these days seems both elitist and out of date, more at home in the age of the empire upon which the sun never sets, rather than in the present.

Magic in the Colonies: India and North America

Rowling's fourth novel, *Harry Potter and the Goblet of Fire*, is where the series really begins to explore the wizarding world outside of Britain as Quidditch fans from around the globe come to watch the final match of the Wizarding World Cup and as schools from France and eastern Europe compete with Hogwarts in the Tri-Wizard Tournament. Notable characters from the schools Beauxbatons and Durmstrang, including Fleur Delacour and Viktor Krum who arrive at Hogwarts in this novel to compete in the tournament, appear as accented caricatures, shown with the casual humor that the British often employ when speaking about continental Europeans. It's interesting to note that the Tri-Wizard tournament, in which foreigners compete with British wizarding students, is "an event that has not been held in over a century" (*GoF* 186), implying that British isolationism has been ongoing in the wizarding world for quite some time.

It's only in this fourth novel, where the idea of foreignness begins to be explored, that South Asian twins Parvati and Padma Patil become slightly more significant characters, with Parvati becoming Harry's date to the Yule Ball. The Patil twins' presence at Hogwarts indicates that British colonization has clearly also taken place in the wizarding world as well as in the Muggle one. As characters, however, Parvati and Padma are not very fleshed out; they provide the image of diversity without much substantial content to back it up. Fan fiction that features the Patil twins thus tends not to focus on the putative romantic relationship between Parvati and Harry (or Padma and Ron), but instead tries to follow through on Rowling's proffered promise of multiculturalism, often exploring the twins' heritage from the Indian wizarding world, as in "Dissipate" (2004) by Pogrebin. Visiting their aunt in India over their summer holidays, Parvati and Padma come to realize that the English magic they've been taught is only one form and that there are other ways to think of their powers. In India, wizarding pictures move only a little, because as their aunt tells them, "Magic is not for such trifles," she says, bending down and continuing to sweep the floor.

> "Who wants to attract *rakshasein* [demons]for a few photographs?" […] Aunty fixes her with cold black eyes, the red swipe of kum-kum at her forehead giving her the look, Padma thinks, of an ancient warrior.
> "Magic is not a plaything, like they teach you at that school. It is life."
> She drops her broom and places her right hand on Padma's chest and Padma feels it flowing between them, magic, magic, no far too weak a word for it. *Jadu*? No. *Jeevan*, slashes of Hindi burn themselves onto her eyes, *jeevan*, life, a thrumming from the depths of the jungle, deeper still until the trees are so dense that the leaves themselves become part of the darkness, rustling and palpable and reaching out with aching limbs.
> Hunger, India is filled with hunger which spills from these secret places into the streets of Bombay, sliding down the blue-grey slats of high-rise buildings and oozing through the bazaars, waiting, waiting, always waiting to be called [LiveJournal.com].

Pogrebin makes magic in this universe culturally contingent, thus rejecting the cultural absolutism of Rowling's Anglocentric universe, while simultaneously illuminating and enlivening minor characters of color, who are not major players in the text.

Left My Heart by Emma Grant (2004–2007) and *Transfigurations* by Resonant (2003) are two examples of fan fiction novels that explore the global wizarding community, particularly the one in the United States. *Left My Heart* (archiveofourown.com) locates the United States' "Diagon Alley" equivalent in the Haight-Ashbury district of San Francisco, where it naturally goes unnoticed surrounded by a community that has become synonymous with counter-culture America. Grant resists the dominant heterosexual master narrative by situating her story within and around the Castro, one of the most famous gay neighborhoods in the United States.

Transfigurations (trickster.org/res/transfig.html), on the other hand, places the U.S.'s wizarding school in Disney World's Magic Kingdom, where it likewise easily escapes notice. As well, Resonant creates a global wizarding culture that is far more clearly laid out than Rowling's. She wonders, for instance, how exactly mail travels across the Atlantic, since owls would clearly not be able to make the trip, and posits the trans-Atlantic goose as the vehicle. Her Native American characters are not ciphers; they affect the narrative in their own right and are no less "civilized" than any other group. Resonant's universe is also less stagnant than Rowling's, including, as it does, Bill's daughter with an Egyptian goblin woman, who has the distinction of being the first

Weasley in Slytherin since the sixteenth century. The story also deftly addresses the problem of "the Goblin Rebellions" that Harry and his class-mates keep hearing about in History of Magic lectures. If we examine Rowling's words closely, we're forced to wonder: who are these Goblins rebelling against—human wizards? Resonant explores how problematic such a depiction is within the context of a series where other species are consistently devalued next to the wizarding "master race." Early resistant readings like those by Resonant and Emma Grant offer a potential for greater diversity in the wizarding world that Rowling's text never fully delivers on.

Meanwhile, to set the stage for *Fantastic Beasts and Where to Find Them* (2016) and its four sequels, Rowling released her own official "History of Magic in North America" (*Pottermore* 2016) to explain the wizarding community that Newt Scamander, the British protagonist of the film, encounters in twentieth-century New York City. In the section titled, "Fourteenth Century—Seventeenth Century" she describes Native American wizarding society before the advent of Europeans on the North American continent. She writes:

> In the Native American community, some witches and wizards were accepted and even lauded within their tribes, gaining reputations for healing as medicine men, or outstanding hunters. However, others were stigmatised for their beliefs, often on the basis that they were possessed by malevolent spirits. The legend of the Native American 'skin walker'—an evil witch or wizard that can transform into an animal at will—has its basis in fact. A legend grew up around the Native American Animagi, that they had sacrificed close family members to gain their powers of transformation. In fact, the majority of Animagi assumed animal forms to escape persecution or to hunt for the tribe. Such derogatory rumours often originated with No-Maj medicine men, who were sometimes faking magical powers themselves, and fearful of exposure. The Native American wizarding community was particularly gifted in animal and plant magic, its potions in particular being of a sophistication beyond much that was known in Europe [www.pottermore.com].

There are many troubling things about this North American "history"—the characterization of Native Americans as having a single, homogenous culture; the stereotypical associations between Native cultures and nature, and so on—but for the purposes of this essay I will simply point out that here actual present-day beliefs of marginalized communities—including "medicine men" and the Navajo tradition of the skin walker—are co-opted as props for Rowling's wizarding world. In contrast, while Rowling's protagonists celebrate Christmas, Christian beliefs never become a part of the invented magic within the novels. Beliefs of Native American tribes and communities, however, are presented as simultaneously fictional, fantastical, and other.

The potential impact of this cultural appropriation on marginalized readers of the Harry Potter generation is profound. On the site nativesinamerica.com, Loralee Sepsee responded to Rowling's piece by writing:

> As Native American youth, we face some of the highest rates of suicide, poverty, poor health, violence, and substance abuse within our communities due to centuries of historical trauma, forced assimilation, genocide, systemic racism, and colonization. For me, and I'm sure for others, Harry Potter was a way to escape these things, or to hold them off for just a little while longer. Do we not deserve respectful representation? Are we allowed to exist without some white woman claiming our mythology and our history and our culture as her own invention? … I want to see the new movie desperately, but I'm so scared that if I do, this beautiful world will become as ruined and as colonized as this one. I'm scared I'll have to leave halfway through, tears streaming down my face, unable to handle sitting idly by [July 2016].

As Sepsee points out, using these beliefs alongside Rowling's invented ones, without differentiation, reduces their cultural legacy by incorporating it into her own.

Rowling continues this section of her history by informing us that:

> The magic wand originated in Europe. Wands channel magic so as to make its effects both more precise and more powerful, although it is generally held to be a mark of the very greatest witches and wizards that they have also been able to produce wandless magic of a very high quality. As the Native American Animagi and potionmakers demonstrated, wandless magic can attain great complexity, but Charms and Transfiguration are very difficult without one [www.pottermore.com].

Thus while raw power may be available to all peoples, the benefits of "civilization" (i.e., the technology and refinement of magic) are invented by white people and only then carried to other parts of the world, providing yet another pathway for Europeans to dominate and colonize.

This, it seems, is exactly what happens in the North American wizarding school, Ilvermorny. Founded by a white Irish witch, Isolt, her English settler husband, James, and their two English adopted sons, Chadwick and Webster (all of whom arrive in Massachusetts on the Mayflower—a heritage linked with upper class American society), the school explicitly mimics the set-up of Hogwarts, just as Harvard, Yale, and Princeton took Oxbridge as their model and just as Phillips Andover and Phillips Exeter took Eton and Harrow for theirs. Although Rowling makes the school expand with the addition of "[t]wo more magical boys from the Wampanoag tribe" and "a mother and two daughters from the Narragansett" (www.pottermore.com/ilvermorny), it's telling that none of these characters even receive a name.

The plot of *Fantastic Beasts and Where to Find Them* does not diverge from this colonialist project, as it brings a Hogwarts graduate, Newt Scamander, to New York City where he solves problems the local American witches and wizards could not have solved on their own, and leaves them better for his presence.

Harry Potter and White Populism

Published in 2013, Gierzynski's book, *Harry Potter and the Millennials*, examines the way in which the Harry Potter generation overwhelmingly supported Barack Obama's election and drew conclusions regarding their opinions on diversity and politics based on this. However, this perception of the generation—and Millennials in general—as a monolithic group, primarily liberal, progressive, and tolerant, is somewhat inaccurate. While very few people agree on why the 2016 U.S. election turned out the way it did, exit polls indicate that many more Millennials voted for Donald Trump than expected; among white members of the Harry Potter generation, Trump secured 48 percent and Hillary Clinton only 43 percent of this demographics' vote (http://edition.cnn.com/election/results/exit-polls). The results of the 2016 election year reaffirm the findings from the 2014 Pew Research Foundation, which showed that Millennials feel unmoored from traditional institutions of authority. The outpouring of support among the white male members of the generation for Bernie Sanders indicates a general state of dissatisfaction with authority, bureaucracy, and the establishment—an institutional dissatisfaction that Harry and his friends share, and that Trump utilized to carry him to victory. Similarly, Harry can be read as the ultimate insider as well as the ultimate outsider: he learns quickly that he is a person of wealth and privilege within wizarding society and that his complete unfamiliarity with the wizarding world doesn't compromise his ability to save it— a narrative position that Trump clearly occupies for his adherents.

Conserving the Potterverse

At the premiere of *Harry Potter and the Deathly Hallows, Part II*, Rowling assured an audience that had grown up with Harry that although her story was now complete "whether you come back by page or by the big screen, Hogwarts will always be there to welcome you home." Of course, she had already made this mythic aspect of her series apparent in numerous ways within the body of the text, perhaps most evidently in her epilogue to the final novel, *Harry Potter and the Deathly Hallows*, where she closes her series with a glimpse of yet another group of eleven-year-old students heading off to Hogwarts, just as their parents, Harry, Hermione, Ron, and Draco had done, seven novels ago. Nineteen years after the climax of the series, we find this new group of first years are replicating their parents' traits: Rose has her mother Hermione's brains, while young Albus Severus appears to be a complete retread of his father Harry. In Rowling's world, character and appearance are entirely inheritable qualities: Harry himself looks identical to his father,

James, except for his eyes, which he has from his mother, Lily. In Albus Severus, this pattern seems to be continuing, and Harry participates fully in this repetition; he has, in fact, named all of his children after extant characters in the series. One receives no sense from this epilogue that the wizarding world has changed in any substantial way over the past nineteen years; in fact, time appears to have merely restored Hogwarts to its status at the beginning of the series, before Voldemort's second rise.

Although she acknowledges that the novel's epilogue is satisfying on the happily-ever-after front, fan critic Astolat nevertheless finds "the awful sense of inertia" troubling. She writes on LiveJournal:

> to me, [Harry's] fight should have been all about diversity and progress, while *Voldemort's* side were the ones wanting to lock them into some kind of false-nostalgia for a time when wizards did things the Good Old Way. At least there should have been goblins in the train station putting THEIR kids on the train too; a tiny little house-elf with giant eyes and quivering ears, timidly getting aboard. […] Or something—just a sign that no, we're not frozen in time [23 July 2007].

And yet, for a universe to be timeless, to "always be there to welcome you home," it *must* remain arrested in a single, repetitive cycle. In fact, Rowling's own history of the wizarding world (as alluded to within the novels) suggests this very cycle, when she indicates that the battle between Harry and the Dark Lord Voldemort is simply a variation on the battle between Dumbledore and his antagonist, Grindelwald. It seems likely that the same cycle will repeat anew, as another Dark Lord arises and another Chosen One is born to defeat him, and it seems likely that Hogwarts is only there to be a home to a select few.

We don't resist this cyclical narrative patterning when we encounter myths, but it becomes more troubling when we imagine history in such terms. In his influential 1917 essay, "History and Chronicle," Benedetto Croce argues that "if it really is history […] if it means something and is not an empty echo, [past history] is also *contemporary* […] for it is evident that only an interest in the life of the present can move one to investigate past fact" (Croce 1921, 12). Building on Croce's idea in her essay, "Harry Potter and historical consciousness," Ann Curthoys suggests that the Harry Potter series rightfully eschews the "empty echoes" of "dead history" (like that taught in Professor Binns's classes), and instead privileges "*living* history" (Curthoys 2011, 8) like the "magical heritage sites" Emily Lohorn addresses in her essay of this collection. After all, Harry becomes involved in the important current events of his day and is aided in this task by the various personal family histories that he is able to access through the pensieve, a magical device that allows its user to literally experience the memories of others. What is this, but *real* history, Curthoys asks (Curthoys 2011, 13–4).

It's a compelling argument. And yet Harry's involvement with the pensieve occurs entirely outside the bounds of the school curriculum. He is the only student at Hogwarts offered access to this "living history," suggesting that this is not a necessary element of universal education, but distributed only to a selected few. Furthermore, Harry uses this knowledge only to defeat a specific antagonist who wants to kill him: he is fighting a personal battle in addition to a war for social justice. We can see evidence of this from the end of the series, which does not address any of the social inequalities endemic in the wizarding world, but instead shows a personal, almost private victory for Harry in which "all is well" with *him*. However, since the wizarding world appears basically unchanged, Harry remains complicit with the system of injustice upon which it is founded.

Progress and Stasis

Mircea Eliade proposes in his book, *Cosmos and History: The Myth of the Eternal Return*, that people often

> defended themselves against [history's terrible apocalypses], [...] by periodically abolishing [history] through repetition of the cosmogony and a periodic regeneration of time.... This traditional conception of a defense against history, this way of tolerating historical events, continued to prevail in the world down to a time very close to our own; and ... it still continues to console... [Eliade 2005, 142].

According to Eliade, there is only one alternative to this conceptualization of time as "cyclic undulation" (144). The *other* defense against the catastrophe of history imagines time as a linear progression, through which the world marches onward and upward, in increasing freedom, reason, and coherence. Marxism, he suggests, embraces this progressivism, reading history not as "a succession of arbitrary accidents," but as possessing a "coherent structure" and even more importantly, a "definite end." The Marxist perspective on religion notwithstanding, Eliade characterizes the philosophy as practically indistinguishable from the Judeo-Christian, except in that its age of gold occurs "only at the end of history" and not also at its "beginning" (149). In other words, Eliade suggests that to exist within the terrible march of history, with its genocides, invasions, and atrocities, humans can either choose to see themselves as part of an inexorable cycle that eternally experiences the desolation of winter and the rebirth of spring in their turn, or they can read their suffering as work that will achieve a better ultimate future. Whichever they pick—the cyclical or the progressive—they must endow their historical trials and travails with meaning.

Eliade, a conservative, seems to prefer the cyclical perspective on history and time for how it inveigles mythic thought into the contemporary present.

More surprisingly, considering Rowling's personal politics, the Harry Potter series subscribes to this view as well. To me, the strangest quality of the Harry Potter books is how little actually happens in them. Although they are exciting adventures filled with giant spiders, dragons, and ghouls, because they are so cyclical, their plots appear to be static from a larger perspective: they have no true forward motion because each book restores the stasis with which it began. Writing in 2003, Nancy Flanagan Knapp describes the then-incomplete series:

> Following this pattern, each book in the series tells the story of one of the years Harry spends at Hogwarts, […] Each year, Harry struggles with […] difficulties of lessons and the vagaries of teachers […] makes friends, […] copes with bullies, […] and enjoys athletic triumphs. […] in each book he must face and overcome Voldemort, who is determined to return to full life and once again dominate and terrorize the wizardly world. Each time, Harry barely defeats him, not through any great brilliance or talent or even luck, but through a sort of dogged holding to what is right [Knapp 2003, 81–2].

Instead of a narrative arc, we get a circle that turns over and over the same ground, repeating endlessly. If, as Croce suggests, the *purpose* of history is to vivify the present, then the meaning of the mythic return, with its fatalism, is dangerous; it encourages us not to act, but to endure. If events merely repeat themselves in endless cycles, then we must simply play out our roles, secure in the consciousness that it doesn't really matter in the grand scheme of things because it's all just another turn of the wheel.

In his article, "Fiction for the Purpose of History," Richard Slotkin writes:

> What we call "history" is not a thing, an object of study, but a story we choose to tell about things. Events undoubtedly occur: the Declaration of Independence was signed on 4 July 1776, yesterday it rained, Napoleon was short, I had a nice lunch. But to be construed as "history" such facts must be selected and arranged on some sort of plan, made to resolve some sort of question, which can only be asked subjectively and from a position of hindsight. Thus all history writing requires a fictive or imaginary representation of the past [Slotkin 2005, 222].

If history, then, *is* at its very core, fiction, it is notable that the only fiction important to Harry and company is myth: a compendium of wizarding fairy tales called *The Tales of Beedle the Bard*, which the main characters sift through to find coded facts that will help them defeat their enemy. Aside from textbooks and other historical manuals, no other kinds of narratives appear to be useful to the protagonists; there are no in-universe stories that help young wizards imagine a new kind of future.

In the Potterverse, the past has always-already happened, and is always-already about to happen again. Harry's timelessness—and his eternal accessibility—means that Hogwarts will always be there to welcome you home—if you want your home to be one where progressive action is sacrificed to timelessness, conservatism, and nostalgia. To go home to Rowling's Hogwarts—as so many members of the Harry Potter generation wish to do—the reader must become someone who wants to escape from time and from history, someone who must reject Croce's "life of the present" in favor of Eliade's "eternal return" to the age of the British empire.

References

Anatol, Giselle Liza. 2003. "The Fallen Empire: Exploring Ethnic Otherness in the World of Harry Potter." In *Reading Harry Potter: Critical Essays,* edited by Giselle Liza Anatol, 163–178. Westport, CT: Praeger.
Astolat. "Deathly Hallows Experience." LiveJournal.com. Accessed March 1, 2017. http://astolat.livejournal.com/156062.html.
Croce, Benedetto. 1921. *Theory and History of Historiography.* Translated by Douglas Ainsley. London: Harrap.
Curthoys, Ann. 2011. "Harry Potter and Historical Consciousness: Reflections on History and Fiction." *History Australia* 8 (1): 7–22.
Eliade, Mircea. 2005. *The Myth of the Eternal Return: Cosmos and History.* Translated by Willard R. Trask. Princeton, NJ: Princeton University Press.
Emmagrant01. 2004. *Left My Heart.* Accessed March 1, 2017. http://archiveofourown.org/works/250282/chapters/387008
Hughes, Thomas. 1857. *Tom Brown's School Days.* Cambridge: Macmillan.
_____. 1868. *Tom Brown at Oxford.* Boston: Ticknor and Fields.
Knapp, Nancy Flanagan. 2003. "In Defense of Harry Potter: An Apologia." *School Libraries Worldwide* 9 (1): 78–91.
Love Actually. 2003. Directed by Richard Curtis. Universal City, CA: Universal Pictures, 2004, DVD.
Pogrebin. 2004. "Dissipate." LiveJournal.com. Accessed March 1, 2017. http://pogrebin.livejournal.com/26088.html
Putney, Clifford. 2001. *Muscular Christianity: Manhood and Sports in Protestant America 1880–1920.* Cambridge: Harvard University Press.
Resonant. 2003. *Transfigurations.* Accessed March 1, 2017. trickster.org/res/transfig.html.
Rowling, J.K. 2002. *Harry Potter and the Goblet of Fire.* New York: Scholastic.
_____. 2014. *Harry Potter and the Order of the Phoenix.* London: Bloomsbury.
_____. 2016. "History of Magic in North America." Pottermore.com. Accessed March 1, 2017. https://www.pottermore.com/collection-episodic/history-of-magic-in-north-america-en.
_____. 2016. "Ilvermorny." Pottermore.com. Accessed March 1, 2017. https://www.pottermore.com/writing-by-jk-rowling/ilvermorny.
Sepsee, Loralee. 2016. "Dear J.K. Rowling: We're Still Here." Nativesinamerica.com. Accessed March 1, 2017. http://nativesinamerica.com/2016/07/dear-jk-rowling-were-still-here/.
Slotkin, Richard. 2005. "Fiction for the Purposes of History." *Rethinking History* 9 (2/3): 221–236.

Fandoms as Classrooms

Harry Potter Online Communities
as Social Intellectual Spaces

AMBER B. VAYO

Sources ranging from NPR to less mainstream outlets often publish headlines depicting Millennials as incompetent—financially, in interpersonal relationships, and in general. The comments on these articles illustrate a generational divide with Baby Boomers and Gen X-ers on one side and Millennials on the other. Millennials frequently respond to their detractors by reminding Boomers (less often, Gen X-ers) that they are usually using media platforms designed by a Millennial while calling Millennials incompetent, or that Boomers and Gen X-ers crashed the national economy. This generational enmity and anti–Millennialism is ubiquitous, but a look at the online fandoms of these Millennials shows that contrary to the popular reliance-on-technology-makes-you-dumber narrative, new technologies are creating social intellectual spaces for this generation to grapple with real world issues through the lens of fan fiction and fan art. A large percentage of Millennials create digital content, and for Millennials, learning becomes a byproduct of content engineering (Palfrey and Gasser 2008, 123). The Harry Potter series is a *bildungsroman* not just in itself but also for a generation of people around the world who grew up on midnight releases, dressing in wizard robes, and trying to fly broomsticks in their backyards. The Harry Potter generation is different from older generations and other Millennials, and as evidenced by examples from the Harry Potter fandom, has experienced a positive educational role of fandoms in an increasingly digital society.

Who Are the Millennials and the Harry Potter Generation?

For my purposes, I will be defining the Harry Potter generation as a cohort of the Millennials. As Dr. Anthony Gierzynski points out in *Harry Potter and the Millennials*: "[a]ge cohorts are made into generations during their formative years by the historical circumstances they find themselves in ... the times ... leave a permanent and unique imprint ... shaping the way its members see and interact with the world" (Gierzynski 2013, 37). There are some discrepancies between Millennials from the 1980s and the Harry Potter generation. The Harry Potter generation is a cohort of digital natives who have a "tendency to express themselves and relate to one another in ways mediated by digital technologies, with a pattern of using the technologies to access and use information and create new knowledge and art forms" (Palfrey and Gasser 2008, 4); older Millennials grew up using technology in high school and college but did not experience the omnipresence of social media in their daily lives until they were much older (Garvey 2015). The three influences that help to define the Harry Potter generation in the United States are political turmoil, the rigidity of K-12 standardized test-based curricula, and the prominence of social networking in their daily lives. While both groups share an affinity for technology and the ability to use it to create thoughtful discourse, the Harry Potter generation largely came of age during a time of political conflict and this helped push them to think critically, if not cynically, about the world around them. Our nation has been at war for most of this generation's lives and this creates a different disposition from that of earlier Millennials.

The mainstream framing of Millennials has focused on the way they are meeting changing economic, environmental, and educational needs. Older generations and those with a vested interest in the *status quo* they have created, deride Millennials for their creative and non-materialist solutions. Members of the Harry Potter generation who make the poor economy work for them by trading on Craigslist or using their collaborative skills to share information and goods are framed negatively both for what is called the "sharing economy" and for not adhering to social conventions. Even when Millennials make responsible financial choices that are designed to suit their environment, such as putting off having children until they can afford them, they are still typically summed up as Reid Cramer of *Time* puts it:

> ... instead of following in the footsteps of their parents who married, bought homes, and had kids, Millennials are renting everything from homes to bikes, phones, and software, signifying a cultural shift that is radically altering their relationship to ownership [June 29, 2015].

Cramer frames this as a choice made by Millennials. He asserts that this a problem because Millennials are unable to earn the type of dividends their parents did from owning property; further, he chides them for not moving into the suburbs and disapproves of their "demand" for better public transportation. Ignoring the burden student loan debt has and will have on this generation, *Time* continues to berate Millennials for not opening up small businesses or buying homes. Comments on articles about student loan debt, which has now surpassed $1 trillion, still claim "today's generation expects everything to be handed to them" (npr.com 2012) other critics suggest that it is because Millennials majored in useless things like "philosophy" and "English" that their student debt is so high, and others still decry raising the minimum wage as a Millennial plot to work less.

When Brooke Donatone discusses her psychotherapy clients with *Slate.com* she is dismissive and glib about the mental health issues that face the Harry Potter generation. Donatone reports asking a patient if the patient thought becoming an adult was scary; the patient said yes. Donatone then notes that the patient is 30 years old and uses this to extrapolate her theory on a generational immaturity. She espouses the theory that the Harry Potter generation experiences an "extended adolescence that delays adulthood." While she fails to define adulthood, according to Donatone, this generation is doing it wrong. She refers to the Millennials as a whole, as a group that "can't think for themselves"; a generation that cannot handle setbacks without becoming suicidal, and one that is afraid of growing up. Her parting thoughts sum up much of the negative attitude directed at those in the Harry Potter generation:

> [m]aybe millennials are narcissistic, like most 14-year-olds are. And maybe they will outgrow their narcissism later in life if 30 is the new 18. We don't have the data on what millennials will be like when they're 40. But more importantly, they need to learn how to cope [Donatone 2013].

That economists would distrust "generation share" is understandable. But that a mental health professional feels comfortable dismissing a whole generation should illuminate the scope of the generational antagonism and intergenerational ignorance facing Millennials. The economy leads to Millennials living at home later in life than previous generations because the housing market and student loan burden preclude early homeownership for this group (Raphelson 2014); rather than those who criticize the systemic burdens they face, those who get published are those who chide this generation as being delayed in adolescence. Yet articles even abound decrying the emotional closeness between this generation and their parents as if the whole generation were suffering Stockholm Syndrome as an after effect of helicopter parenting.

Let Them Speak: The Harry Potter Generation Defies Negative Stereotypes

One of the more compelling reasons to study the Harry Potter generation is their reliance on technology to form groups and facilitate messages, which shows a level of collaborative learning where around "64 percent of online teens in the United States have created some sort of content on the Internet" (Palfrey and Gasser 2008, 112). The Harry Potter fandom is massive with websites like *Pottermore*, the official Harry Potter website, boasting millions of pupils from around the world as of October 2014. Unofficial sites gather even larger numbers of people who create their own blogs, fan art, vlogs (video blogs), and cosplay, including the popular YouTube parody *A Very Potter Musical.* In the same way that Hermione Granger created coins for Dumbledore's Army to communicate secretly (*OotP* 398–9) this group communicates through various allusions both textual and extratextual to identify each other. They create hashtags, memes (typically, shared elements of culture that can be passed around, on the internet that in fan culture tends to be an image or poster that references popular, fan, or political culture) and references to fan fiction and art that form the *lingua franca* for the fandom. The label fandom itself is usually attached to subcultural groups seen as obsessed with nerdy or geeky areas of interest. As Palfrey and Gasser note, while "not all Digital Natives are participating in the creative renaissance that is happening … what stands out is … the extent to which this creativity represents an opportunity for learning, personal expression, individual autonomy, and political change. These examples of self-expression through digital media point towards a greater engagement in remaking content" (113). For the Harry Potter generation, online fandoms are an immersive culture where students can spend hours talking with peers in their fandom—memes abound with the phrase "they're not my fandom, they're my family."

Due to my study of fan fiction, my Tumblr account, made for this study, is populated with memes and comments generated by high school and college age women. These teens, mainly British and American, speak openly on this platform, and their observations about the futility, racism, and classism of standardized testing and school culture substantiate many similar assertions from professional scholars. Their content outlines why they feel they need to turn to fan fiction and online communities for support in the education process. Further, they include information about student culture and learning habits that outside researchers can easily miss. For instance, while "[c]hildren raised on new media technologies are less patient with filling out worksheets and listening to lectures" (Collins and Halverson 2009, 3) we can approach this as a different culture of learning, rather than a lack thereof. Just "because

Digital Natives learn differently from the way their parents did when they were growing up doesn't mean that Digital Natives are not learning" (Palfrey and Gasser 2008, 240). Arguably, they are taking a more proactive role in their education because often they go beyond school to learn. Students of the Harry Potter generation have come to feel comfortable reaching out to strangers for scholastic engagement when they will not reach out to people they know in real life, through engaging with fan fiction, fan art, and fan communities. Outside of the industrialized framework of standardized testing, fans in the Harry Potter generation are supplementing and in some cases developing their own pedagogy, especially in terms of writing. Online fandoms and the intellectual spaces they provide have become integral parts of the lives of many people throughout the digital world with "[m]ore than a quarter of all online Americans (and especially younger ones) … us[ing] the Internet to tag content" (Palfrey and Gasser 2008, 123).

Since so many high schools are devoid of civics and current events courses, this real-world engagement that fandoms provide is actually a crucial component of global citizenship; thus, participation in a fandom can pick up where formal education leaves off in the critical engagement arena (Pope 2003). Members of the Harry Potter generation learn about each other and others in a way that helps break down traditional identity and group barriers, "[m]uch of the way we talk about identity assumes it is a personal attribute, but society maintains control over the use of identity as an associational tool" (Shirky 2008, 204). The Harry Potter generation is changing the toolbox, by using online tools to engage in collaborative production despite the difficulty of navigating diverse groups (Shirky 2008, 50). These "[i]nteractive learning environments would also provide contexts where students could tackle real-world problems beyond the scope of the projects they can carry out in the community" (Collins and Halverson 2009, 28). For those in the Harry Potter generation who are also in the fandom, the Harry Potter series contextualizes political situations by grappling with issues similar to those they could see on the news, since there are allegorical elements in the series that can be used to make relatable modern concerns. What Harry Potter and its fandom does is allow people from different backgrounds to discuss these divisive political issues in a safe context. For example, one meme addresses an economic situation many young Millennials are anxious about: it is a barn owl, referencing the owls of the series, standing sadly in the rain with the caption "Harry Potter is over. Can't find new job" (Memester 2013).

Self-made intellectual spaces like fandoms become necessary as school curricula are constantly changing, making it difficult to discuss contemporary issues or even have space in school to discuss non-tested subject areas (Pope 2004; Abeles and Congdon 2010). The American members of the Harry Potter generation have been raised in country that values standardized tests more strongly than ever. It has been some time since the No Child Left Behind Act (NCLB) started; this means that the students now in high school and those in the first years of college have always been in an educational system that emphasizes specific quantifiable outcomes (Abeles and Congdon 2010; Levine 2006). Compared to earlier generations, this creates a different view of not only what education is, but how it is acquired and applied. This generation has been pressured into career choices and college courses early on leading to a generation with rising rates of anxiety and depression (Donatone 2013). Here the culture and parents in a bad economy, are pushing the Harry Potter generation to "do well" which tends to be defined as college and a good paying job (Abeles and Congdon 2010). The need for a "practical" degree, or a professional degree, is pushed onto these students; hence, members of the Harry Potter generation are at once told writing is an important part of school because they need to pass standardized tests; and that majors in the humanities, where skilled writing is essential, do not matter in the 'real world" or college degree programs (Levine, 2006). For such students who struggle to resolve this contradiction, Harry Potter fandom represents a subversive type of education: like Harry and the rest of Dumbledore's Army, they learn by doing what they enjoy, without the supervision of the school and without the quantifiable outcomes of standardized tests. This autonomous education is not formalized by the establishment or entrenched in the traditional "grade grubber" trophy-hoarding view of Millennials purported in both articles and comments sections on media outlets. Rather, fan fiction and fan art create a lens through which students study other content areas—creating memes about the economy, physics, chemistry, and other works of literature that all allude to Harry Potter. The fandom functions as the gateway to other pursuits and Hogwarts really is serving in an educational role that will lead young readers to future intellectual endeavors.

How the Harry Potter Generation Learns: Communities and Cultivation Theory

For the seven-book series, J.K. Rowling created four Houses into which each Hogwarts student is Sorted. Each house has its own identity: Ravenclaw the wise; Hufflepuff the hardworking and loyal; Gryffindor the brave; and Slytherin the ambitious, and the Rowling-approved site *Pottermore* refers to some students—including Harry and Hermione as the books suggest, and Professors Flitwick and McGonagall—as hatstalls. These characters are not as easily classified and have more of a choice in the matter than characters who are Sorted immediately. Members of the fandom grapple with this by creating Raven-Puffs, Gryffin-Claws, Slyther-Puffs, Slyther-Claws and other combinations. The common trend of hybridizing Hogwarts Houses is a reaction against black-white distinctions that reflects the discomfort with traditional notions of identity that the Harry Potter generation seem to feel (Tierney 2014).

While students engaging in this trend may seem to be dwelling on something they know—themselves, or the four Houses—they are also using their agency to create communal identities that are mediated in part by other group members. Being a Raven-Puff means something different to me than it does to every other Raven-Puff, which is the point. The mediation between identities is especially interesting in students who choose to create hybrid version of Gryffindor and Slytherin—traditional nemeses. Here the fandom members engage with each other to ask when ambition can be a good or even brave trait, or if bravery is inherently ambitious (questioning the Slytherin/Gryffindor distinction altogether). Further, to create house slogans, the lists of house traits, mottos and the like, "involves knowing how to use language to discursively construct identities and … affiliation with other members of a space, and, thus, access to further learning" rather than the accumulation of facts and information (Black 2008, 45). Fandoms create spaces and communities that allow students to share knowledge in a way that is inclusive and show a remarkable ability to aggregate and disseminate information (Palfrey and Gasser 2008, 241). The interactive nature of this community—one person creates art, asks for others to help edit it, and then shares it for comments—does what classroom group work cannot always do by encouraging both participation and best effort. In certain fandoms some members have become "internet famous" and are requested by their peers to create certain pieces of art or stories with certain themes or involving specific characters or character groups. These communities can help fans develop and further their own creative identities and endeavors, which in turn creates more interaction and immersion within the community itself. Some memes and pictures have tens of thousands of "likes," "shares," "pins," and "notes." Even for those with a more modest reach "technology creates real opportunities for students to improve their performance over time by building opportunity for reflection into learning environments" (Collins and Halverson 2009, 27).

This immersive attitude allows students to learn about self-expression and writing for an audience while discussing their chosen fandom. Harry Potter is especially useful for educational purposes because there are so many avenues to discuss different subjects from sports to law, colonialism to liberalism, and boarding school to genocide, as Lauer and Basu discuss in the first essay of this volume. As cultivation theory suggests: "When we become immersed, we truly experience all that the fictional world offers and take to heart the lessons that our heroes learn. In doing so, we internalize those characteristics and lessons" (Gierzynski 2013, 78). So as fans revisit these sites and revise their work, the fandom becomes a place for analytic depth and members help each other re-engage in the educational process. As they engage with fan spaces, they develop more questions; confirming information and persuading each other online by citing examples and creating an analysis, (i.e., the general work of academic research) are things they do on their own.

If we take cultivation theory seriously, we see the way their fandoms begin to inform the students' notions of themselves since "[c]ultivation theory hypothesizes that repeated exposure to a media source leads audiences to internalize the perspectives of that source and to see the world as similar to the world portrayed in that media" (Gierzynski 2013, 29–30). It also affects the way those in the Harry Potter generation view their education, since "Being part of a community strengthens the learning of values shared by that community. Indeed, social relationships have the 'most important impact ... on motivational processes of social learning theory'" (Gierzynski 2013, 39). However positive this may seem, there may be a "participation gap" between those who engage and those who do not: "The digital world offers new opportunities to those who know how to avail themselves of them. There[,] opportunities make possible new forms of creativity, learning, entrepreneurship, and innovation.... Young people need to learn digital literacy—the skills to navigate this complicated hybrid world" (Palfrey and Gasser 2008, 15). It is important to be aware of populations for whom digital spaces remain inaccessible and who thus cannot participate in these forms of learning. Educators may do well to consider how such spaces might be duplicated in the classroom and how they can teach digital literacy, as we continue to expand digital access for all.

Scribbling Students: Why Fan Fiction?

Like Hawthorne complaining about the scribbling women, angered by both their choice of topics and the economic threat they posed to him, many academic and professional writers tend to look skeptically at fan participation for the same reasons. But "educators need to accept that the mode of learning is changing rapidly in a digital age ... it's necessary to expand the frame to all learning, not just the kind that happens in the classroom" (Palfrey and Gasser 2008, 239). This is true in no small part because fan fiction and fan art tend to be relegated—in popular misconceptions—to gossip that is concerned with character relationships, actor worship, or shipping (to ship is to hope for or believe in a romantic relationship between or among characters). But giving cause for optimism, fan fiction and fan art typically rely on tools we associate with literary study: allusion, summary, or parody; and conversations in fan spaces range from literary criticism (discussion of archetypes, style) to critical thinking and philosophy (can the ends justify Dumbledore's means?). Further, both fan art and fiction "rely on inter-textual knowledge to interpret text and context" (Sandvoss 2007, 25). Fan art can be anything from hand or computer-drawn pictures of a character or celebrity, to memes that play on cultural context and literary allusion, and to re-imagining what characters would look and dress like. There are illustrations for cosplay (i.e., costumed play) that people wear in their daily lives, and in the Harry Potter fandom, tattoos that range from house emblems to new symbols made from an amalgamation of Harry Potter icons.

In part, a scholarly disregard for fan fiction and fan art stems from a difficulty in assessing what fan art is, what it means, and why it matters. According to critics, "Blurring the lines of these formerly distinct categories [commercial fiction and fan or amateur fiction] has led to a decline in analytic depth and an ideological stagnation" (Sandvoss 2007, 20). However, in our increasingly digital society with so many young adults and teens spending time online with their fandoms, to ignore or demean fan fiction is to lose an opportunity to develop new pedagogical models.

Aside from fandom's ability to foster personal identity and creativity, the freedom both from pedagogical constraints and from the difficulties in discussing controversial issues makes a fandom ideally suited to young people who seek to explore complex issues that may not be viable to discuss in person. Fandoms challenge the implicitly self-interested model of test-based advancement in schools by focusing on extracurricular collaborative learning and non-quantifiable peer-engagement. In a zero-sum socioeconomic structure where the highest test scores theoretically get the payoff of the "best" colleges, collaborative learning is subversive. Intellectualism and overwhelming interest are commonly viewed as geeky and antisocial traits, but fandoms are far from antisocial. The Millennials in general and the Harry Potter generation specifically are "Digital Natives [who] are good at collaboration" (Palfrey and Gasser 2008, 233).

As Henry Jenkins repeatedly illustrates in his foundational work *Textual Poachers: Television Fans and Participatory Culture,* many traditional scholars disregard fan fiction as the jurisdiction of young female writers who are concerned with interpersonal relationships among characters on a television show. Jenkins, on the other hand, reinforces the notion of fan space as political and intellectual and demonstrates that understanding the controversial, via a fictional lens, has always been a hallmark of the fan fiction experience and allure. Individuals from different perspectives and backgrounds can discuss "hot button" topics in a calmer context by using the characters or fictional worlds as a medium through which they discuss these issues. Jenkins uses the specific example of abortion through Counselor Troi in *Star Trek: The Next Generation* (Jenkins 1992, 85), but Harry Potter *also* has its share of social issues from slavery to genocide to authoritarian governments and propaganda, terrorism and torture, to many others. We see social intellectualism manifest itself in the discussion students have in their questions on fan forums and in the alternate universe stories they create. Feminist issues ranging from sexual assault awareness and prevention, equal pay, representation, and women in the workplace versus the home are all dealt with through the lens of fan fiction, posters, and group discussions. There is an ongoing fan art series on sexual assault that includes posters stating "Love Potions do not equal consent. Coercion through magic is illegal, combined with the use of love potions it is rape." Here the fandom comes together and uses the Potter world to discuss a serious issue that many of them have faced and are facing. While the Harry Potter generation spans the range politically and religiously, a study of the readers themselves shows "Harry Potter fans to be more accepting of those who are different, to be more supportive of equality, to be less authoritarian.... Potter fans are more likely to exhibit these perspectives that parallel the lessons and character traits prominent in the series" (Gierzynski 2013, 6). Millennials may be more justice/equality oriented than other generations (Tierney 2014), but regardless of the exact causal effect of the series, the generation illustrates these qualities in their fandom by creating safe spaces for difficult and intellectual discussion.

The ubiquity of the internet and social networks have allowed fandom members to support each other academically and socially, creating a generation whose members work with each other both inside and outside of traditional education structures. In part due to fan communities and celebrity geeks like Simon Pegg, Joss Whedon, and David Tennant, "[t]he public recognition and evaluation of the practice of being a fan has itself profoundly changed over the past several decades" (Gray, Sandvoss, and Harrington 2007, 4). Fandoms have come to serve as support systems for self-identified loners and geeks, allowing many more students to engage in the process of creating and distributing fan fiction and fan art. Studies of online groups have shown that "students were more likely to be friends if their interests overlapped, and that the likelihood rose if the shared interests were more specific ... it's easier to like people who are off in the same way you are off, but it's harder to find them" (Shirky 2008, 200).

If the primary purpose of education is to teach students to think critically about the world around them and their place in it, then we need to teach to them rather than at them, but breaking the code of the Harry Potter generation can be intimidating to those who are not familiar with media technologies, are not comfortable with mixed media classrooms, and do not understand the stress heaped upon this generation by their parents. The Harry Potter generation are good at understanding all of these things: "[s]tudies show that children who have the most extensive access to the Internet are more likely than their less experienced peers to take a skeptical view of the kinds of information that they draw from Web-based sources" (Palfrey and Gasser 2008, 166). To this end the Harry Potter fandom has created an outlet to engage in both personal reflection and thoughtful, global critical thinking for many of the generation. In his article "Rethinking Thinking About Higher Level Thinking" Reed Geertsen notes: "To think well is to impose discipline and restraint on our thinking—by means of intellectual standards—in order to raise our thinking to a level of perfection or quality that is not natural or likely in undisciplined, spontaneous thought" (Geertsen 2003, 2). So frequently schools focus on knowing answers to questions rather than knowing how to find the answer or what questions to ask. The skill-and-drill approach to testing creates boredom and a sense of disengagement with intellectual abilities because students are trained to passively receive a schooling, rather than to actively engage in earning an education. According to the National Public Radio article "Testing: How Much is Too Much?" American students "take an average of 113 standardized tests between pre–K and grade 12" (Kamenetz 2014). Fandoms, on the other hand, bring students together to share multiple and varied perspectives on a subject that inspires a passion for learning rather than adhering to testing. Due to both NCLB and the role of digital technology "[t]eachers worry that they are out of step with the Digital Natives they are teaching, that the skills they have imparted over time are becoming either lost or obsolete, and that the pedagogy of our education system cannot keep up with the changes in the digital landscape" (Palfrey and Gasser 2008, 8).

As Rebecca Black states in her book *Adolescents and Online Fan Fiction:* "at a time where to be competitive U.S. students must begin to 'major' in innovation, creativity, and problem solving, not just in passing paper-and-pencil tests of factual knowledge, our students are majoring in test preparation" (Black 2009, xiii). For education "[t]o prepare students to communicate in this emerging world requires not simply the traditional reading and writing, but learning how to communicate using different media with people who do not share the same assumptions" (Collins and Halverson 2009, 13).

However, "[t]he things that schools and teachers do best should not be scrapped in the rush to use technologies in the classroom…. The way that students learn to think critically, much of the time, is through old-fashioned dialogue" (Palfrey and Gasser 2008, 246). But to add moderate technology and widen a student's audience, "[s]tudents' work in schools has always faced the artificial barrier of being legitimate only within the confines of the classroom. When student work is seen only by teachers, students do not experience the authentic feedback that results from exposing their work to a real audience" (Collins and Halverson 2009, 25). The intricacies in fan fiction, in the questions members of the Harry Potter generation who are engaged in fandom ask about magical law, the scope of Dumbledore's vision, or the socio-moral complications of politics between wizards and house elves, all demonstrate an awareness of the grey area in which so much scholarly thought takes place and fit the disciplined thinking that leads to creative solutions. The fandom's reaction "against" having to Sort into one of Rowling's four predetermined identities—or Houses—does help us see students thinking about identity and agency in ways that can be used to supplement important scholastic lessons.

Because so many current fandoms are television or movie based, it is easy to relegate them to a certain type of scrutiny, but as professors and researchers Jonathan Gray, Cornel Sandvoss, and C. Lee Harrington write in *Fandom: Identities and Communities in a Mediated World* (2007) the term "fandom" could be equally applied to lovers of theatre, football, specific celebrities, or even the opera. Fandom has been a pejorative term in the past, but as social media has helped create gathering spaces, people have seen the power of fandoms to resurrect media properties that were killed by producers and production companies. Members of the Harry Potter generation "are putting into practice the idea of bottom-up innovation" (Palfrey and Gasser 2008, 233). There can be no doubt then that "[d]igital natives will move markets and transform industries, education, and global politics" (Palfrey and Gasser 2008, 7). Fandoms know they can have a voice and that their voices can create a fan culture from a subculture because online sharing is "inherently social and collaborative. In many respects, it's about the power of communities" (Palfrey and Gasser 2008, 118).

Community Discourse in Harry Potter Fandom

One interesting form of collaborative learning comes when students are discussing the cult of Albus Dumbledore. Dumbledore was a hero to many, but a close reading of his actions causes even a staunch Dumbledore supporter a little discomfort. The fan fiction surrounding Dumbledore often addresses the question "is Dumbledore a shady dude?" (Junega 2013). Some webpages talk about Dumbledore's secrets from Harry and his abuse of authority (Theowyn 2007). The memes labeled "The books according to Draco" nicely point this out. Year one becomes "The year we won the House Cup but Dumbledore gave it to Gryffindor," which fits when fans consider the effect of not only the public shaming of Slytherin, but the unfairness of Dumbledore's action. The Slyther-Puff fandom (Hufflepuff/Slytherin) makes memes dedicated to kind Slytherins who can't get into their own common rooms because they refuse to say passwords that are racist. The Slytherin-leaning fandom notes in *Sorcerer's Stone* (1997) that Dumbledore knew before the feast that he would award Harry, Ron, Hermione, and Neville those points, but waited to do so until after everyone thought Slytherin won (*SS* 305–7). It may have made Neville finally feel useful, but fans are concerned that Dumbledore would publicly and with forethought be cruel to Slytherin House, a quarter of his student body. What is or is not owed to Slytherin House is a recurring concern for the fandom. Equally recurring are the questions surrounding Professor Snape. The discussions about and fan fiction portrayals of Severus Snape range from sympathetic and bullied youth, to malicious, obsessed stalker. The notion that Harry would name his son Albus Severus and that he claims Snape is "probably the bravest man I ever knew" (*DH* 758) has generated substantial, largely negative, sets of fan fiction, fan art, and various memes. Albus Severus Potter's name has not only memes and commentary but also its very own fan fiction called "You Have Got to Be Kidding me" (CaseyLynn1 2014). At issue is the question of Snape's bravery as compared to other characters. Some stories include Teddy Lupin overhearing Harry's claim and responding with "excuse me?" as his father, Remus Lupin, wrestled daily with the social stigma of being a werewolf and despite this, still fought on the side of the Order of the Phoenix and died at the Battle of Hogwarts, unlike Snape. The fandom takes up this problem and provides Albus Severus with a collection of new names taken from house elves ("Dobby Kreacher") and other creatures ("even Aragog Fang, just please!"). A sub-series of posts deal with Snape's reasons for treating Harry (because he was James Potter's son and Sirius Black's godson) badly; regardless of his poor experiences with Harry's older relatives, he is still an adult male who takes out his own childhood and life trauma on his young students. The ways the fandom connects this discussion to contemporary issues and tries to parse out both the causes and effects of bullying, cyberbullying and bullying by teachers are inventive and encouraging.

Beyond his bullying personality, though, another subset of the fandom also rejects the Snape-as-brave myth specifically because of his treatment of Lily (Evans) Potter. As the media reports on the sexism and rape threats women face online and homicidal misogyny, you see these issues addressed in the fandom when it comes to talking about Snape's "love" for Lily. When Snape asks Voldemort to protect Lily at the expense of Harry and James Potter (*DH* 677), fans, especially (encouragingly) teenage girls, realize that this scene represents a crucial element to Snape's character. There is a schism between fandom members regarding the Lily/Severus relationship. One group is the "Always" romantic group who see Snape as a victim of his circumstances and a romantic hero; the other notes that Snape's love was obsessive and unhealthy, not tragically romantic. Harry Potter fans who grew up with the protagonists of the books are actually struggling with issues they face as new adults—dating and relationship boundaries—within the confines of the narrative, and many use personal narratives and quantifiable statistics to make their points. The fandom also studies the system of government in the magical world. House elves are clearly enslaved, but they technically are not human; perhaps it is in their nature to serve. Fan boards discuss whether Hermione is using her privilege to push a form of colonialism on them by freeing them. On the other hand, the treatment of Dobby, Kreacher, and the house elves whose heads are mounted on the wall at 13 Grimmauld Place (*OotP* 62) show us that unchecked authority over these beings is a moral problem that most of the wizarding world overlooks. The fandom discusses the moral importance of S.P.E.W., while grappling with it as an organization promoted by the wizarding class to "free" one of the under-classes. Readers are not presented with enough information about house elves in the books to know what level of their service is nature and what is nurtured by wizarding society. Either way, Hermione's decision to force freedom on them by hiding clothes around Gryffindor Tower (*OotP* 255, 385) is regarded negatively.

Fans thus question how Dumbledore, purported hero of the downtrodden, allows house elves to continue laboring in Hogwarts under his Headmastership. That Dumbledore lets this continue calls two things into question. The first is the problem of elf enslavement. If Dumbledore is the bringer of justice to the masses, would he not have freed all the Hogwarts elves? Is Albus Dumbledore complicit in one of the longest oppressions in the magical world? Here fans are speaking to each other and engaging in a public and communal philosophical conversation. Fandom discussions and stories premised on the notions of Dumbledore as anti-hero or even proto-villain respond to each other in addition to responding to the seven books of the series. Conversations about literature, morals, ethics, history, law, psychology, society, and contemporary issues of slavery flourish in the fandom through both critical and creative writing. Watching the fandom grapple with this in the wake of race-based violence is an interesting look into how teens and young adults view what it means to have privilege. This is the wonder of the Harry Potter fandom. The fan art and fan fiction in a sense constitute a secondary—albeit non-canonical—source that students start to quote and cite and paraphrase, tools that will ultimately need to be honed for proper academic writing but that are already showing impressive sophistication considering the age of many of the writers.

Collaboration, or Meeting the Students Where They Are in the Digital Age

Ultimately, "the changing nature of social and cultural life requires a new understanding of interconnections among types of audience experience"

(Longhurst, Bagnall, and Savage 2007, 125) because as new technology and internet platforms emerge or update, a person's virtual presence becomes part of their identity. Academia is slow to change, but we can capture some of the momentum and enthusiasm of change by accepting a less hierarchical view of education and what constitutes a text allowing students some access to their identity they choose and not simply relegating academic discussions of online identities to Facebook narcissism.

The breadth and depth of online fan fiction shows us that students can be motivated to do detailed, research oriented writing and thinking on their own time. It is easy to demonize the internet and the influence social media has on actual socialization and information literacy, but

> it is possible to envision school spaces where new media … 'have the potential to enhance and expand teacher repertoires by taking tremendous pressure off their shoulders to be the sole sources of classroom knowledge and interpretation [Luke 2000 qtd in Black 2008, 46].

Using the tools at our disposal with our students in a way that can mirror their engagement with fandoms or at least allow us access to the kind of learning they find effective, can lead us to a "teachable moment" on how to come to valid conclusions or create research questions. Recognizing this, teachers across the country are requiring class blogs. Additionally, discussing with our students how they use the internet can show them how to search with information literacy and intellectual rigor,

> [s]tudents are learning while using these sites. And that is worth tapping into. And, although fan fiction authors … engage in a range of school-related literary practices … they are all part of authentic social and communicative activities that are meaningful and contribute positively to powerful identities in these shared learning spaces [Black 2008, 27].

In our students, lack of agency manifests itself not only in a lack of responsibility, but in a lack of investment in their own education, in which they see themselves as merely passive participants. What fandoms and their communities do is create an attitude of engagement and excitement on the part of their members individually and communally. Additionally, as the article "Hope on PhD Attrition Rates—except in the Humanities" for *Inside Higher Ed* delineates, one of the main reasons for our anti-intellectual culture is the isolation we associate with modern types of studying and formalized education (Jaschik 2007). The semi-monastic approach to studying, "the isolationist view of thinking in the Euro-western tradition epitomized by a solitary man turning inward" (Geertsen 2003, 5), no longer appeals to highly networked students. Fandoms are creating spaces of social intellectualism—though they may not fit our traditional view of the term.

Our anti-intellectual culture creates plenty of space for itself in the form of reality TV, celebrity competitions, anti-intellectual representations in the media (those geeks who have no social skills), and the glorification of "bros" who focus on sports and sexual prowess. The cult of machismo in the media defines "cool"—or the "in crowd"—specifically to exclude those gathered for the purpose of discussing ideas and philosophies. But fandoms formed around a collective area of interest, or obsession, are geared towards critical analysis and in-depth understanding of that interest. For many in the Harry Potter generation, the fandom became a matter of interest not only in the stories themselves or in comparing the movies to the books, but also as a touchstone for discussing the political, social, and economic issues that affect this generation beyond the texts and into the real world. The online space creates a safe and encouraging place for readers to come together and ask nuanced, tough questions about the texts and even their own personal beliefs.

"[S]tudents are accustomed to active participation ... where graphic art and online publishing software enable new forms of semiotic engagement and symbolic manipulation of media" (Black 2008, 1). We use the pedagogical maxim: meet the students where they are. As it turns out, they're on Tumblr trying to develop their own voices and creating a space for their own agency. This complicates traditional teaching and learning models that ignore student-driven content and for some faculty members, teaching these digital natives presents challenges. They are sometimes referred to as the *Sesame Street* generation because they expect to be entertained as well as educated. While this adds a burden to the classroom teacher, it also reinforces what we know about education: students do better and enjoy themselves more when they are interested in what they are learning. We do not all have to be Big Bird, but reorganizing some of our pedagogies and reevaluating our biases against popular literature or fan fiction might allow us to foster attitudes of inclusion and social intellectualism.

The voluntary engagement in a fandom where one can learn from many different sources "can be juxtaposed with many classrooms, where literacy is often viewed as a mere tool for content area learning ... learning is viewed as an individual process" (Black 2008, 27). There should be an authority in the classroom, but students should be allowed to develop authority as well. A fandom provides mutual earned respect and uses cooperative and dialogic learning rather than adherence to traditional pedagogy. A classroom of twenty-plus students needs discipline, and so too does a fandom. I'm not promoting anarchy, but we can have discipline and mutual respect (indeed, as Professor Umbridge's failures remind us, we cannot have real discipline without respect). In addition to developing an intellectual community, Harry Potter fans in the Harry Potter generation create a network to help each other navigate the digital world in the same way that Hogwarts Houses help students navigate the magical world. If we learn one thing from fandoms, it should be the attitude towards collaborative learning created in that space. The fandom comes together to participate, to engage, and to share knowledge, or create new knowledge, about something they enjoy. American educational expert John Dewey believed that "the attitude of the thinker ... [is] more crucial than knowledge of reasoning skills. He believed that in the absence of a thoughtful and perceptive disposition, knowledge of how to think ha[s] limited value" (qtd in Geertsen 2003, 4). The typical hierarchical model of top-down teaching is complicated by the disposition of digital natives, while fan perspectives lend themselves to such a disposition.

To this end, a wildly popular series like Harry Potter rewards a perceptive disposition, and it is J.K. Rowling's gift to us that this disposition seems to be in a perpetual state of evolution rather than being doomed to a quick burst of life and then eventual anonymity as forecasters of "Pottermania" mistakenly suggested a decade ago.

In a world that is constantly assessing what justice means when faced with news of genocides, Guantanamo Bay detainees, other crimes and post-war nation building, the Harry Potter fandom discusses these issues. They also bring them into the intellectual/anti-intellectual world by discussing bullies and whether or not, or how, to create justice in schools. The limits of the Ministry of Magic are analogous to the limits of justice in our world. As Emily Lauer suggests in her essay, *Harry Potter and the Book Burners' Mistake*, growing up with this series can lead to an activist outlook on the world. One of the most poignant elements of fan fiction analysis is to follow a fan fiction writer as she (or less often, he) begins to make the connections between the wizarding world's social problems and those in the real world. These connections lead to individual comments about *The Daily Prophet* as a government-supported news outlet, and later news propaganda in the lead up to Voldemort's rise to power. Fans discuss what justice looks like for students who have committed suicide due to bullying and the teachers who allowed that to continue. The discussion is at once heart wrenching and incredibly thoughtful. The same can be said of discussions about sexist teachers: Tumblr user Queen-NatashaRomanoff discusses a moment at her German high school when her teacher noted that they didn't need to discuss feminism because women haven't contributed that much to society. A fandom can allow users to meld the personal and the political, the fictional and the real, the educational and the entertaining, to develop talent, intellect, and passion. That is the Harry Potter generation's greatest hope for a magical legacy.

REFERENCES

Abeles, Vicki and Jessica Congdon, directors. *The Race to Nowhere: The Dark Side of American's Achievement Culture.* Reel Link Films, 2010.
Black, Rebecca W. 2008. *Adolescents and Online Fan Fiction.* New York: Peter Lang.

Caseylynn1. 2014. "Albus Severus Potter, A Harry Potter Fanfic." *Wattpad*. Accessed March 1 2017. http://www.wattpad.com/37736862-albus-severus-potter-a-harry-potter-fanfic-you.

Collins, Allan and Richard Halverson. 2009. *Rethinking Education in the Age of Technology: The Digital Revolution and Schooling in America*. New York: Teachers College. Cramer, Reid. 2015.

Donatone, Brooke. 2013. "Why Millennials Can't Grow Up: Helicopter Parenting Has Caused My Psychotherapy Patients to Crash Land." Slate.com. 2 Dec. http://www.slate.com/articles/health_and_science/medical_examiner/2013/12/millennial_narcissism_helicopter_parents_are_college_students_bigger_problem.html.

Garvey, A. 2015. "The Oregon Trail Generation: Life Before and After Mainstream Tech." *Social Media Week Blog*. 21 Apr. Accessed March 1, 2016. http://socialmediaweek.org/blog/2015/04/oregon-trail-generation/.

Geertsen, H. Reed. 2003. "Rethinking Thinking about Higher-Level Thinking." *Teaching Sociology* 31(1): 1–19.

Gierszynski, Anthony. 2013. *Harry Potter and the Millennials: Research Methods and the Politics of the Muggle Generation*. Baltimore: Johns Hopkins University Press.

Gray, Jonathan, Cornel Sandvoss and C. Lee Harrington, eds. 2007. *Fandom: Identities and Communities in a Mediated World*. New York: New York University Press.

"How the Sharing Economy is Hurting the Millennials." Time.com. 29 June. http://time.com/3939850/sharing-economy-pitfalls/

HP According to Everyone Else. n.d. Tumblr.com Accessed 18 Sept. 2011. http://hpaccordingtoeveryoneelse.tumblr.com/.

Jaschik, Scott. 2007. "Hope on Ph.D. Attrition Rates—Except in Humanities." Inside highered.com. 7 December. Accessed 2 Dec 2014. https://www.insidehighered.com/news/2007/12/07/doctoral.

Jenkins, Henry. 1992. *Textual Poachers: Television Fans and Participatory Culture*. New York: Routledge.

Junega, Sahil. 2013. "Who Thinks That Dumbledore Was a Shady Character?" Quora.com. 10 June. Accessed March 1, 2016. https://www.quora.com/Who-thinks-that-Dumbledore-was-a-shady-character.

Kamenetz, Anya. 2014. "Testing: How Much Is Too Much?" *NPR*. 17 Nov. Accessed 18 Nov 2014. http://www.npr.org/sections/ed/2014/11/17/362339421/testing-how-much-is-too-much.

Levine, Madeline, PhD. *The Price of Privilege: How Parental Pressure and Material Advantage Are Creating a Generation of Disconnected and Unhappy Kids*. New York: HarperCollins, 2006.

Longhurst, Brian, Gaynor Bagnall, and Mike Savage. 2007. "Place, Elective Belonging, and the Diffused Audience." In *Fandom: Identities and Communities in a Mediated World*, edited by Jonathan Gray, Cornel Sandvoss, and C. Lee Harrington, 125–138. New York: New York University Press.

Memester. 2013. "Harry Potter Over: Can't Find New Job." Memestorage.com. 11 Oct. Accessed 15 October 2014. memestorage.com/news/harry_potter_is_over_can_t_get_new_job/2013-11-10-4916

Palfrey, John and Urs Gasser. 2008. *Born Digital: Understanding the First Generation of Digital Natives*. New York: Basic.

Pope, Denise Clark. *"Doing School": How We are Creating a Generation of Stressed Out, Materialistic and Miseducated Students*. New Haven: Yale University Press, 2001.

Raphelson, Samantha. 2014. "Some Millennials—and Their Parents—Are Slow to Cut the Cord." NPR.org. 21 October. http://www.npr.org/2014/10/21/356951640/some-millennials-and-their-parents-are-slow-to-cut-the-cord

Rowling, J.K. 1998. *Harry Potter and the Sorcerer's Stone*. New York: Scholastic.
_____. 2003. *Harry Potter and the Order of the Phoenix*. New York: Scholastic.
_____. 2007. *Harry Potter and the Deathly Hallows*. New York: Scholastic.

Sandvoss, Cornel. 2007. "The Death of the Reader? Literary Theory and the Study of Texts in Popular Culture." In *Fandom: Identities and Communities in a Mediated World*, edited by Jonathan Gray, Cornel Sandvoss, and C. Lee Harrington, 19–32. New York: New York University Press.

Shirky, Clay. 2008. *Here Comes Everybody: The Power of Organizing Without Organizations.* New York: Penguin.

Theowyn. 2007. "The Life and Lies of Albus Dumbledore." *Scribbulus* 21. http://www.the-leaky-cauldron.org/features/essays/issue21/lifeandliesalbusdumbledore/

Tierney, John. 2014. "How to Win Millennials: Equality, Climate Change, and Gay Marriage." *The Atlantic.* 17 May. Accessed March 1, 2017. https://www.theatlantic.com/politics/archive/2014/05/everything-you-need-to-know-about-millennials-political-views/371053/.

Harry Potter and the
Male Student Athlete

JULIA D. MORRIS

One late fall afternoon in 2014, a football player entered the office where I was working at the University of North Carolina at Charlotte as an academic advisor for student-athletes, a student population that typically has trouble balancing the heavy demands of their sport with their educational requirements. A new freshman, this particular student was still getting accustomed to the university experience—one week excited by history and stumped by algebra, and the next week, the other way around. As we began our conversation, I watched this ordinarily lively student visibly tense up as he always did when we had to discuss a reading assignment for his English class. When I asked him why this was, he gave a response I had grown sadly accustomed to: he said that he "hated" to read.

Trying to make him more comfortable, I inquired after his weekend plans, which surprisingly (to me) turned out to include a Harry Potter themed event. I asked if he liked Harry Potter, expecting a reply about the films. "I love Harry Potter," he said instead. "I've read all the books." As always, I was happy to meet another Harry Potter fan, but it was unclear to me how someone who "hated" to read and who claimed with assurance that he "never" read could finish and love Rowling's seven-volume series. When I asked why this didn't count as "reading" to him, he said with certitude: "Harry Potter is not a real book … like a novel, or whatever." It was then that I began to realize that the issues this student and many other male student-athletes were facing had nothing to do with their hatred for reading *per se*.

Student athletes do not hate reading in my experience; rather, they hate giving a poor performance of their abilities. Athletes, male athletes in particular, are generally competitive both on and off the field. The English classroom, too, is an arena for competition and student athletes tend to believe their performance and potential is measured in numbers, in this case, by the grades they receive. Thus, within the literature classroom, they recognize that they do not give a performance of their finest skills and, unfortunately, develop apathy towards their classes, unable to believe that reading is a practical and practicable skill that they can acquire, use, and perhaps even enjoy.

In this essay, I argue that it is possible for such students to learn to appreciate reading through the context of play, which already occupies such a large portion of their lives. Harry Potter, which ushered in the second golden age of children's and young adult literature, made it possible for this generation of college athletes to re-access reading without the stigma that reading "kids' books" might previously have held. In broader terms, encouraging college students to study children's and young adult literature can help student athletes build their reading skills, invest in their education, and most importantly, build confidence in their ability to perform in an academic arena.

Getting a Generation of Boys to Read

In their childhood and adolescence, girls often acquire literacy much faster than their male classmates. In Michael W. Smith and Jeffery D. Wilhelm's *Reading Don't Fix No Chevys: Literacy in the Lives of Young Men*, the authors detail this gap between male and female readers in secondary classrooms as "widening" as girls "greatly outperform" their boy counterparts in language arts classrooms (Smith & Wilhelm 2002, 20). While Smith and Wilhelm's study does not concentrate on college students or athletes in particular, the authors do examine forty-nine male readers of varying race, ethnicity, economic status, background, school setting, and ages. The respondents demonstrate that the reading issues amongst male readers are ongoing and persist through young adulthood. While these young men and boys often recognize that reading is a theoretically important skill for the distant future, they feel completely disconnected from the reading they are asked to do at school—apart from earning a passing grade—or at home. In their conclusion, Smith and Wilhelm suggest that to combat this lack of connection, teachers need to engage male readers in what they call the "inquiry process" (Smith & Wilhelm 2002, 209). Looking at what young male readers *are* reading (i.e., magazines, video games, articles both online and in print, etc.), it seems that they need to be allowed to search for their reading material. They state that "every case where true inquiry environments were introduced in school in place of asking students to report on what the teacher already knew, they were embraced" (Smith & Wilhelm 254). In other words, male readers need to form a personal relationship with the text so that it fits within the "context" of their lives in order to develop their appreciation of reading (Smith & Wilhelm 2002, 256). Finding this point of access allows young male readers to invest, the same way all readers hope to, in their reading material—both in a pedagogical setting and outside it.

Finding Context for Student-Athletes

In *Flow: The Psychology of the Optimal Experience*, Mihaly Csikszentmihalyi writes that "happiness … is a person's best moments which are not passive, receptive, or relaxing time … the best moments occur when a person's body or mind is stretched to its limits … to accomplish something difficult" (2008, 3). The culmination of these experiences, for Csikszentmihalyi, creates "mastery" which leads to happiness, or "flow" (Csikszentmihalyi 2008, 2–3). Male athletes are familiar with Csikszentmihalyi's principles of "flow"; they have "stretched" their bodies in a way that enhances them and leads them to a sense of accomplishment and "mastery." But, as *Reading Don't Fix No Chevys* details, only one of the forty-nine male participants in their study saw any relation between reading and "flow." By and large, the participants were not able to see themselves stretched to accomplishment inside school the same way they were while "mountain biking" or "playing hockey" (Smith & Wilhelm 2002, 91). Male student athletes are a concentrated sector of the male literacy issue Smith and Wilhelm uncover, and they are unable to access Csikszentmihalyi's "mastery" because they are not engaging in the process of "stretching" their minds.

According to the National Collegiate Athletic Association, more than 60 percent of student athletes identify themselves as "athletes" before they see themselves as students (NCAA). While identifying as an athlete does not indicate poor academic performance, not identifying as a student can and does. The trick to academics for those male student athletes who resist the classroom may be to remind them that they do not have to leave their athletics at the door. I believe the solution for male athletes is to draw an analogy between their bodies and their minds. By learning that they are able to play with their minds in much the same way they use their bodies, they will see the avenue to "flow" through reading in a much more relatable, or "contextual" way. My concentration on student athletes should serve as a case study for the issue of male literacy while also highlighting the need for "context" for male readers. Athletics serves as the "context" for this group of male readers, who are not only capable of reading but also studying themselves in characters such as Rowling's Potter.

For these students, the magic of Harry Potter is not wand waving or drinking potions; rather, for student athletes, the magic has to do with the book series' engagement with competition in the form of both war and play. Harry and his friends use competitive play throughout the series to accomplish their goals, just as these students use what is ostensibly just a game to determine their futures. The student-athlete watches as Harry and his friends use play explicitly on the Quidditch field and then use the principles of competition as play to accomplish a revolution, connect with a sense of self, and create a sustainable future. For the student-athlete reader, just as for Harry, competitive play on the field can function as a substitute for real-world concerns off of it.

Rowling's *Harry Potter* series joins the "play" of the body with the "play" of the mind. Male student athlete readers will see themselves in Harry, who himself is a male student and an athlete, and will begin to utilize reading to stretch their minds towards a greater mastery of reading.

Harry Potter: Student-Athlete and Child-Soldier

To explore this topic, I will concentrate on the content of the fifth book and movie in the Harry Potter series: *Harry Potter and the Order of the Phoenix*, which is arguably the key turning point for the series in a number of ways. The first question that appears to surround the narrative of *Order of the Phoenix* is: does it still count as children's literature? Is a story where children form their own army, prepare themselves for battle, and simulate revolution truly a children's story?

Amateur and parental watch-dog critical sites, such as "isthismoviesuitable.com," take on this issue. In his review for this site, Michael Record makes several interesting observations about J.K. Rowling's novel that had to be addressed when filming the motion picture version. Record asserts that Harry's fifth year at Hogwarts is, fundamentally, a tale about teenage angst and isolation. He rates the movie's "emotional distress" category as "4/5" for the emotionally charged horrors Harry experiences during his visions of Voldemort's mind. Most interesting is the concept that this book and its film adaptation, although marketed as children's literature—are not actually meant for children; rather, he adamantly advocates that *Order of the Phoenix* is, "for adults." Record states that this is due to the content of the novel, which grapples with teenage loneliness and feelings of powerlessness. However, his implications beg readers to ask what the "real" message reaching children might be. He suggests that the material is only "of adult interest" even though he admits there is no material that could be considered as "not child friendly" (Record 2013). Thus, his reader understands that the story is for child audiences and that the message is for adults. But what happens if, and when, children are able to read between the lines? And what about the category of adolescent, between child and adult?

In contrast to Record's assessment of *Order of the Phoenix* is *The New York Times* book review by John Leonard, published in July of 2003. Leonard's article, entitled "Nobody Expects the Inquisition," calls *Order of the Phoenix* "the witching hour," implying that Rowling's fifth installment is her "most magical." He finds the book to be "mystery-novel-esque," and wonders if Rowling perhaps channeled Agatha Christie. The grit of the novel, according to Leonard, is that Harry and his friends experience the normalities of prepubescent teenagers becoming pubescent teenagers. His review attributes the overarching theme of subverting authority as a naturally evolving issue: teenagers will be teenagers.

Record believes that the novel's content implies a message of gravity that is "beyond child appropriateness," while Leonard's review states that children evolve out of childhood in Rowling's text. But according to both layperson and critic, *Order of the Phoenix* transcends childhood concerns. While Record and Leonard can agree that Rowling brings more adult content to the world of her child characters, both stop short of addressing what it is that is "too much" for child audiences. What is the distinction that renders *Order of the Phoenix* inappropriate for monkey-bars-chat or blacktop talk?

I consider the fifth volume to be the turning point of the series because war in *Harry Potter and the Order of the Phoenix* surpasses the play-space of children, and not just with weapons, bloodshed, or violence. Rather, the novel establishes the way in which war can take place within the parameters of the playground and implies that children can be on the forefront of war before they pop their first pimple. The majority of *Order of the Phoenix* takes place within the confines of the magical school, Hogwarts, just as the preceding installments do. But Rowling's fifth novel does not distinguish between the war building in the outside world and the safe space of school for children. The school becomes a battleground.

Further, war, inherently a competition between opposing sides, becomes a game for children to play and attempt to win. Rowling pushes the disparate themes of childhood-play and warfare together. War, within the context of the novel, is accessible to children. The game of war is not only real, but it is a *real game* to be played by the characters in *Order of the Phoenix*. I believe the novel identifies warfare as a playable game for children. Children in the novel are unwillingly recruited and psychologically manipulated into participating in war, and before they or the readers realize, the war of Rowling's novel becomes a children's crusade. It is not necessarily a graphic story; no bedtime nightmares disclaimer is required. But the most disturbing effects of war are not always blood stained.

War on the Playing Field

The Hogwarts cohort emulates the wizarding world war that is brewing outside the school's walls. For student athletes, this grand scale game of simulation will ring particularly true. Rowling's text provides a story to accompany what children do in real life: imitate adult situations. The battleground turned playground mirrors the way in which student athletes' locker rooms become living rooms, team members become family members, and real-world anger can be turned into organized aggression. Rowling's text exposes the need for student athletes to sublimate their inability to affect change in the real world for success in their athletic arenas.

On our college campuses, the male student athlete is also fighting a metaphorical war on the field of their sport. Beyond the analogies that exist between fighting and on-the-field violence is the primary premise behind competitive sports: to win. Athletics teaches participants, and spectators, to pick a side and root for its success no matter what. Being the performers on the field, student athletes are not only charged with the task of hoping for their own success but also the opposing team's defeat; there is always an enemy during an athletic competition.

As in Rowling's *Order of the Phoenix*, student athletes are simulating real-world issues. Sporting events require more than just two teams to go head-to-head; they also require fans and spectators. While these supporters mean well (e.g. they hope for their team's success) they are concurrently promoting violence. Especially prevalent in contact sports is the praise of a "good hit" or a "hard block." Commentary from the sidelines includes rallying in the form of "hit harder" or "finish them off." The divide between the teams, while premised on good fun, simultaneously promotes a dislike for anyone who does not support the "correct" team. In *Order of the Phoenix*, Potter's "army" is trying to enact change within their school by mimicking the adult members of the "order" who are hoping to kill off the enemy. The lines between play and violence are closely tied in both the novel and on the field.

The tragic "Battle of Hogwarts" actually takes place in the seventh book, with many favorite characters dying as a result. So why throw the light on *Order of the Phoenix* to discuss child warfare instead of on the final installment, when the war for the magical school actually occurs? The answer is that war is placed within Hogwarts in Book Five. *Harry Potter and the Order of the Phoenix* turns out to be the most potent example of child warfare, although the final installment, *Harry Potter and the Deathly Hallows*, makes the culture of war much more obvious. Hogwarts is the metaphorical playground of the series, and the war infiltrates that space before any other. This clearly implies that no childhood space is safe from the threat of violence and no weapon is too potent for children to use. Even more disturbing, war breaks out amongst the students before it does amongst the adults. It is plain that war is far easier for children to manifest and compete in than was made clear before Rowling's publication of the fifth book. Still, Rowling's depiction of this impending war and the students' preparation for this war resembles the training of Quidditch players before an important game or match.

Critics on *Harry Potter* and Childhood

Critics vary wildly in their assessment of Rowling's originality in her treatment of the safe space of child readers. In *Sticks and Stones: The Troublesome Success of Children's Literature from Slovenly Peter to Harry Potter*, Jack Zipes opens by claiming that he does not wish to undermine Rowling's works, which have "reinvented childhood reading," but instead, wishes to do the author a service by examining how such a literary "convention" became such an international sensationalized "phenomenon" (Zipes 2002, 175), pointing to a formulaic plot that constitutes an identical progression in each installment (i.e., confinement, call to arms, the adventure, and the return home) and identifying Harry as only distinguishable by his lightening-bolt scar since his "white, Anglo-Saxon, athletic, and honest" qualities are run-of-the-mill and "classic Boy Scout" (Zipes 2002, 171). Zipes's critique, which damns with faint praise, quotes cultural critic Christine Schoefer's impression of *Harry Potter* as a reinforcement of "men who run the world" ("Harry Potter's Girl Trouble," 2000). Sara Ann Beach and Elizabeth Harden Willner disagree vehemently in "The Power of Harry: The Impact of J.K. Rowling's Harry Potter Books on Young Readers," in which they praise Harry as a literary hero for children. Both pieces refer to Harry as "Arthurian legend" (Zipes 2002, 171) and "Arthur-like" (Beach/Harden 2002, 104); however, where Beach and Harden find Harry's abilities remarkable, Zipes finds Rowling's ordinary representation of remarkableness to be "conventionally predictable" (Zipes 2002, 177).

As we can see, Zipes' discussion is inherently critical of Rowling, despite his desires to "not undermine" her literary triumph. Regardless, he is forced to confront Rowling's obviously "successful formula" to access child readers (Zipes 2002, 175). *Order of the Phoenix* contains the elements Zipes points out in each installment: "confinement," "call to arms," "the adventure," and "the return home" (Zipes 2002, 175). Thus, according to the "formula," this fifth adventure of Potter's should garner the same cogency for child readers. And yet Zipes states that Harry's inevitable growing up is a "difficulty" in reading the fifth novel, where the Beach and Harden team render Harry's growing up as a "hindrance" for young readers. There is clearly something about the later books that critics from all sides find difficult to fit into their assessments of the series as a whole. I assert that this is not because it deviates from Zipes' formula; rather, because it brings calamity within the formula. However, both Zipes' and Beach and Harden's articles, despite their differing opinions on the worth of Harry Potter as a "hero," establish that Rowling's novel normalizes Harry's experiences as universal, going so far as to find him "essential" to the reinvention of children reading: Harry Potter continues to be a very real presence in the lives of twenty-first century children.

Dumbledore's Army and Other Games of War

Harry Potter and the Order of the Phoenix immediately establishes war as a competition in which one must pick a side. The title indicates such, as "The Order of the Phoenix" is a very real society within the magical community. "'It's a secret society,' said Hermione," in response to Harry's confusions about the Order. She continues by saying, "'Dumbledore's in charge, he founded it. It's the people who fought against You-Know-Who last time'" (*OotP* 67). This establishes that the Order is an active combatant against the forces of evil in the novel. However, it also makes clear that the Order was the forces of the battle from "last time," rather than the pending war climate. As the discussion continues, Harry learns that, though his friends are not privy to the meetings as they are happening, they have "the general idea" of what occurs (*OotP* 68). Thus, the meetings are not secretive; rather, they are held in the very house Harry, Ron, and Hermione are living in for the time being. The reader should note that the main characters are fifteen or younger, as in the case of Ron's younger sister, Ginny Weasley, who is also very much involved.

The adult members of the Order are Ron's parents, select Hogwarts professors, and Harry's godfather, who is the only parental figure the orphan boy has after his parents were killed. Thus, it is not at all paradoxical that the children should also look to join and align themselves with the Order. Harry even states, despite the warnings of the adults around him that he wishes to join the fight against evil, and thus engage in the culture of war. "'Why not?' said Harry quickly. 'I'll join, I want to join, I want to fight'" (*OotP* 96). But the conversation ends abruptly, as the adults do not want to divulge—yet—the identity of the secret "weapon" the evil side is in possession of. This "weapon" is described as "powerful" and "something that [Voldemort] didn't have last time" (*OotP* 96–97). The children do not yet realize that they are the weapon(s) the adults are too afraid to discuss.

By introducing the Order of the Phoenix in the first chapters of the novel, Rowling immediately normalizes the culture of war. She gives clear delineations between the two "sides": those who join the Order, and those who align themselves with Voldemort (referred to as "Death Eaters" in the novels). Thus, despite the impending violence, the children have already declared themselves "good," and any fighting and/or casualties are pardonable because they are enacted on behalf of the "good side." This brings the formation of "Dumbledore's Army" into discussion. The moniker asks readers to note the usage of the terminology "army," which denotes an armed infantry. The "DA," as it is referred to, is a kid's club within the Hogwarts School. Harry and his friends found the club for the purpose of "taking matters into [their] own hands" (*OotP* 339). As Hermione explains to the group of more than twenty-five students, who voluntarily gather to join, the army is meant to "'study Defense against the Dark Arts … and by that [they] meant to learn how to defend themselves properly, not just theory but real spells'" (*OotP* 339–340). This is a concrete establishment of warfare within the school of Hogwarts. The club is meant to allow the children to practice "real" spells, or violence, in order to train themselves in defensive action.

Enacting a team, much like forming the DA, is meant to simulate "real" competition, not just learn "theory," as Hermione states (*OotP* 339). Sports, especially contact sports such as football, boxing, wrestling, rugby, or soccer, are characterized by "necessary bodily contact between players" according to the National Collegiate Athletic Association (NCAA). In essence, contact sports, like Dumbledore's Army, are organized violence. Team sports present a regulated opportunity to "properly" learn to defend oneself against an enemy; or, in this case, the opposing team (*OotP* 339). But athletics extend beyond the goals of Dumbledore's Army, as players not only intend to defend themselves, but also play offensively by attacking the facing team.

Dumbledore's Army thus brings war within Hogwarts, with all of its vital components. They have a cause to fight for, a leader to follow, and an enemy to vanquish. In the case of Dumbledore's Army, the opposing team is Professor Umbridge, a vastly unpopular Hogwarts teacher. The children enact their own revolution, much like the Order of the Phoenix waiting to respond to the eminent threat of war. But the children go farther than their adult counterparts, as their group begins to take decisive action against Professor Umbridge's authority. The group forms as a retaliation against Umbridge's imposition of new school rules. Professor Umbridge is appointed "High Inquisitor of Hogwarts," and is thus given "an unprecedented level of control at Hogwarts School of Witchcraft and Wizardry" (*OotP* 306). Harry complains throughout the first chapters of *Order of the Phoenix* that he is frustrated by the lack of action the Order has taken against the return of the magical community's greatest foe, Voldemort. Thus, he and his friends waste none of the time their adult counterparts do and decisively act against their enemy.

Harry is elected into a position of leadership because of his veteran status as a rule breaker and his previous experiences with danger. As the others observe, it seems "only natural" that Harry would assume the role as team leader (*OotP* 343). The other members of the group peg him with questions about his past brushes with combat: "Can you really produce a corporeal Patronus"? "Did you kill a basilisk with that sword in Dumbledore's office"? "He saved the Sorcerer's Stone … and not to mention, all the tasks he had to get through in the Triwizard Tournament last year—getting past dragons and merpeople and acromantulas and things…" (*OotP* 340–343). This harkens back to the power rankings within organized athletics, as the team captain is usually a senior with the most significant experience, although here, too, Harry is a prodigy on the playing field, making his school team and captaining it long before what ought to have been his expected year. Harry's group is seen to absorb and internalize the battle of the outside world into their organization. This happens within the world of sports, as well. Consider some of the greatest college athletic rivalries: Army versus Navy, Ohio State versus University of Michigan, Clemson versus South Carolina. Often these rivalries are more than isolated incidents of a great win or an untimely loss. Rather, animosity between two universities is long standing and extends beyond the world of sports. But the only admissible battle between two rivals is on the football field with rules that supposedly govern the organized violence of contact sports. Too often, teams carry the culminated pressure of a university's hatred for the opposing school on their shoulder to the effect of aggressive consequences. This is made evident by the Entertainment and Sports Programming Network's claim that rivalry games are "some of the most violent" of the season, with an entire week of college football coverage and tens of thousands of dollars dedicated annually to "rivalries week" (ESPN).

College athletics receive an unending stream of broadcasting attention. For example, ESPN broadcasts their NCAA Division I FBS college football coverage through at least seven media platforms that run on a 24-hour loop during the season. Additionally, the Internet boasts more than 111,000,000 results when the searcher enters "college football" into the inquiry box (Google). If the searcher were to attempt to limit the results by filtering the search by only one year (i.e., 2015), the results double with 222,000,000 returns (Google). Arguably, this is also a form of psychological warfare. College athletes have more than 200,000,000 opportunities to become psychologically infiltrated with discussion about their past and future performances, including pre-game predictions, statistics, and unfounded conjectures for success or failure. While sports broadcasters present their information as factual, usually donning suit and tie and delivering statistics of how impossible odds are completely possible, the bottom line is that this information is subjective and entirely opinionated. But college students, who have unlimited access to media, cannot help but be psychologically affected. They may see themselves losing prematurely simply because a sportscaster is being paid to entertain the masses with his (often unsubstantiated) opinion.

As mentioned previously, the adult members of the Order of the Phoenix believe that Voldemort has access to a detrimental weapon of warfare: the children. For Harry, war is internalized when Voldemort is able to manipulate his mind. He is able to make Harry feel and see certain things at various points in the novel. Harry states that he is overcome with emotions he has no control over. He describes, "an odd feeling in his stomach … a strange, leaping feeling … a *happy* feeling…" (*OotP* 381–382). Ron, panicking, asks Harry if he has a "vision" of Voldemort (*OotP* 380). Harry responds that, no, these sensations are beyond visions; he is able to read Voldemort's moods.

Harry is able to link his emotions with that of the enemy, and they manifest physically in the young hero. It is important to note that Harry does not have any control over this connection; the effects of war are organic and unavoidable. Harry's internalization of war implies that there is no escape of war, even for children. It is a universal affliction from which even the world's playgrounds are not safe. We cannot pick the "good" side in the hopes of rescuing our children from the turbulence.

Margery Hourihan's book, *Deconstructing the Hero*, dives into this very idea of heroic representation, or, in other words, who the "winner" is, and how to decipher their characteristics. She delves into children's literature in the section entitled, "Action and Violence." Here, she describes a hero of literature as being a character "of action." Heroes, Hourihan states, are "neither contemplative nor creative" (Hourihan 2005, 96). Instead, they are naturalized towards violence and we, as readers, are conditioned to search for that violence in order to indicate whom the story's hero is: the one who wins. The reader wonders, after reading Hourihan's account, whether children are ever totally separate from the adult world. If violence seeps into children's literature in the form of active play, the idea that children are training for the adult world becomes evident. Furthermore, children are training each other, as their playmates are regularly other children. Hourihan's discussion of what makes a "hero," specifically a child hero, generates the discussion of whether literature that involves games, contests, competition, and pretend can or should be read as an instruction manual for adulthood.

This idea of survival, as established in Hourihan's book, is manifested in Rowling's usage of prophesy. Towards the end of the fifth novel, Harry learns that there is a preordained contract that ties his life and Lord Voldemort's together. It states that, "neither can live while the other survives" (*OotP* 841). On the surface, this prophecy establishes rules for the game that is Harry's life, and the life of his childhood friends: they will have to play to survive, and survival is not enough. It is not enough for Harry to fight against the opposing side; Voldemort "must die at [his] hand" (*OotP* 841). Children, thus, are established as incapable of being spectators of war. Neither can they simply live within the environment of war. They must actively participate, *and* produce fruitful results. They must not only play the game of war; they must win.

Student athletes are plagued by a similar prophesy. It is a very simple formula. If a student athlete wishes to be successful, they must win. It is not enough to have a good time, or to put forth a "good college try." Winning is essential in the world of college sports. Players are put through tests of both physical and mental ability to test their tenacity for playing their desired sport before they are selected for the team. But the pressure has only just begun at this point. In order to keep a spot on the team, the athlete must also produce fruitful results, scoring points, rounding bases, and gaining yards. Playing an organized college sport ensures that one side will win and one will lose.

Harry and his friends may not fully realize that they are taking war into their own young hands, forming a training resistance that will better prepare them for battle. Student athletes similarly may not realize that they are internalizing the same struggle as Harry and his friends. As Harry's group brings the war into their childhood space of play, athletes also sublimate real world issues into the opportunity to participate in organized violence. Thus, Rowling raises the daunting question of what happens when the sacred play sphere of children is burst as happens so frequently in war-ravaged regions. The answer quite possibly lies within the world of college athletics. When young people are allowed to bring the real world into an area of simulated violence, that simulation begins to signify real world issues. In the context of *Order of the Phoenix,* this violation recruits children into the game of war. It also teaches them that childhood games have a practical application. War is not only played, it is played to be won in *Order of the Phoenix* and on the field of student athletes. The "natural subversion of authority" that John Leonard observes in *Order of the Phoenix* is really a natural inclination to the warfare campaign, and the innocent are not irreproachable in their competitions: playing at war or sports.

Conclusions and Implications

Male athletes on the college campus can be characterized as a student population embarrassed to admit they need help learning. For many such students, their decision to attend a university is separate from academics. Rather, they elect to attend college based on a desire to play their designated sport. They are not interested in specific classes, professors, or academic incentives. Instead, they see college as the next step in their athletic careers. The greater implications of this are that college athletes are stigmatized as a group of students who do not perform well in reading-intensive courses. Additionally, they feel they are unable to incorporate their experiences as athletes in the classroom. For the Harry Potter generation, J.K. Rowling's series—with its student-athlete hero, who substitutes Quidditch for football—can serve as a gateway to long-term academic achievement for male student-athletes when its appeal is understood by instructors.

REFERENCES

Beach, Sara Ann and Elizabeth Harden Willner. 2002. "The Power of Harry: The Impact of J.K. Rowling's Harry Potter Books on Young Readers." *World Literature Today* 76 (1), 102–106.

Csikszentmihalyi, Mihaly. 2008. *Flow: The Psychology of Optimal Experience.* New York: HarperCollins.

Hourihan, Margery. 2005. *Deconstructing the Hero: Literary Theory and Children's Literature.* London: Routledge.

Rowling, J.K. 2003. Harry Potter and the Order of the Phoenix. London/New York: Bloomsbury/Scholastic.

Schoefer, Christine. 2000. "Harry Potter's Girl Trouble." *Salon.* Accessed 2017. http://www.salon.com/2000/01/13/potter.

Smith, Michael W. and Jeffery D. Wilhelm. 2002. *Reading Don't Fix No Chevys: Literacy in the Lives of Young Men.* Portsmouth, NH: Heineman.

Zipes, Jack. 2002. *Sticks and Stones: The Troublesome Success of Children's Literature from Slovenly Peter to Harry Potter.* London: Routledge.

Lumens and Literature

Teaching Harry Potter in the College English Classroom

CHRISTINA A. VALEO

Over six summers in the past eight years, I have had the opportunity to teach a 300-level elective class on the Harry Potter series. Most of the students know the novels well before the course begins; all of them know the novels are popular. Some of my students have an encyclopedic understanding of Rowling's wizarding world, but almost without exception, those readers have never *studied* the novels. The students who have not read the books before the course are drawn to the class because of the series' popularity. Some come to see what all the fuss is about; others follow enthusiastic friends; still others are electing to read books they had been prohibited from reading as children. Beyond encouraging their reading, my role is to encourage their thinking. This essay considers the suitability of the Harry Potter series for encouraging a shift in collegiate-level readers from simply reading popular books to also thinking about them. We know this series is popular, but is it literary? Does it stand up to serious academic analysis?

In discussions of reading—or teaching—we distinguish our terms in order to articulate to students what exactly we expect. It is not enough, for example, that students are "reading" the assigned texts; we expect also that they are "engaging" or "critically thinking." In my class students have been primarily "readers" of the Harry Potter novels before enrolling in the course. They have read the books in what Louise Rosenblatt (1978) calls an "aesthetic" mode. They have been reading for pleasure. Their books are unmarked (however well-loved); they have not been reading from any particular theoretical position; they have rarely considered social or cultural contexts beyond the world of the novels. Rosenblatt (1978) identifies "aesthetic" reading as when "the reader's attention is centered directly on what he is living through during his relationship with that particular text" (25). We reach for idiomatic expressions like "getting caught up in a book" to describe that relationship.

One of my objectives for my course is to support my students' efforts to read the books in a thoughtful, engaged way that college readiness scholarship is now calling "Critical Reading." Here we are considering a different reading posture—closer to what Rosenblatt called "efferent" reading—i.e.: reading for information. According to Rosenblatt (1978), efferent reading is the mode readers choose when "the primary concern of the readers is with what he will carry away from the reading" (24). If, in reading for fun, people in my course identify themselves as "fans" of the series, I want them to also become "scholars" of the series: to read with an intent to "carry away" something particular from the text beyond cultural literacy. Through writing assignments, sample articles, and class discussions, I help them to understand what it means to approach these novels in a scholarly way. The series thus becomes our example text for scholarly critical reading as a practice.

It helps my academic agenda that the books are quite literary. We can, of course, study "popular culture"—and popular novels—with remarkable (and publishable) scholarly success. Often in such cases we study the phenomenon—the popularity itself—rather than the text. I attribute the quality of the academic work in my own course, however, to the literary quality of the series; that is, its complexity and depth in the hands of a writer skilled enough in her craft to communicate clearly.

The success of this course—the student learning that unfolds—is due to three conditions: the disposition of the students, the work of the course, and the literary quality of the series.

The Disposition of the Students in the Course

Whatever their experience with the Harry Potter series, the students in my class come prepared to do college-level work. The course is offered at the 300 level, which translates roughly into the third year of a four-year degree program. It is worth five credits (of the 180 students must earn for a Bachelor's Degree), but it applies to no particular major, minor, certificate, or program. Most students are taking it "for fun." The only prerequisite is our ENGL 201: College Composition: Analysis/Research/Documentation (required of all students to graduate) or its equivalent. Most students who take the class are traditional-aged undergraduates (18–22 years old), but some are older adults who are returning to school later in life. I have also had high school students taking the course and a middle-aged librarian in a local school district who was taking the class for continuing education credits. That means that over the eight years I've taught the class, the majority of my students have been of the Harry Potter generation, or just following in it, aged as the younger siblings of the Harry Potter generation and influenced by them.

My students' knowledge of the Harry Potter series varies widely. Some have never read the series or seen the movies, either because they intentionally resisted the trend or because they were forbidden as children from reading the books or seeing the movies. The latter are approaching the series now as young adults with the freedom to choose. Students who were not allowed to read the books typically come from a religious community that identifies as Christian; they are sometimes also home schooled rather than having attended public or private schools. Many of my students who were home schooled or who identify as Christian know and love the series, by the way; but among those who were prohibited, those descriptors often fit. Whatever the reasons may be that students arrive in the course without having previously read the books or seen the movies, they always have an awareness of the phenomenon, including the theme parks, merchandise, vocabulary from the novels, Rowling as a public person, and some of the story lore. Many students have seen the movies but not read the books. Because so many characters and subplots have necessarily been culled from the film scripts (not to mention the actual changes from the novels that the films sometimes portray), the students who have only seen the film have nowhere near a comprehensive understanding of the series, as aptly demonstrated by Dion McLeod and Elise Payne elsewhere in this volume. They may have a very different impression of characters from the movies than they will see in the novels (the film versions of Ron and Hermione, for example, are quite different from their book counterparts). We spend some time in class viewing and discussing scenes from the films, but for the most part our focus is on the novels themselves and students in this category have much to discover.

Finally, most students in the class have read the books previously. Some have read them only once—often in their childhood, as the books were released. At the time of writing, a 21-year-old student was born in 1995; *Sorcerer's Stone* (the American version of *Philosopher's Stone*) appeared in 1998, while *Deathly Hallows* was published in 2007. Students in this category will say by way of introduction, "I grew up with Harry Potter" or "I grew up with these books."

Other students in the class have not only read the books previously, they have read them multiple times. Some continue to reread on a regular basis.

This range of reading experience makes for some dynamic class discussions. While many students are experts on the series in some ways, many have never thought critically about it and almost none have completed any thoughtful literary or theoretical analysis. They may well recall particular plant names, for example, but never have thought about the Latin associations

178 Part III: Pedagogy

of those names, the wordplay involved, or the considerable knowledge of scientific and spiritual plant lore behind Rowling's choices. Others come to the series with strong intertextual connections from one particular discipline such as world mythologies or psychology, but have examined the series only through that lens. The class offers those students an opportunity to broaden their approach and to become students of the text in areas that do not match with their previous expertise. The chance to challenge or complicate their own previous readings or viewings is one of the best learning experiences the class can offer them. They move from being able to articulate the nuances between house-elf magic, goblin magic, and wizard magic powers, to also being able think about those differences with a critical lens. What differences do those distinctions make in the story world? What implications might there be for issues of social justice in the real world? To again invoke Rosenblatt, what might a student carry away?

Evidence of this new skill—to think about the books in a deeper way rather than just to consume them—comes in many forms. My students often begin their commentary with the phrase, "I never noticed…" as their attention is drawn to significant details like the relative position of the various statuary figures in the fountain at the Ministry of Magic. From these observations they move to adopt analytic postures, consider a variety of interpretations, and factor context into their consideration of this treasured series.

The Work of the Course

Whatever their previous reading or viewing experience, students have elected to take the course and are paying tuition to do so, and they will earn credit for the course. As a 300-level class, it carries considerable weight in terms of student work both in number of pages read and in number of pages students will write. My intent is to move students quickly away from any sense that this eight-week course taught in the abbreviated summer term will bear too much resemblance to a book club encounter. When students mention on the first day that they "have always liked the books" or "love these books," I offer a gentle correction: I don't really care whether they like the books or not. I certainly do enjoy rereading them, but some of the smartest and most successful students to whom I have taught Harry Potter did not "like" the books at all. In some ways, their refusal to be swept away by the phenomenon helped them adopt the stance of a critical reader and thinker.

Those highly successful students who are not—and who never have been—fans of the series helpfully complicate the easy pedagogical binaries I was attempting to distinguish early in my introduction. While, I argue, fans are usually able to function as students in my course, it is absolutely true that some students are never fans. They are critical readers from the start and have no aesthetic reading stance to move beyond; the popular nature of these novels has often heightened, rather than abated, their thoughtful (even skeptical) approach to the series. I have not found, however, that the converse is true: becoming scholars of the series does not seem to have dampened the enthusiasm of long-time fans.

The Literary Quality of the Series: My Role in the Class

My role as the course instructor is complicated by my dual positions as fan and scholar. I initially read the series for fun and only later did I undertake scholarship and teaching about the series. In the class I have a strict "no spoilers" rule: we do not, as a large class, talk about happenings in subsequent novels. "No spoilers" certainly sounds like a "fandom" rule, but it also serves as an intentional pedagogical practice to help students shift from fans to students or scholars. Much like we proofread most effectively if we read from the last sentence of our essays back to the first sentence, we read and discuss more thoughtfully if our enthusiasm for the series as a whole is curtailed by the fact that we cannot discuss beyond the current book's end.

Other class procedures are similarly intended to move students into a scholarly mode. The Response Paper requires students to write a one-to-two-page paper for each week (i.e.: every novel after the first). Students may write about a particular novel or take on a topic that threads among novels. They may also choose to respond to a scholarly article, and I demonstrate how to find appropriate articles through our school's library database. Whether they respond to novel or scholarship, they must formulate a claim and support it with textual evidence. For most students, the process of writing down their thinking about the book formalizes that thinking. The additional requirements of a claim and evidence in their paper encourage a critical distance: they must articulate their primary thought, organize their evidence, and proofread their work. All of these elements move students into a formal engagement with the series, more so than does solo reading or casual chat with friends without any academic stakes.

In addition to assigning writing tasks that require students to support claims with textual evidence, I construct classroom discussions that are also formatted so students will first mimic then adopt scholarly behaviors. Several times over the course students must come up with the discussion questions that engage scholars when they talk about a text together for that class meeting. Further, providing students with disciplinary vocabulary (even terms as simple as "plot," "character," "conflict," "setting," and "style") shifts their thinking and their discourse from reading-for-pleasure to reading-for-analysis.

Asking my adult students how younger readers might respond or have responded to the novels also helps them move toward a more sophisticated reading stance. Whether they draw on their own youthful reading of the series or imagine it in the hands of other young readers, they can readily see how the novels work on young readers. One fruitful topic for this kind of discussion is Rowling's use of the redirect and the misdirect. She uses this plotting move frequently in the first three books, so we have several opportunities to talk about how this device impacts younger readers and how it affects adult readers in the series. Frequent readers of the series note the change in their experiences between the first time they read the three novels, when they may have suspected that they were being misled about the perpetrator but could not be sure, and their second time through, when they can see the red herrings for what they are. Their recognition of their increased reading sophistication also allows them to cultivate a critical thinking approach to reading the series.

I give students practice thinking and speaking from multiple interpretive perspectives, as they do when they work in "jigsaw learning" groups. They are assigned a topic to discuss in a small group environment, but at the conclusion of that first discussion, I reconstitute the groups so that each new group has one "expert" from each of the previous group. That expert is responsible for reporting to the new group whatever understanding was gained in the work of the first group. A crucial element of this reporting task is that the student will need to convey not only whatever conclusions she came to in the first conversation, but the observations of her group-mates as well. This seemingly simple task emulates the more formal work of scholars who acknowledge the different opinions (even contrary opinions) of other scholars in their work.

In the second class meeting (on *Chamber of Secrets*, 1998), I offer a mini-lecture on "ways of reading," focusing on the spiders and snakes in the story. I present interpretive possibilities through reader response, gender studies, myths and archetypes, multiculturalism, the hero's journey, structuralism, and biological/anthropological considerations. I have found that students innately tend to read from one or another of these theoretical perspectives, but that unless they are English majors who have taken a critical methods course, they may not realize that their points of focus or patterns of inquiry are actually disciplinary practices with labels and language that distinguish them.

Similarly, I want our fourth class (on *Goblet of Fire*, 2000) to show students how to approach the series profitably with either a micro- (focused on detail) or macro- (focused on "the big picture") approach, so I juxtapose the two in the first hour of the class. I begin by leading a discussion on the house-elf Winky, using that character's subplot to consider some of the dominant tensions of the series and to practice the reading methods of reader response, feminism, Marxism/cultural materialism, and psychoanalysis. I then switch deliberately and abruptly back to a larger view of the series, suggesting that *Goblet of Fire* represents the end of Act One, and we should pause to review what we know about the series so far. Students who have long understood narrative structure (conflict, climax, resolution—whether in drama or in fiction) have usually not applied that understanding to this series, although they know the books so well in other ways.

Our class discussion about *The Order of the Phoenix* (2003) usually exhibits the shift from "reading" to "thinking," from "fandom" to "scholarship." By this week, the fifth of the eight-week course, students' improved reading and analytic skills are evident as they work to unpack this key symbol and motif of the series. Soliciting students' current knowledge about what a phoenix is (or "activating schema" in pedagogical parlance) results in information about its mythical status and its resurrection cycle. Now students are ready to apply that framework to what they know of the Potter series as a whole: resurrection, death, rebirth, cycles, and healing all come into the conversation. Further, students are able to recall and consider the ramifications of versions of resurrection, transformation, and rebirth that we have seen in the series so far. They treat such instances as more than plot points, recognizing the pervasive theme that runs through the series. They also now can situate the conversation in the Judeo-Christian context from which the author—and her novels—originate. For students whose upbringing intersected with that culture this is a chance to consider the "Christianity" of the series and its messages. The discourse has shifted considerably from the fan-like wonderings of why Sirius Black does not return to the world of the living after he is killed; now students deliberate what difference a "Christian" label makes to the series, its author, or its reception.

To further illustrate how a theoretical approach can complicate—and ultimately enrich—our experience of the series, I bring scholarly articles into the class on relevant days and guide students through reading the articles. These are texts that everyone reads—in addition to those that students have elected to read as material for their writing assignments. Articles such as Tenille Nowak's (2013) "The Nuances of Rule-Breaking," help my students to understand reader response theory because they highlight how youthful readers differ from adult readers of the series. Whether they read the series as children or were prohibited from reading it, they are now in the position to 1) reflect on the impact that moral quandary might have had on them as young consumers and 2) consider whether, when, and how they would introduce the series to the children in their lives (their own children, their future children, children in their families, or children in their future classrooms). Again, without any changes but maturity, they can see the series from a whole new perspective, and that sensation helps them understand what other altered and altering points of view might be out there for them to consider.

As younger—or first time readers—my students were frequently caught up in the plot and had not stopped to analyze Rowling's structure or her craft. An article like Susan Nelson Wood and Kim Quackenbush's (2001) "'The Sorcerer's Stone': A Touchstone for Readers of All Ages" or Edward Duffy's (2002) "Sentences in Harry Potter, Students in Future Writing Classes" helps them to establish critical distance. After we discuss the romance-laden *Half-Blood Prince*, we read Tison Pugh and David L. Wallace's (2006) article "Heternormative Heroism and Queering the School Story in J.K. Rowling's Harry Potter Series" to help students see spaces for readings between and beyond the heterosexual pairings with which the adolescent characters are so preoccupied. These articles both model and encourage the efferent reading stance; they move these students into modes where they read in order to find a promising theme or evidentiary thread that they can "carry away" to further discussions on paper and in person.

As the course progresses and students' analytical fluency builds, they can take on the question of literary merit in more thoughtful ways. It has been my experience in other courses on popular genre (dystopian fiction, for example), that the more expert the students become as readers, the more dissatisfied they are with the popular novels they had "loved" (sometimes the same titles that initially drew them to the course). The opportunities to discuss the seven books in the Harry Potter series—individually and collectively—have certainly made my students more discerning, but their enthusiasm is untarnished. Often, in contrast, their delight in the series grows with their informed regard of its qualities.

Conclusions

Enthusiastic students and compelling tasks are not in and of themselves enough to result in serious academic work: the texts must stand up to weeks of serious analysis and discussion for hours at a time. Texts that are formulaic or repetitive; or too simple in language, structure, or style will not support this kind of learning. Stories that rely so heavily on plot that they ignore the ethical and social implications of characters' choices are quickly talked through and over. Books that reveal nothing new in the rereading will obstruct generative class conversation as soon as any participant has read them through.

My students' learning in the course is inextricably linked to its subject, and their success is supported by the considerable substance of the series. The final class assignment, and the one that most reveals my students' growth as readers and their regard for the series, is their Learning Letter, a final essay in which students reflect on what they have learned in the course. In these essays, students' observations settle into several discernable trends, and many turn to metaphors of "depth" versus "surface" to articulate their perception of their growth and gains in the course. One student noted:

> I took this course because I am [sic] huge fan of Harry Potter, to the extent where I have read each book at least five times.... I had read these books many times at different times in my life, but I realized after reading them in class I only read the surface of the books and never went deeper. Before this class I knew all the little facts about the books now I know these books in the literary sense [Heather, Learning Letter, Summer 2011].

This student's reflections point to several issues relevant to our discussion. First, she notes that rereading independently did not have the same effect as reading the series in a classroom environment. Next, she articulates the shift I frequently see as students move from encyclopedic—almost trivial—knowledge of the minute details to critical thinking capacity that allow them to evaluate the books on a grander scale. Finally, this student's word choice highlights my assessment of the literary nature of these books: students cannot as easily expand their own ability to think more deeply about a text if the text does not offer them depths to explore.

Another student carefully charted the changes in her own maturity level from when she first encountered the books to when she reread them for class, and she notes the impact of that shift on her reading:

> I feel that since I started reading (and rereading, and rereading...) the books when I was eight years old, I was stuck in my eight year old mindset. Not only did I realize I had held back from rereading the final three books in the past because of their darker themes and how uncomfortable my "inner eight year old" had felt reading them, but I had completely missed certain themes, especially in the first three books. I was able to explore characters in a deeper, more thoughtful way than I had in the past, and that was incredibly insightful [Sarah, Learning Letter, Summer 2011].

As the decades move on from this generation who waited eagerly to read the books as they emerged and attacked them immediately, it will be interesting to observe when future young readers find their ways to the novels—and when they choose to take them on. In this final writing assignment, many students focus on their own growth as readers, sometimes specifically as readers of this particular series. But intertwined with that assessment I frequently find a reassessment of the books themselves. They note the complexities and contexts they have discovered, as one student did in Summer 2011: "When we discussed the books in class, I made the leap from story to literature" (Andrea, Learning Letter). Andrea seems to be noting a shift in herself, but her labels nod toward a shift in her regard for Rowling's writing from "story" to "literature." Another student also reaches for the descriptor "deeper" to articulate her realizations about the reading:

> We delved deeper into the issues of the books in this class, which I enjoyed and felt were scholarly endeavors because it wasn't just discussing who our favorite characters were or what happened or how 'cool' a certain scene was, it was actually discussing motivations for characters and the deeper moral, social, and political issues of Rowling's world [Justine, Learning Letter, Summer 2012].

It is those rich contexts and textual complexities, I will close by arguing, that make this course—and this series—work. The relation between students' reading skills and their regard for the series is inextricably connected. The additional light that a dedicated college-level course shines on the series does nothing to diminish students' regard for the books—or the pleasure they take in consuming them. A student from the Summer of 2013 who has since gone on to graduate-level work in English reflected at the end of the class that he found

> this to be an extremely immersive and comprehensive course that beautifully kept the series enjoyable while still deconstructing the text. Many times the process of deep analysis and discussions in a classroom format removes some of the enjoyment of the series, however this was not the case here, which I applaud [Aaron, Learning Letter].

In the six summers that I have taught the course, I have seen many of our college teaching objectives realized in this literary intersection between childish enthusiasm and collegiate skill. While there is no doubt that Rowling's Harry Potter series is unique—and a seemingly irresistible combination of fantasy, mythology, allusion, and coming-of-age—it seems evident to me that we can leverage students' enthusiasm for quality literature that has been labeled "popular" and let that energy light their way to measurable academic achievement.

REFERENCES

Duffy, Edward. 2002. "Sentences in Harry Potter, Students in Future Writing Classes." *Rhetoric Review* 21(2): 170–187.

Nowak, Tenille. 2013. "The Nuances of Rule-Breaking." In *Teaching with Harry Potter: Essays on Classroom Wizardry from Elementary School to College,* edited by Valerie Estelle Frankel. Jefferson, NC: McFarland.

Pugh, Tison, and David L. Wallace. 2006. "Heteronormative Heroism and Queering the School Story in J.K. Rowling's Harry Potter Series." *Children's Literature Association Quarterly* 31 (3) : 260–281.

Rosenblatt, Louise. 1978. *The Reader, the Text, the Poem: The Transactional Theory of the Literary Work.* Carbondale: Southern Illinois University Press.

Rowling, J.K. 1997. *Harry Potter and the Philosopher's Stone.* London: Bloomsbury..

_____. 1998. *Harry Potter and the Chamber of Secrets.* London: Bloomsbury.

_____. 1999. *Harry Potter and the Prisoner of Azbkaban.* London: Bloomsbury.

_____. 2000. *Harry Potter and the Goblet of Fire.* London: Bloomsbury.

_____. 2003. *Harry Potter and the Order of the Phoenix*. London: Bloomsbury.

_____. 2005. *Harry Potter and the Half-Blood Prince*. London: Bloomsbury.

_____. 2007. *Harry Potter and the Deathly Hallows*. London: Bloomsbury.

Wood, Susan Nelson, and Kim Quackenbush. 2001. "'The Sorcerer's Stone': A Touchstone for Readers of All Ages." *The English Journal* (90) 3: 97–103.

"Harry Potter changed my life"

Students and Educators Reflect on the Harry Potter Generation

LAUREN HAMMOND *and* LINDA PERSHING
with ALLISON BIANCO, RACHAEL DOHRN,
CATHY GUTIERREZ, SHELBY M.M. KACIREK,
HARMONY OWEN, ANGELO JOHN REYES
and ERIN L. SOUTHAM

With over 400 million copies sold worldwide and translations in 80 languages, the Harry Potter books are among the best-selling publications in world history ("Meet Author" and Rowling). Although it has been over ten years since the publication of the final novel (2007), we continue to hear references to Harry Potter in casual conversations, social media, TV shows, theater, and movies (with the *Harry Potter and the Cursed Child* stage play and a Fantastic Beasts film series franchise), testimony to the pervasive influence Harry Potter has on contemporary popular culture. Author Joanne Rowling has been compared to other popular authors like the Inklings, J.R.R. Tolkien and C.S. Lewis, with their focus on narrative, fantasy, and "imaginative literature." Moreover, Rowling's series has inspired a new generation of writers. While waiting for the release of each successive book, fans created their own Harry Potter stories, and many of today's popular young adult fiction writers got their start by participating in Harry Potter fandom. For example, Harry Potter fan fiction author Cassandra Clare (*The Mortal Instruments)* got her start with her wildly popular *The Draco Trilogy*. Other authors, such as Maureen Johnson (*The Shades of London*) and John Green (*The Fault in Our Stars*), also emerged from Harry Potter fandom. Four years after the release of the last Harry Potter film (2011), the 2015 San Diego Comic

Convention featured a Harry Potter panel. Madhuri Shekar, author of *In Love and Warcraft,* discussed the influence that the Potter series has had on her writing. Two additional panelists, authors Justin Zagari (*Snape and the Marauders)* and Sunny Williams (*Harvey Putter and the Ridiculous Premise*), have written screenplays inspired by the Harry Potter books. At the 2016 Comic Convention, Director David Yates and many of the cast members of *Fantastic Beasts and Where to Find Them* shared their insights about the film to a sold-out audience of Potter fans ("A Day at San Diego Comic-Con").

As the series' popularity continues to grow, scholars have become increasingly interested in the Harry Potter phenomenon. Rowling's creation of her magical realm has sparked considerable analysis within academic circles. Educators have used Harry Potter as a framework and vehicle to teach a wide variety of subjects from science to literature, and scholars are attempting to understand the many dimensions and meanings of the enthusiastic fandom around the world, blockbuster film series, social media and fan websites, attendance at the MGM Studios tour outside of London, extensive merchandising, fan conventions, and wildly popular Harry Potter attractions in Universal Studios theme parks in Florida and California, and in Osaka, Japan. Commentary about culture, social inequalities, death and dying, societal institutions, loyalty and friendship, and the meaning and value of love are just a few of the themes in Harry Potter debated by educators in many disciplines. In addition to the novels' literary value, current research has brought to light another noteworthy aspect of the Harry Potter phenomenon: the Harry Potter narratives have played an important, often surprising, role in the lives and worldviews of fans. Through personal reflections and critical analysis, this essay explores some of the ways in which the Harry Potter series has helped shape a generation of readers. In what follows, students and teachers investigate how Harry Potter has influenced and affected their lives in meaningful and profound ways.

Dr. Linda Pershing, a scholar of folklore and cultural studies, recognizes the rich material and creative possibilities of using Harry Potter in her teaching. Having witnessed the enormous impact the series has had on this generation of students, she developed a Harry Potter course using pedagogy that focused on student participation, empowerment, and peer learning.

Linda Pershing, university professor and instructor of a study abroad course on Harry Potter, discusses her initial interest in the series as an educational tool

My work with the Harry Potter series didn't begin until Fall, 2012. Gloria Diaz, an exceptional student, was sitting in my office discussing her plans to apply to graduate school. As many other students had done in the previous few years, she mentioned her love of the Harry Potter books during our conversation. At the time, I had not read them. My daughter was a teenager when *Sorcerer's Stone* was published in 1998 and read the series on her own. Foolishly, I dismissed the books as a passing fad for young readers. Gloria's comments finally grabbed my attention. First in her family to complete high school and attend college, she had shared stories with me about the many hardships her family of four faced as Mexican immigrants in Escondido, California, sharing a one-bedroom apartment along with several relatives, each adult working two or three jobs, and she and her sister scrambling to learn English and acclimate to Southern California culture and anti-immigrant bias in the public schools. Feeling inadequate and like an outsider, she struggled to find her way, particularly as a first-generation university student. Knowing her family history, I was fascinated when she mentioned that Harry Potter helped her survive.

When I asked Gloria *why* she loved the books so much, she became very quiet and tears welled up in her eyes. After several moments, she explained: "When I was growing up, Harry Potter saved my life!" From that moment onward my life changed dramatically. I decided to read the books over the winter break, and I got hooked. I loved the characters and was fascinated by the life lessons and rich imagery and symbolism in the narrative. During the Spring semester of 2013, I asked ten undergraduates to join Gloria and me in conducting background research on the many themes, constructions of and commentary on culture and society, and the mythology and folklore (two of my areas of expertise) in the Harry Potter novels. Together we explored academic and popular analysis of Harry Potter, sharing our findings each week in a small seminar and creating a database of information. The next semester we worked together to create a course on culture and folklore in the Harry Potter series, focusing on the principle concepts and themes, and investigating the complex ways in which J.K. Rowling had woven folklore and mythology into her tales.

The students in the project were enthusiastic and passionate about it. Many continued the next semester as "prefects," or student assistants, in a classroom of 120 students. In our course, Harry Potter: Culture and Folklore in J.K. Rowling's Magical World (Interdisciplinary Studies 370, which fulfilled an upper-division general education requirement in social science), I met weekly with a group of 12–20 prefects. All had taken the course before, and we planned each future class session together, building on our past experiences. In addition to the presentations and classroom activities I led, the prefects who had experience in public speaking worked with me to offer short presentations about the reading or co-led class discussions. Together we explored various types of pedagogy to keep the course engaging and interesting. I purchased lots of posters and props (i.e., cauldrons, owls, a Marauder's Map); before each session, we decorated the room to create the feeling of a Hogwarts classroom. Several students made large canvas paintings of a great wooden door framed by a stone wall, and we hung these over the entryway, so students felt like they were walking into the magical space of Hogwarts Castle. Prefects wore black academic gowns and Hogwarts House ties, and I dressed in a long witch's gown and hat. We sorted students into Houses (Gryffindor, Hufflepuff, Ravenclaw and Slytherin); within each House we assigned students to a Hogwarts class (Potions, Transfiguration, Defense Against the Dark Arts, etc.). A prefect was assigned to sit in each of these "classes" in order to create a sense of smaller group identity and lead discussions. During games and activities, members of the Houses competed for house points. We staged a Yule Ball (many students dressed in formal attire) and an End-of-Term Feast. Teaching the Harry Potter course was the most engaging, innovative, and by far the most fun experience of any course I've taught in my 27 years as a university professor.

These students loved to read and discuss Harry Potter. The course resonated with them more than anything else I've taught, including other types of popular culture. Much of my teaching focuses on issues of social justice and the politics of culture, and Harry Potter offers ample opportunities to explore these issues. Themes of particular significance in the series include social inequality and injustice, class, race, gender, sexual identity, the value of relationships, love and family, adolescence and the pain of growing up, the news media, and government bureaucracy and the tendency of those in power to support the status quo. In *Harry Potter and the Millennials: Research Methods and the Politics of the Muggle Generation*, Anthony Gierzynski (with Kathryn Eddy) define the Harry Potter generation as "the Millennials" or anyone born between the early 1980s to the early 2000s (Gierzinski 2013, 39–40). In their analysis of interviews and surveys, Gierzynski and Eddy find that members of the Harry Potter generation tend be more open to diversity and political tolerance, less authoritarian, less likely to support the use of deadly force or torture, and more politically active (see also the related study by Italian psychologists Loris Vezzali et al. [2015], with their finding that reading Harry Potter improves attitudes toward stigmatized groups, such as immigrants, gays, and refugees). Harry Potter books and films have not only influenced students' personal lives but also helped shape their worldviews as members of the Harry Potter generation. Co-authoring this chapter with students, I have been moved by the reflections of these young people about how deeply the series has saturated their lives and thinking, as well as their ideas about social inequality, ethics, and the value of life.

Lauren Hammond, lead author of this essay and co-creator of Linda Pershing's Harry Potter university course, discusses her introduction to the HP series and her insights about the Harry Potter generation phenomenon

Unlike most of the Harry Potter readership in my generation, my interest in the series did not grow from my childhood experiences with the books. I first read *Sorcerer's Stone* when I was nine years old. However, I was not an avid reader at the time and soon lost interest. In the fall of 2012, when I was a 23-year-old undergraduate student of literature and writing at California State University San Marcos, Professor Pershing (we call her Linda) began to gather a select group of students in the hopes of working together to craft a folklore and cultural studies course based on the Harry Potter novels. I was not one of them, at least not at first. Over winter break, just a few weeks before the group started working on the project, a student friend of mine who had been asked to participate invited me to meet Linda. Soon thereafter Linda offered me a position as a student researcher on the team. I was hesitant because my familiarity with the series was limited; I was not one of the Harry Potter enthusiasts who knew every book very well and could quote chapter and line in the text. I soon recognized that other students in the project considered me a neophyte; there was an elitist mentality in the group. I also noticed a competitive tension during our meetings, a battle of wits as group members tried to impress each other with their detailed knowledge of all things Harry Potter.

However, in addition to my initial discomfort with feeling inadequate, I soon became enthralled by the quality of the debates and the extent of all participants' commitment to the project. I was surprised to discover such depth in the Harry Potter narratives. Most exciting was our collaborative ability to explore the parallels and contrasts between Rowling's magical realm and our own society. A Harry Potter newbie, I soon found myself on a level playing field as we sought out more complex understandings of Rowling's universe. Our discussions also focused on sharing our experiences in relation to analysis of Rowling's narrative. Many of the other students began to trace the impact the series had on their childhoods. For what seemed like the first time, we attempted to define what the novels had meant to us at different stages of our youth, and then analyze those experiences through theoretical lenses. Many students were able to pinpoint specific, meaningful Harry Potter-related events during their adolescence, often stating that the decisions they made were influenced directly by the actions of specific characters in the novels. As university juniors and seniors with a variety of interests and majors—including anthropology, communication, liberal studies, literature and writing, psychology, Spanish, and women's studies—we drew on our differing academic training. Applying varied theoretical concepts to Rowling's work, we began to discover and share new perspectives on the Harry Potter novels.

After teaching the course for two consecutive semesters, Linda created a Harry Potter study abroad course, traveling with 27 students in June 2015 through England, Edinburgh, and the Scottish Highlands to visit locations related to the Harry Potter books and films. All participants were avid Harry Potter fans, and together they explored the history and related cultural sites of Great Britain, such as cathedrals and castles used to film scenes of Hogwarts, traditional boarding schools in the UK, museums with artifacts that inspired Rowling's writing, Edinburgh cafés where Rowling sat and wrote (by hand) parts of the first books in the series, as well as the Warner Bros. Studios in Leavesden, where the films were made. These helped participants develop a richer understanding of Harry Potter and the fandom. The study abroad course also enabled students to connect their personal experiences of Harry Potter with the history and culture that informed the books and films.

Allison Bianco, participant in the study abroad course, is enthusiastic about the series' appreciation of cultural traditions, and its ability to bring people together

I will always remember being a fourth grader and picking up my first copy of *Harry Potter and the Sorcerer's Stone.* I had already seen the first three movies and was hopelessly obsessed with them. I compared everything around me to the world of Harry Potter, often thinking "what would Harry, Ron, and Hermione do?" and using the series to inform my decisions. Growing up alongside them made me feel like I was never alone. No matter what was happening in my life, I could turn to these stories for support. It is rather hard to describe how much Harry Potter means to me, like trying to explain why someone is your best friend. In addition to all I learned about British and Scottish culture and history, the study abroad course opened my eyes to the exciting exploration of other nations, cultures, and new experiences. Now I want to keep traveling and see other parts of the world. This all happened because of Harry Potter. The books and films have the power to bring people together around a shared love of the stories, and these form a common bond and language among us.

In their essay, "A Magically Nice Guy: Parasocial Relationships with Harry Potter across Different Cultures," psychologists Hannah Schmid and Christoph Klimmt describe the connections that readers make with Harry Potter characters as "parasocial relationships" (Schmid and Klimmt 2011, 253). Young readers like myself felt like they were going through the adventures and experiences along with the characters. We experienced anxiety when one of the characters was in danger, embarrassed with them through the awkwardness of puberty, and angry when they were bullied. Schmid and Klimmt observe that when readers admire and hope to acquire the physical and emotional traits of the characters, they often develop parasocial relationships with them. Harry, in particular, is brave, values friends and family, and opposes the evil and destruction that Voldemort represents. When fans come from societies and cultures that share these values, they are able to develop parasocial relationships with Harry Potter characters, even across widely varying racial and ethnic backgrounds, religions, and countries. Fans in the Harry Potter generation such as myself have developed bonds to the novels that are so strong that they continue to shape our lives well into adulthood. Around the globe there is a generation of young adults who may not know each other but share a common feature: personal identification with the narratives and experiences of Harry Potter characters and their struggles and triumph.

Lauren Hammond reflects on readers' shared experiences with the series

In her article, "Final Film is Bittersweet for the Harry Potter Generation," Rhian Evans describes how "the release of each new book or film is linked to [readers'] memories of being a certain age" (Evans 2011). Young fans who were close in age to Harry when the first book was published often talk about "growing up" with Harry and his peers. Another participant in the study abroad course, Cathy Gutierrez, noted that shared experiences among fans in this age cohort were a significant factor for the 27 students who traveled together. Cathy noticed that many study abroad course participants who read the novels as children felt as though they themselves were students at Hogwarts, along with the young witches and wizards described in the novels.

During the trip, the students often commented that the books were helpful in coming to terms with troubling dynamics of growing up, peer pressure, and coping with the world around them. Angelo John Reyes, a participant in the study abroad course, reflected that as a young reader he learned from Harry the importance of being a "standup person," i.e., to stand up for what he believes in and what matters to him, despite peer pressure to do otherwise. Angelo noted that throughout the book series, Harry faced obstacles and ostracism that many children encounter during adolescence. Harry had to make friends in a new social setting, cope with being unpopular at times, and learn how to deal with those who became his enemies. As a boy Angelo was drawn to these narratives, particularly those describing schoolyard politics and bullies. He also appreciates the fact that J.K. Rowling described

Harry's physical appearance as nothing extraordinary—an average-looking boy with messy hair and glasses—which helped Angelo accept himself and identify with Harry more closely.

Members of the Harry Potter generation also commented that the books were instructive to them when they were young adults. Particularly during difficult or troubling times in their lives, participants recalled turning to Harry Potter novels for comfort and advice. Participants in the study abroad program often commented that they joined the course in the hopes of better understanding their personal relationship to the series.

Shelby M.M. Kacirek, participant in the study abroad course, notes that her relationship to the series served as a coping mechanism during difficult times

I started reading *Sorcerer's Stone* when I was ten years old. I didn't like it at first because it was nothing like any of the other books I had read, and it scared me. However, as more of my friends started reading it, I decided it was time to give the series another try. Perhaps because of peer support and participation, this time I began to fall in love with the world that Rowling crafted. My best friend and I started reading the books together, creating a strong bond between us. Many of my childhood friendships that grew from our shared love of Harry Potter have lasted to the present day. The books taught us about the value and tenacity of friendships and offered models for relationships in our own life.

Harry Potter also helped me survive my parents' divorce. I vividly remember the night we were sitting at the dinner table; my younger sister and I sensed that a serious and uncomfortable conversation was about to take place. Finally, Mom and Dad told us they were separating. I remember feeling that our world suddenly turned upside down. My sister started crying and my head was spinning. I gathered every ounce of courage I could muster, took my sister's hand and announced, "Taylor, whatever happens, no matter what, I will take care of you. I don't care if we have to find a way to live or if we live by ourselves. I will *always* be there for you." Our parents were shocked. In that moment I drew on one of the most important lessons in the Harry Potter series: the importance of *being there* for the people you love, even in the bleakest of circumstances. By this time in my childhood, Harry Potter already deeply informed my thinking.

During my research in the study abroad course, I began to understand how the experiences of fictional characters in Harry Potter novels shaped my reaction to my parents' divorce. Throughout the novels, Harry and several others (including Hermione Granger, Luna Lovegood, Neville Longbottom, Sirius Black, Remus Lupin, and Severus Snape) go through difficult and troubling times. The choices, pain, triumphs, doubts, and failures they experience made a lasting impression on me, giving me a framework for my own behavior and decisions. Neville stands up to his friends when he thinks they are in the wrong, demonstrating the importance of speaking out when one feels strongly about an issue or problem, despite the disapproval of others. Luna demonstrates that appearances can be deceiving; she has special talents and is steadfast in the battle against Voldemort and the Death Eaters. Sirius reminds us not to judge people on a surface level or by popular reputation, because they may be much more than they initially appear to be. Through her portrayal of Snape and Dumbledore in the final novels, Rowling also blurs the line between good and evil, suggesting to young readers that life is complicated, it is important to understand the world in depth and in multiple dimensions, and that the choices we make are essential. Most importantly, the novels teach us that love and friendships have the power to overcome hatred and evil, even in the face of overwhelming odds.

Lauren Hammond reflects on visiting the Harry Potter sites as "sacred spaces" for study abroad participants

The Harry Potter stories are alive and ever present for many members of the Harry Potter generation. During their travels, Linda noted that students often spoke about feeling a sense of reverence and deep emotion when they visited sites that served as Hogwarts hallways and classrooms in the films, the same numinous feelings that Dennis J. Siler details in his essay of this collection. At Warner Bros. Studios north of London, when students entered the room with the massive model of Hogwarts Castle, participants in the study abroad course paused, grew quiet and reflective, and had tears in their eyes, as if they had entered sacred space. When they visited the Elephant House café in Edinburgh, everyone wanted to sit at the same table where Rowling sat as she wrote the first books and have their picture taken in the same location where Rowling was photographed while she was writing. For participants on the trip, this was a pilgrimage; fans have internalized and love the story so deeply that they were compelled to visit the locations related to the books and films just to feel closer to the novels and the characters.

Harmony Owen, participant in the study abroad course, illuminates the positive impact that male and female characters within the series had on her understanding of gender relations

As I sat during our study abroad course, slowly sipping my Earl Grey and looking up at the High Table of Middle Temple Hall in London—its walls decorated with enormous portraits, rows of armor, and stunning stained-glass windows, all covered by a magnificent wood ceiling—I thought to myself: *this* feels like Hogwarts. I had the same thought many times over in the days that followed as we made our pilgrimage across the United Kingdom, visiting various locations related to the films and novels, including Oxford University, Gloucester Cathedral, and the Scottish Highlands. I am a 27-year-old university graduate and one of the fortunate students who participated in the Harry Potter study abroad course offered by California State University San Marcos. The excitement I felt when I was admitted to the program was like receiving my acceptance letter to Hogwarts. I realized how emotionally connected I am to the series while standing in front of the magnificent film set for Professor Dumbledore's Office at Warner Brothers Studios in Leavesden, goose bumps rising on my arms and sending chills down my spine.

My mother convinced me to pick up *Sorcerer's Stone* in 2001; starting when I was eleven years old, I grew up with Harry, Hermione, and Ron and the other Hogwarts students. As I have gotten older, rereading the series and watching the films still arouses feelings of happiness and well-being. This brings me comfort, like baking on a rainy day. Akin to suddenly smelling the perfume of someone I once knew and cared for, I feel nostalgic when I hear the tinkling bells of the Harry Potter theme song "Hedwig's Theme" (Williams 2001); I also feel nostalgia for my childhood adoration of all things Harry Potter. Psychologists Constantine Sedikides and her co-authors describe nostalgia as "a sentimental longing for one's past, a sentimentality that is pervasively experienced." They suggest that across a variety of cultures, nostalgia "transcends social groups and age," both among "well-functioning adults" (Sedikedes et al. 2008, 304–5) and children.

Rowling created a safe space where I, as a child, could connect with the characters on an emotional level and escape what was sometimes the scary and confusing reality of the world around me. The relationships between Hermione, Ron, and Harry were far from perfect, yet they ultimately proved their loyalty to and love for one another. It is part of the human condition to make mistakes and sometimes disagree with others, including those we love. To move beyond this, we must have the desire and ability to empathize with the feelings of others. Many of Rowling's endearing characters, including Harry, Dobby, Snape, and Tonks, rely on empathy and love to overcome evil. As an adolescent I learned from the series about the struggles of building friendships and the consequences of alienation. I also felt an immediate connection to Hermione, relating to her desire for acceptance by her peers, as well as frustrations with sexist gender expectations. At times, Hermione's friends, including Ron and Harry, picked on and trivialized her. I have a twin brother, and as a child I was constantly battling with my brother's friends. One minute they shunned me for having "cooties," and the next, they tried to kiss me. Hermione helped me negotiate this confusing terrain by realizing I could be smart, motivated, and define meaningful relationships with boys and men on my own terms. German scholars Katrin Berdnt and Lena Steveker observe in their introduction to *Heroism in the Harry Potter Series*:

> At the close of the twentieth and the beginning of the twenty-first centuries, the Harry Potter series has invited a reassessment of the concept of heroism, for it suggests that the protection and careful adjustment of what has been achieved should be deemed just as heroic as traditional notions of masculine courage and action. One of the most distinctive features of Rowling's visions of heroism is, we believe, that they thrive on sympathy and compassion rather than merely resulting from physical strength, dominance or superior power of any kind. In a time in which artistic excellence is often synonymous with an artist's preoccupation with the dark side of life and its representation in art, Rowling dares to portray a hero who is, above all, kind [Berdnt and Steveker 2011, 2].

In her portrayal of human struggle Rowling places great emphasis on the significance of choices and the importance of everyday acts of empathy and heroism. Although the story of Harry Potter is at its core a retelling of earlier narratives, it also reframes what it means to be a hero and supports a more positive interaction between males and females.

I was inspired by Rowling's message that courage is an important element of friendships. At the End-of-Year Feast in the *Sorcerer's Stone*, Dumbledore awards Neville Longbottom ten house points for telling the Trio they should not go out at night, risk danger, and break the rules. Dumbledore reminds students that "it takes a great deal of courage to stand up to your enemies, but just as much to stand up to your friends" (*SS* 306). This helped me develop my thinking about how to interact with peers; it also made me recognize that doing the right thing might not make me popular, but was important, nonetheless. The struggles and triumphs of characters in the Harry Potter novels guided me in making sense of my own experiences. They also helped me think critically about social justice in the real world. I wasn't pulling screaming mandrakes out of pots or swishing a wand to levitate a feather, but the books enabled me to recognize the Weasleys, Malfoys, and the injustice of economic inequality in the world around me.

Lauren Hammond suggests that virtue and heroism are redefined throughout the series in ways that are especially appealing to female readers

As highlighted by Allison, Shelby, and Harmony, through Rowling's fantasy world we see a metaphorical reflection of evolving understandings of race, class, and culture. In his analysis of the Harry Potter series, psychologist Neil Mulholland and contributors to his edited volume examine how Rowling uses her writing to convey a refreshing new outlook on social and political concerns (Mulholland et al. 2007, 207). Children and adult readers alike are encouraged to consider moral dilemmas by encountering issues of race (or species), economic inequality, and ethnocentrism in Rowling's narratives. Harmony's reflections, in particular, touch on Rowling's critique of a hero whose status is derived from class, blood status, or physical prowess. Male and female heroes are not established through social hierarchies; rather, they earn recognition through the kind, empathetic, and courageous choices they make. The reader experiences the heroism of a mother's love, a friend's loyalty, or a stranger's empathy. This reconceptualization of heroism is particularly appealing to female readers because it offers an alternative to the dominant discourse, going against the grain of the violent, hyper-masculine male hero.

Rachael Dohrn, a high school teacher and participant in the study abroad course, discusses her identification with Hermione and this character's empowering actions

I would like to express my gratitude to Hermione Granger and J.K. Rowling for my current social position and occupation as a teacher. Distracted by other concerns and ignorant about the value of education, I found in Hermione, the best and brightest student at Hogwarts, the inspiration to change the trajectory of my life. I was a delayed reader of Harry Potter. Actually, I was delayed in every aspect of public education. In elementary school I was not interested in reading, and I failed in most subjects. I was bored and did not pay attention. During math, I faked understanding the fundamentals of multiplication and division by copying my neighbors' work. By the end of second grade, this habit spread to all areas of my learning. I was forced to attend summer school to try to compensate for my poor work during the regular academic year.

During spring break in sixth grade, my family forced me to watch the DVD of *Harry Potter and the Chamber of Secrets*. The magical moment happened for me at the end of the film, when Ron and Hermione had their awkward "I really want to give you a hug right now, but I'm going to shake your hand, instead" moment. My reaction was: Wait! What? They have a crush on each other? I immediately bought the next book in the series (*Prisoner of Azkaban*) and finished it by the next evening. My uncle was so proud of me that he bought me *Goblet of Fire*, which I completed within days. Over the next two months, I went back and read *Sorcerer's Stone* and then reread *Chamber of Secrets, Prisoner of Azkaban,* and *Goblet of Fire*. Come June 21, 2003, I was *so* ready for the release of *Order of Phoenix*, which I had already pre-ordered. Before Harry Potter, I had never been excited about reading.

So my summer went, enjoying the many adventures, duels, magical creatures, and tasty sweets along with Harry, Ron, and Hermione. More than any other character, I latched on to Hermione. Driven to achieve, studious, quick to grasp what others missed, she was the smart student I never imagined I could be. Hermione opened a door for me. I knew I wanted to become like her, my new role model. Feeling motivated by this, I decided that seventh grade was going to be *my year*. Taking to heart Dumbledore's reminder: "It is our choices, Harry, that show what we truly are, far more than our abilities" (*CoS* 333), I made the choice to prioritize my education, just like Hermione. I graduated from high school and went on to earn a bachelor's degree and a teaching credential. Today I teach high school language arts and am working towards a master's degree. I owe this to Hermione and J.K. Rowling.

In her analysis of Hermione and her accomplishments, Tara Foster suggests that "young readers of the series clearly see Hermione not as a stereotypically 'weak' girl but as an example to emulate" (Foster 2012, 121). Hermione has no inclination to abandon her academic achievements in order to be accepted or attract boys. Instead, she prioritizes her education above all things, exemplified in her amusing comment to Harry and Ron after the three of them were nearly pulverized by an enormous troll, "I hope you're pleased with yourselves. We all could have been killed—or worse, *expelled*" (*SS* 162, emphasis mine). During a final exam in Defense Against the Dark Arts, she articulates her greatest fear:

> Hermione did everything perfectly until she reached the trunk with the boggart in it. After about a minute inside it, she burst out again, screaming.
> "Hermione!" said Lupin, startled. "What's the matter?"
> "P-P-Professor McGonagall!" Hermione gasped, pointing into the trunk. "Sh-she said I'd failed everything!" [*PoA* 319].

Hermione complicates the stereotypical portrayal of the damsel in distress. Although there are several situations in which the boys must come to her rescue, there are many times when Hermione proves to be emotionally and intellectually independent. She often exemplifies self-sufficiency in conducting research and finding information. Drawing on her example when I teach, I model this in my high school classroom by encouraging students to do research motivated by curiosity and a desire to learn more. When my students ask questions I can't answer, I respond by instructing them to search for the information. This encourages young learners to pursue answers and knowledge, even when they are not immediately available.

In *Deathly Hallows,* Hermione, quite uncharacteristically, abandons her education during her final year at Hogwarts in order to assist Harry in his quest to destroy horcruxes. Why would she choose such a path? Many critics conclude that Rowling needed Hermione to fill the role of the sidekick aiding the hero. Foster, however, contends that Hermione knew she needed to help save her world in order to ensure her continued educational endeavors:

It is neither fair nor accurate to allege that by the end of the series, Hermione "has only exercised her gift to aid Harry's quests rather than focusing on her own career. He is the hero; she is but an assistant" (citing Elizabeth E. Heilman and Trevor Donaldson, "From Sexist to (Sort-of) Feminist: Representations of Gender in the Harry Potter Series," in *Critical Perspectives on Harry Potter*, 2nd ed., ed. Elizabeth E. Heilman [New York: Routledge, 2009], 139–161). One might wonder what kind of career Hermione could possibly have had under Voldemort's regime as a Muggle-born witch, an enemy of the Head of the Muggle-Born Registration Commission, and a close associate of Undesirable Number One. Her moral reasoning tells her that her own advancement must come after ensuring the survival of her world. Whenever it is a question of defeating Voldemort, Harry's quest must also be the quest of every witch and wizard who would not be murdered or enslaved by evil [Foster 2012, 121].

Hermione's character is not the only way the novels communicate the value of education. The story takes place primarily at Hogwarts School of Witchcraft and Wizardry. Rowling dramatizes various threats to Hogwarts, including incompetent teachers (e.g., Professors Binns and Lockhart), outdated and draconian (no pun intended) administrators (like Dolores Umbridge), administrative policies and pressure from the Ministry of Magic, and Voldemort's threat to destroy the school. Many Hogwarts students take their education seriously enough to be upset or outraged; they are willing to fight back when their education is threatened. For example, when "grotesque, punitive, abusive ogress Dolores Umbridge, who is repeatedly pictured as a toad" (Wolosky 2014, 289), takes over the Defense Against the Dark Arts class, Hermione works with Harry to create their own Defense Against the Dark Arts course, which becomes Dumbledore's Army. In her analysis of *Order of the Phoenix*, Jennifer Flaherty contends: "Despite her inherent respect for authority, Hermione is one of the most rebellious students in the school when the freedom of knowledge is challenged" (Flaherty 2004, 96). Harry and Hermione are the leaders; other students look to them for directions and information. Hermione gains so much knowledge that she becomes a valuable resource to others; she becomes a walking library of information.

In their study of the empowerment of girls through various genres of young adult literature, Joanne Brown and Nancy St. Clair suggest, "Empowered girls in young adult literature … come to know themselves well, both their strengths and their weaknesses, and they resist letting themselves be defined by others" (Brown and St. Clair 2002, 49). When discussing Hermione with friends and colleagues who identify as members of the Harry Potter generation, I often hear that she was a role model for their younger student-selves, as well. Others remark that they were already driven to be studious in school, and that Hermione was a reassuring companion, a character to whom they could relate, who showed that it was possible to prioritize academics and still have friends and romantic relationships. Emma Watson, who played the role of Hermione in the Harry Potter films, has herself become a champion for the empowerment of girls and women. After the movies, she earned a bachelor's degree at Brown University and completed a year of study at Oxford University. She then became a Goodwill Ambassador at the United Nations, heading the "He for She Campaign" that focuses on empowering girls and promoting gender equality throughout the world.

These important lessons have shaped my perceptions of the world and my goals in life. I am a proud member of the Harry Potter generation. I credit Rowling's novels for the important decisions I made to seek an education and become a high school teacher. I will be forever grateful for Hermione's influence in my life, encouraging my desire to continue learning as a lifelong process.

Lauren Hammond challenges the common exclusionary descriptions of the Harry Potter generation and advocates for a broader definition

Much has been made of the Harry Potter generation: what it is, who is included, and conversely, who is not. Purists believe that the Harry Potter generation, strictly speaking, includes only those fans who grew up at the same time as Harry and read the books during this period. As one blogger wrote, "Age is the most obvious credential for a member of the Harry Potter generation. Many fans recall starting the books at age 10 or 11 and virtually growing up alongside Harry and his friends" (Jennette 2013). This definition would exclude me, because I did not read the books until I was older, as well as some other contributors to this article. If that is the accepted definition of the Harry Potter generation, we will have to console ourselves with just being a part of the larger Harry Potter fandom. However, the participants' reflections in this essay point to a much broader understanding of the composition of the Harry Potter generation, suggesting that we define the Harry Potter generation more fluidly to include upcoming, young Potter fans, who also grew up reading the books and have been similarly affected by the series. The beauty and power of Harry Potter is that it often seeps into the real world, whether readers realize it or not. Diverse groups of readers and viewers come together around their love of the tales. Many feel as though they will always have a home at Hogwarts. Rowling's magical world that so often serves as our escape from troubled times continues to be a safe haven, often transcending cultures and generations.

Erin L. Southam, middle school librarian and teacher, discusses her role as a Harry Potter enthusiast and her work with younger generations of fans

In June 2015 my daughter and I participated in the Harry Potter study abroad course that took us from London through England to Edinburgh and into the Scottish Highlands. We visited and learned about film locations and sites related to the book and film series. In Edinburgh, for example, we visited the Elephant House café, where Rowling wrote portions of the first books. Thousands of Potter fans have visited this special place to pay homage to Rowling and Harry Potter. They have left their thoughts and heartfelt thanks in graffiti messages that cover every possible inch of the walls in the restroom entryway and women's restroom, as well as letters that fill the drawers of tables in the café. My daughter and I sat at the table where Rowling sat when she was writing (there are photos showing her there), an experience that was pure *magic!* Looking out the window, I spotted Greyfriars Kirkyard, where Rowling took walks, and gravestones that inspired character names, such as McGonagall ("the world's worst" poet, William McGonagall, died in 1902), and perhaps Riddle (Thomas Riddell, Esq., died 1806, and descendants). I saw the beautiful and majestic Edinburgh Castle atop Castle Rock, towering over the city and perhaps sparking Rowling's imagination as she described the castle of Hogwarts School of Witchcraft and Wizardry.

As a middle school teacher and librarian, I have a finger on the pulse of adolescent readers. While new book series gain popularity each year, some remain tried and true. Harry Potter is one of those series. Hardly a day goes by when I do not hear a reference to Harry Potter and Rowling's magical world, testimony to how deeply these books have affected young readers. At the beginning of each school year, the Rowling shelf empties quickly and stays that way until June. New copies must be purchased every year due to wear and tear. Some students pick up Rowling's books from the library because their families cannot afford to buy their own copies. Others check them out because they have enjoyed the movies and are ready to read the novels. Some read them for comfort; having read them multiple times, they are drawn again to these heartwarming stories about heroes, adventures, love, and magic.

At the heart of the Harry Potter series is the Hero's Journey, a narrative pattern of many steps delineated by Joseph Campbell, among others. This journey begins in the "ordinary world" as the hero encounters a situation or problem that must be solved; it ends when the hero "returns with the elixir" and the power of transformation (Vogler 2015). The hero's journey often incorporates lessons of friendship, love, and courage, a story in which the reader can find some reflection of her/himself, as well as a story about conquering hardships that many people encounter and must overcome in their own lives. Whether it is a conflict with friends or the death of loved ones, the Harry Potter narratives shine a light on creative ways to cope with difficult situations in our own lives. My students are also attracted to the element of magic in the stories, magic created by witches and wizards and magic arising from the human experience. Once a week I lead a Harry Potter book club that meets to discuss the books and various aspects of fandom. The club grows each year; we now have approximately 25 students. We read and discuss two chapters each week, and students volunteer to serve as discussion leaders. I am often amazed by the depth of the conversation and pleasantly surprised by the talking points the student discussion leaders raise in our sessions. They share their perceptions of the world and how it works, often leading to vigorous debates. While recently discussing the chapter entitled "The Firebolt" in *Prisoner of Azkaban*, students were divided about whether or not Hermione had done the right thing by reporting to Professor McGonagall Harry's anonymous gift of the Firebolt broomstick, which resulted in Harry losing possession of the broomstick for several months (while it was thoroughly examined for jinxes or other possible evil spells). This led to lively discussion. Middle school students are usually excited to share their thoughts and perceptions, and I find that they often articulate sympathetic and empathetic perspectives about differing points of view when they talk about Harry Potter. This makes the series particularly valuable for group discussions that expand critical thinking. Working with the next generation of Harry Potter readers has convinced me that the fandom is alive and well.

Lauren Hammond, closing thoughts

What does this all mean for the future of Harry Potter? The theme park attraction, the Wizarding World of Harry Potter at Universal Studios, Orlando, has been so popular that park executives added a new area for "Diagon Alley," a second version was built in Japan, and another park in Burbank, California, opened in 2016. Rowling wrote the first screenplay for a series of movies based on the Harry Potter companion book, *Fantastic Beasts and Where to Find Them*, which premiered in November 2016. Harry Potter conventions continue to draw thousands of fans, including LeakyCon (recently dubbed GeekyCon to incorporate other fandoms), the 2016 Leviosa Convention in Las Vegas, and the bi-annual MISTI-Con in Laconia, New Hampshire. Many major cities have some form of a Harry Potter meet up, with Los Angeles having the world's second largest, known as "Dumbledore's Army." Around the globe, Live Action Role Plays (LARPs) are based on Harry Potter, including the "College of Wizardry," in which participants travel to a castle in Poland to experience life at a magical school. Harry Potter study abroad courses and specialized tours are offered throughout the United Kingdom, focusing on the books and films. There is crossover between the Harry Potter fandom and others, such as Lord of the Rings and Sherlock Holmes, creating new fan fiction and podcasts. Universities across the U.S. and in other countries are offering Harry Potter courses, focusing on topics as varied as neuroscience and politics. Harry Potter will contribute to popular culture for years to come as the next generation of readers is drawn to the books and films. Will people continue to read these books a hundred years from now? When the Harry Potter series moves beyond copyright, will other versions of the narrative emerge and be widely published?

Good stories often teach lessons about ethics, morality, and the meaning of life. For us, the contributors to this essay, Harry Potter helped us define essential human experiences, such as courage, social justice, friendship, and love. The books also helped many of us navigate childhood, playing a particularly important role in our thinking and development as we moved to adulthood. We believe that Rowling's tales of adventure, magic, good, evil, virtue, and the power of love resonate with the human heart. They remind us to rely on kindness and empathy in our dealings with friends, strangers, and enemies alike. We believe that the Harry Potter tales have the staying power to entertain, instruct, and most importantly, touch the hearts of generations to come.

REFERENCES

Berdnt, Katrin and Lena Steveker. 2011. "Introduction." In *Heroism in the Harry Potter Series*, edited by Katrin Berdnt and Lena Steveker, 1–5. Farham, England: Ashgate.

Brown, Joanne, and Nancy St. Clair. 2002. *Declaration of Independence: Empowered Girls in Young Adult Literature*, 1990–2001. Lanham: Scarecrow Press.

"A Day at San Diego Comic-Con with the Cast of Fantastic Beasts." 2016. Pottermore.com. Accessed October 29, 2017. https://www.pottermore.com/news/san-diego-comic-con-2016-with-cast-of-fantastic-beasts.

Evans, Rhian. 2011. "Final Film Is Bittersweet for the Harry Potter Generation," *Western Mail*. Accessed July 7 2015. http://www.genios.de/presse-archiv/artikel/WMAL/20110715/final-film-is-bittersweet-for-the-h/MDNP2011071515F15458.html, July 7, 2015.

Flaherty, Jennifer. 2004. "Harry Potter and the Freedom of Information: Knowledge and Control in *Harry Potter and the Order of the Phoenix*." *Washington and Jefferson College Review* 54: 93–102.

Foster, Tara. 2012. "Books! And Cleverness!: Hermione's Wits." In *Hermione Granger Saves the World: Essays on the Feminist Heroine of Hogwarts*, edited by Christopher E. Bell, 105–124. Jefferson NC: McFarland.

Gierzynski, Anthony and Kathryn Eddy. 2013. *Harry Potter and the Millennials: Research Methods and the Politics of the Muggle Generation*. Baltimore: The Johns Hopkins University Press.

Heilman, Elizabeth E., and Trevor Donaldson. 2009. "From Sexist to (Sort-of) Feminist: Representations of Gender in the Harry Potter Series." In *Critical Perspectives on Harry Potter*, edited by Elizabeth E. Heilman, 139–161. New York: Routledge.

Jennette, Alyssa. 2013. "Defining the Harry Potter Generation" (blog). *Mugglenet.com*, September 29. Accessed July 18, 2015. http://blog.mugglenet.com/2013/09/defining-the-harry-potter-generation.

"Meet Author J.K. Rowling." 2017. Scholastic.com. Accessed October 29, 2017. http://harrypotter.scholastic.com/jk_rowling/.

Mulholland, Neil, ed. 2007. *The Psychology of Harry Potter*. Dallas: BenBella Books.

Rowling, J.K. 2017. "Harry Potter to Be Translated into Scots." Jkrowling.com, June 28. Accessed October 29, 2017. https://www.jkrowling.com/harry-potter-translated-scots/.

Schmid, Hannah, and Christoph Klimmt, 2011. "A Magically Nice Guy: Parasocial Relationships with Harry Potter Across Different Cultures," *International Communication Gazette* 73 (3): 252–269.

Sedikides, Constantine, Tim Wildschuit, Amy Arndt, and Clay Routledge. 2008. "Nostalgia: Past, Present and Future." *Current Directions in Psychological Science* 17 (5): 304–305.

Vezalli, Loris, Sofia Stathi, Dino Giovannini, Dora Capozza, and Elena Trifiletti. "The Greatest Magic of Harry Potter: Reducing Prejudice." *Journal of Applied Social Psychology* 45 (2): 105–121.

Vogler, Christopher. n.d. "Hero's Journey." *Storytech Literary Consulting.* Accessed July 18, 2015. http://www.thewritersjourney.com/hero's_journey.htm.

Williams, John. 2001. "Hedwig's Theme." *Harry Potter and the Sorcerer's Stone: Original Motion Picture Soundtrack.* Atlantic 7567–93086-2, CD.

Wolosky, Shira. 2014. "Foucault at School: Discipline, Education and Agency in Harry Potter." *Children's Literature in Education* 45: 285–297.

About the Contributors

Balaka **Basu** is an assistant professor at the University of North Carolina at Charlotte, where she works on fanfiction and digital narratives. She holds a Ph.D. from the Graduate Center of the City University of New York. Her first coedited collection, *Contemporary Dystopian Fiction for Young Adults* (Routledge, 2013) won the Best Edited Book from the Children's Literature Association.

Allison **Bianco** is pursuing a BA in linguistics at California State University–Long Beach and hopes to become a speech pathologist. The Harry Potter series has had an immense influence on her education, and she has been particularly interested in Rowling's use of etymology since she discovered that *accio* means "I summon."

Rachael **Dohrn** graduated from Colorado State University in Fort Collins, Colorado, with a BA in English and a certificate in teaching. As a child, she wandered into a bookshop, picked up a copy of *Harry Potter and the Sorcerer's Stone*, and was so engrossed by the novel she finished it that night. She has since read it more than twenty times.

Cathy **Gutierrez** is pursuing a double major in biology and nursing, with a minor in Spanish, at California State University–San Marcos. In June 2015 she took a Harry Potter study-abroad course in England and Scotland, which included a broomstick flying lesson at Alnwick Castle and a tour of Warner Bros. Studios in Leavesden. Her goal is to become a registered nurse and a physician's assistant.

Lauren **Hammond** is a Ph.D. student at the University of California–Riverside. In 2013, she presented her research on Harry Potter at the annual conference of the American Folklore Society. In her continuing studies as a graduate student, She enjoys teaching English, tutoring writing, researching, and presenting at academic conferences.

Shelby M.M. **Kacirek** is a content creator and videographer and she helps clients share their own stories and effectively reach their targeted audiences. She has a longstanding interest in visual storytelling and hopes one day to work in the film industry. She actively raises money for the Malala Fund and continues to seek out her inner Hermione Granger by standing up for what is right every single day.

Emily **Lauer** is an associate professor at Suffolk County Community College–SUNY, and is a past president of the CAITY Caucus of NeMLA. Her publications include work on Spider-Man, young adult dystopia, and *Alice's Adventures in Wonderland*, and her current work addresses adaptations into and out of the comics form.

Emily **Lohorn** is an adjunct professor, teaching English and education courses at Southwestern College. She holds an MA in children's literature from San Diego State University, and her main research interests include the role of history in children's literature and the intersection of fantasy and technology.

Dion **McLeod** completed his Ph.D. in English literatures at the University of Wollongong, Australia, in 2016. His research interests include social justice and children's literature, queer theory, and reception studies. His publications include an article on Rowling's function as author/fan in the Potter universe and queer romance in John Green and David Levithan's *Will Grayson, Will Grayson*.

Julia D. **Morris** is a Ph.D. student at Old Dominion University, studying curriculum and instruction for literacy studies and educational psychology. Her research deals with literacy in higher education classrooms and university athletic academics. She serves as the program evaluator and research coordinator for a National Science Foundation grant, studying peer review practices through various technology mediums.

Harmony **Owen** is a public information officer in Canyon Lake, California. In 2015, she earned her BA in communication at California State University–San Marcos. She is a Harry Potter enthusiast who began reading the series when she was 11 years old and continues to draw strength from her favorite childhood characters.

Elise **Payne** is a Ph.D. candidate specializing in English literature. Her research focuses on character studies, and specifically on how concentrating on supporting characters when engaging with texts can change the meanings and messages we get out of them.

Linda **Pershing** is a retired professor of folklore and cultural studies and was the founding faculty member of the Women's Studies Department at California State University–San Marcos. An avid Harry Potter fan, she taught university courses on the folklore and cultural messages in the novels and a study abroad course on Harry Potter folklore and culture in England and Scotland.

Angelo John **Reyes** earned a BA in political science from California State University–San Marcos and attends Thomas Jefferson School of Law in San Diego, California. He remains as passionate about the Harry Potter series as he was when he first discovered it more than a decade ago.

Dennis J. **Siler** holds a Ph.D. from the University of Arkansas. He teaches at the University of Arkansas–Fort Smith, where he is the founding director of the honors international studies program. His books include *Channeling Ovid* and *Parley P. Pratt and the Making of Mormonism*. His areas of expertise include Shakespeare and Renaissance drama, Harry Potter, pop culture analysis and pedagogy.

Erin L. **Southam** holds an MA in reading education from San Diego State University and an MS in library science from Texas Woman's University. She is fortunate to indulge her passion for Harry Potter in her daily job as a teacher and librarian for elementary and middle schools. She runs a Harry Potter book club and assists club members in organizing an annual school event called "Pottercon."

Heather **Urbanski** holds a Ph.D. in English and is an associate professor at Fitchburg State University. Her published works include *Plagues, Apocalypses, and Bug-Eyed Monsters*, the edited collection *Writing and the Digital Generation*, and *The Science Fiction Reboot*, all of which combine her fandom interests in science fiction and scholarly focus on rhetoric in popular culture.

Christina A. **Valeo** is a professor at Eastern Washington University, where she has taught courses in English literature, children's literature, dystopian fiction and English education since 2003. She has published on Romantic writers, romance writers, and children's literature. Her contribution to this collection grew out of her teaching on the Harry Potter series.

Amber B. **Vayo** is a public law Ph.D. student in the political science department at the University of Massachusetts–Amherst. Her research interests include trauma-sensitive yoga (which she teaches) and protocols for making legal institutions more accessible to lower income communities. Her interest in Harry Potter stems from the series' focus on sociopolitical issues.

Isaac **Vayo** is a lecturer in cultural studies and comparative literature at the University of Minnesota–Twin Cities and an instructor of arts and letters at Concordia University–St. Paul. He has written extensively on 9/11 and terrorism, popular music, and literature. With Todd Comer, he edited the 2013 volume *Terror and the Cinematic Sublime*. His work also explores the manifestations of late capitalism.

Marian **Yee** is a teacher, scholar, and writer residing in Brookline, Massachusetts. She teaches literature, composition, film, and contemporary art at the Boston Conservatory at Berklee. Her scholarly writing includes papers on composition pedagogy, anthropology and performance, and studies of works by Woolf, Orwell and Pym. She also loves Harry Potter and writes young adult fiction.

Index